READING LAW AS NARRATIVE

Society of Biblical Literature

Ancient Israel and Its Literature

Steven L. McKenzie, General Editor

Editorial Board

Suzanne Boorer
Victor H. Matthews
Thomas C. Römer
Benjamin D. Sommer
Nili Wazana

Number 5

READING LAW AS NARRATIVE
A Study in the Casuistic Laws of the Pentateuch

READING LAW AS NARRATIVE

A Study in the Casuistic Laws of the Pentateuch

by

Assnat Bartor

Society of Biblical Literature
Atlanta

READING LAW AS NARRATIVE
A Study in the Casuistic Laws of the Pentateuch

Copyright © 2010 by the Society of Biblical Literature

All rights reserved. No part of this work may be reproduced or transmitted in any form or by any means, electronic or mechanical, including photocopying and recording, or by means of any information storage or retrieval system, except as may be expressly permitted by the 1976 Copyright Act or in writing from the publisher. Requests for permission should be addressed in writing to the Rights and Permissions Office, Society of Biblical Literature, 825 Houston Mill Road, Atlanta, GA 30329 USA.

Library of Congress Cataloging-in-Publication Data

Bartor, Assnat.
　Reading law as narrative : a study in the casuistic laws of the Pentateuch / by Assnat Bartor.
　　p. cm.—(Ancient Israel and its literature / Society of Biblical Literature ; v. 5)
　Includes bibliographical references.
　ISBN 978-1-58983-480-4 (paper binding : alk. paper)—ISBN 978-1-58983-481-1 (electronic library copy)
　1. Narration in the Bible. 2. Narration (Rhetoric) 3. Bible. O.T. Pentateuch—Criticism, Narrative. I. Society of Biblical Literature. II. Title.
BS1182.3.B37 2010
222'.1066—dc22
　　　　　　　　　　　　　　　　　　　　　　　　　　　　　　2010007839

17 16 15 14 13 12 11 10　　5 4 3 2 1

Printed in the United States of America on acid-free, recycled paper
conforming to ANSI/NISO Z39.48-1992 (R1997) and ISO 9706:1994
standards for paper permanence.

Contents

Abbreviations vii

Acknowledgments ix

Introduction 1

1. The Laws of the Pentateuch as "Embedded Stories" 17

2. The Lawgiver as Narrator 23

3. Representation of Speech: The Mimetic Illusion 85

4. Representation of Inner Life: The Lawgiver as Psychologist 133

5. Point of View 163

Conclusions 183

Bibliography 189

Indexes
    Authors 201
    Passages 204
    Subjects 215

Abbreviations

AB	The Anchor Bible
ANET	*Ancient Near Eastern Texts Relating to the Old Testament,* edited by J. B. Pritchard (3rd ed.; Princeton: Princeton University Press, 1969).
BDB	*The New F. Brown, S. R. Driver, C. A. Briggs, Gesenius, Hebrew and English Lexicon of the Old Testament* (Peabody: Hendrickson, 1979).
CAD	*The Assyrian Dictionary of the University of Chicago* (Chicago: Oriental Institute, 1956—).
CBQ	*Catholic Biblical Quarterly*
HL	Hittite Laws
HUCA	*Hebrew Union College Annual*
ICC	International Critical Commentary
JANES	*Journal of the Ancient Near Eastern Society*
JAOS	*Journal of the American Oriental Society*
JBL	*Journal of Biblical Literature*
JNES	*Journal of Near Eastern Studies*
JPS	The Jewish Publication Society
JQR	*Jewish Quarterly Review*
JSOT	*Journal for the Study of the Old Testament*
JSOTSup	Journal for the Study of the Old Testament Supplement Series
JSS	*Journal of Semitic Studies*
LE	Laws of Eshnunna
LH	Laws of Hammurabi
LL	Laws of Lipit-Ishtar
LU	Laws of Ur-Namma
MAL	Middle Assyrian Laws
OTL	Old Testament Library
NCBC	New Century Bible Commentary
NJPS	The New Jewish Publication Society Translation
RB	*Revue Biblique*
RSV	Revised Standard Version
SBL	Society of Biblical Literature
SBLDS	Society of Biblical Literature Dissertation Series

SBLWAW	Society of Biblical Literature Writings from the Ancient World Series
SVT	Supplements to Vetus Testamentum
VT	*Vetus Testamentum*
ZAW	*Zeitschrift für die alttestamentliche Wissenschaft*

Acknowledgments

This study has its origins in a doctoral dissertation I completed at Tel Aviv University. I would like to express my deep gratitude to my dissertation advisors, Professor Gershon Brin and Professor Ed Greenstein, for their constant aid, dedication, encouragement, and kindness. Their meticulous reading, which did not leave out any detail; their insightful comments; and the stimulating questions that were asked as well as the fruitful answers that were offered evoke great admiration.

Special thanks to Professor Greenstein for his good advice and assistance, in substantive as well as technical matters, during the preparation of the manuscript. My study has been greatly improved by his ideas and suggestions.

I would like to thank Tel Aviv University and the Memorial Foundation for Jewish Culture for their support during my Ph.D. studies. I would also like to thank my colleagues—teachers and students of the Department of Bible at Tel Aviv University—for showing favorable interest in my research.

Last but not least my family. I am grateful to my husband, Sami, and my children, Noam, Rea, and Yaara, for being considerate and understanding during my long and demanding project.

Introduction

Several years ago, when I began to formulate my general ideas about the narrative reading of the laws of the Pentateuch, my teacher, Ed Greenstein, told me a story. His friend, the biblical scholar Joel Rosenberg, used to deliver a weekly Torah lesson to his prayer group, but when he arrived at the Torah portion *Mishpatim* (Exodus 21–23), he observed a certain disappointment in his audience. The dramatic stories about the exodus from Egypt and the revelation at Mount Sinai—stories that fired the imagination—gave way to "dry" legal material, a law collection extending over three chapters. But when he was able to show his audience that the cases described in the law collection were actually miniature stories, the transition from narrative to legal discourse was no longer so clear-cut. This is when I understood (not coincidentally through the narration of this story) that my intuition was correct and that it was not only possible but also appropriate to read law as story.

When I read the laws of the Pentateuch, I sensed that stories were poking out through the repeated patterns and linguistic formulas. And when, despite the parsimonious language, the minimalist descriptions, and the paucity of detail, I was able to imagine what had befallen the Hebrew slave; when I found myself speculating about the twists of fate of the captive woman, or envisioning the tale of horror concerning a jealous husband, a suspected woman, and a stern priest (Exod 21:2–6; Deut 21:10–14; Num 5:12–31), I realized that I ought to read the laws as they are—as narrative laws. However, recognizing that I could not proceed with only intuition, feeling, and personal insight as guides, I searched for a theoretical ground and methodological anchor that would allow me to turn my personal reading into a method of reading that could be generalized and shared. My search was fruitful, and it is the results of this search that I hope to present to my readers in this introduction; to explain how the narrative reading of the laws of the Pentateuch came into being.

The narrative reading of biblical law is an interdisciplinary interpretive method. It examines legal biblical texts with the principles and the research tools of literary theory and narratology (i.e., the study of storytelling), thus reflecting contemporary trends in jurisprudence. This approach is known as the "law and literature" school. This school of thought emerged as a common framework for innovative interdisciplinary research in jurisprudence; it then expanded and escaped the confines of the academy until it became an intellectual, social, and political movement leading to the democratization of the legal world.

In the 1970s and 1980s, new voices began to be heard in the United States in the field of legal theory. The law, so it was argued, is social literature—a way of speaking about people and about the relationships between them.[1] The world in which we live is a normative world in which law and narrative are intertwined.[2] These statements and other similar ones were the harbingers of studies to come that investigated the mutual connections between law and literature.

Some of these studies were not innovative and continued a time-honored theoretical tradition that had its roots in nineteenth-century England when legal theorists began to examine the way in which the legal world was represented in the works of William Shakespeare, Charles Dickens, and other authors. It continued in the twentieth century in the analysis of the legal narratives that occupy the center of classical works of literature, such as Fyodor Dostoyevsky's *Crime and Punishment*, Franz Kafka's *The Trial*, or Albert Camus' *The Stranger*.[3] The law, interrogated within a larger cultural context, serves as an instrument for understanding the human condition in its social and existential aspects.

The study of law and literature did not end there, however. These earlier studies led to a growing recognition of the importance of literary texts as a means of understanding the legal world. The unique insights that literature affords into the human spirit, so it was claimed, enable the legal scholar to arrive at a more profound understanding of the intricate relationships between human beings and the law, and helps us to cultivate a moral and humanistic climate within the framework of legal discourse. Those engaged with the law, it was argued, should use literature as a humanizing device; they must distance

---

1. James Boyd White, *The Legal Imagination: Studies in the Nature of Legal Thought and Expression* (Boston: Little, Brown, 1973), 243–44.
2. Robert Cover, "Nomos and Narrative," *Harvard Law Review* 97 (1983): 4–10. Those familiar with Hebrew literature may notice how this title echoes Hayyim Nahman Bialik's famous essay "Halakhah and Aggadah." Bialik examined the unique literary model of rabbinic literature, which combines law (*halakha*) and narrative (*aggadah*), and saw it as a perfect paradigm for the fusion of the forces at work in culture in general. See Chaim Nachman Bialik, "Halacha and Aggadah," in *The Complete Works of C. N. Bialik* (2nd ed.;Tel Aviv: Dvir, 1939); an English version was published in *Contemporary Jewish Record*, vol. 7 (trans. L. Simon; New York: American Jewish Committee, 1944).
3. Many books have dealt with the legal aspects of Shakespeare's work. I mention only two here: Edward J. White, *Commentaries on the Law in Shakespeare* (2nd ed.; St. Louis: F. H. Thomas Law Books, 1913); Paul W. Kahn, *Law and Love: The Trials of King Lear* (New Haven: Yale University Press, 2000).

themselves from cerebral and analytical ways of thinking and adopt a mode of thought that makes room for emotion and takes into account the vulnerability of the other. This kind of empathic thinking will develop and cultivate a more worthy concept of justice—"poetic justice."[4]

The intermingling of these two fields that suddenly evolved, and the recognition that they held much in common (both construct reality through language, both employ rules of wording and require interpretation) led legal scholars and literary scholars to join forces. Scholars from each discipline began to examine the law and to analyze and critique legal texts with tools and interpretive principles borrowed from literary theory. This new branch of legal theory became known as the "law as literature" school, and it rendered what was a remote and arcane legal discourse more intelligible and accessible, and therefore also more socially efficacious.[5] The school of "law and literature" and its various branches gave rise to a new and different view of the law and of justice.

---

4. This is the name of a book by Martha Nussbaum, one of the leading scholars in the field known as "literature in the law": Martha C. Nussbaum, *Poetic Justice: The Literary Imagination and Public Life* (Boston: Beacon, 1995).

5. See Ronald Dworkin, "Law as Interpretation," in *The Politics of Interpretation, Critical Inquiry* 9 (1982–83): 179–200; idem, *Law's Empire* (Cambridge: Mass.: Belknap Press, 1986), 228–39; Stanley Fish, "Working on the Chain Gang: Interpretation in the Law and in Literary Criticism," in *The Politics of Interpretation, Critical Inquiry* 9 (1982–83): 201–16; idem, *Doing What Comes Naturally: Change, Rhetoric and the Practice of Theory in Literary and Legal Studies* (Post-contemporary Interventions; Durham, N.C.: Duke University Press, 1989); Sanford Levinson, "Law as Literature," in *Interpreting Law and Literature: A Hermeneutic Reader* (ed. Sanford Levinson and Steven Mailloux; Evanston, Ill.: Northwestern University Press, 1988), 155–73; Richard Weisberg, *Poethics and Other Strategies of Law and Literature* (New York: Columbia University Press, 1992); Robin West, *Narrative, Authority, and Law* (Law, Meaning, and Violence; Ann Arbor: University of Michigan Press, 1993); Ian Ward, *Law and Literature: Possibilities and Perspectives* (New York: Cambridge University Press, 1995); Guyora Binder and Robert Weisberg, *Literary Criticisms of Law* (Princeton, N.J.: Princeton University Press, 2000).

One of the severe critics of the school of "law and literature" is the legal scholar Richard Posner. He claims that the two disciplines are fundamentally different, as evidenced by the different type of language each employs. While the language of law is scientific, neutral, and accurate, the language of literature is rhetorical, multifaceted, and ambiguous. See, e.g., Richard A. Posner, *Law and Literature: A Misunderstood Relation* (Cambridge, Mass.: Harvard University Press, 1988). Posner's adamant position appears extreme, if merely for the fact that as early as 1930 the American Justice Benjamin Cardozo wrote an essay entitled "Law and Literature," in which he analyzed the writing style of his colleagues and pointed out the literary and rhetorical means they used in their decisions. See Benjamin Cardozo, *Law and Literature and Other Essays and Addresses* (New York: Harcourt, Brace, 1931).

It was in the most recent developments in the field of law and literature that I found a methodological basis for the literary reading of biblical law, as I will elaborate below. But here I must venture out of the literary field and invoke another discipline—cognitive psychology.[6] Both of these fields, literary theory and cognitive psychology, are engaged in the systematic attempt to penetrate and decipher the meta-code of our culture—the narrative, the story.

Narrative is the leading genre in all literary composition. It is also a major mode of expression in other artistic media, and even in nonartistic forms of writing. It is therefore given serious attention within two separate frameworks: within the general domain of literary theory and within the field of narratology, a subdivision of literary theory devoted specifically to all aspects of narrative as such.[7] In recent years, however, the study of narrative has extended beyond the boundaries of these two frameworks. The fact that stories are not only a literary genre or a mode of expression but also a central component of the human perceptual system places narrative squarely in the realm of research in cognitive psychology. Stories—this much is agreed upon—are the main means through which we understand and attribute meaning to things; they are the basic and typical form we use to organize our experiences in the world and to frame our knowledge of reality.[8]

These insights soon spilled over into other fields of knowledge, and historians, philosophers, anthropologists, art historians, and scientists began to

---

6. Cognitive psychology deals with the study of cognition and of the mental operations that form the basis of human behavior. Among other things, it is interested in the ways in which people decipher their experiences and lend meaning to their environment. See Derek Edwards, *Discourse and Cognition* (London: SAGE, 1997), 28–43.

7. See, e.g., Seymour Chatman, *Story and Discourse: Narrative Structure in Fiction and Film* (Ithaca, N.Y.: Cornell University Press, 1978); Gérard Genette, *Narrative Discourse: An Essay in Method* (trans. J. E. Lewin; Ithaca, N.Y.: Cornell University Press, 1980); Gerald Prince, *Narratology: The Form and Functioning of Narrative* (Janua linguarum, Series maior 108; Berlin: Mouton, 1982); Mieke Bal, *Narratology: Introduction to the Theory of Narrative* (trans. C. van Boheemen; Toronto: University of Toronto Press, 1985).

8. According to Walter Fisher, communications scholar and founder of the "narrative paradigm," humans are "narrating animals"—*homo narrans*. See Walter R. Fisher, *Human Communication as Narration: Toward a Philosophy of Reason, Value, and Action* (2nd ed.; Columbia: University of South Carolina Press, 1989), 57–68. See also Edwards, *Discourse and Cognition*, 266–71. Recognition of the importance of narrative to the entirety of cognitive operations has led to the development of a subfield within cognitive psychology, known as narrative psychology, which focuses on the way narrative works as a rational-cognitive means of constructing reality and understanding it. See Jerome S. Bruner, *Acts of Meaning* (Jerusalem-Harvard Lectures; Cambridge, Mass.: Harvard University Press, 1990), 35, 55–56; idem, "The Narrative Construction of Reality," in *Narrative Intelligence* (ed. Michael Mateas and Phoebe Sengers; Advances in Consciousness Research 46; Amsterdam/Philadelphia: John Benjamins, 2003), 41–62.

look at the ways in which stories were embedded in their research topics, and to consider the extent to which narrative is used even within the discourse of research.[9] This broad development did not pass unnoticed by legal theory, and scholars began to look increasingly at the narrative dimensions of legal discourse, describing the rhetorical and narrative techniques used by participants in legal proceedings, and analyzing the narrative and rhetorical elements that make up legal decisions.[10]

The present study applies a narratological approach to one area of the law—the field of legislation. It identifies the narrative elements that exist in the laws of the Pentateuch and exposes the narrative techniques employed by the authors. It examines the poetics of biblical law and its effects on the cognition and awareness of those addressed by the laws and on ourselves, the readers.

Do Legal Texts Really Contain Narrative Elements?

All laws deal directly or indirectly with human affairs. They deal with realistic events that occur in time and in space and use true-to-life characters to establish norms and formulate policy. Laws present and represent stories about people, about their property and their ties to their communities, and about interpersonal relationships and the relationships between communities. At the same time, not every law can serve as the object of a narrative reading, because it may not always describe a series of events or contain characters; not all laws present conflict, development, or change.[11] And when the language of the law is brief and laconic, or when it is punctilious and laden with technical jargon,

---

9. See, e.g., W. J. Thomas Mitchell, ed., *On Narrative* (Chicago: University of Chicago Press, 1981); Hayden White, *The Content of the Form: Narrative, Discourse and Historical Representation* (Baltimore: Johns Hopkins University Press, 1987); Mieke Bal, "The Point of Narratology," *Poetics Today* 11 (1990): 727–53; Cristopher Nash, ed., *Narrative in Culture: The Uses of Storytelling in the Sciences, Philosophy and Literature* (Warwick Studies in Philosophy and Literature; London: Routledge, 1994).

10. These narrative studies were variously designated as "storytelling in the law," "law as narrative," or "narrativity of the law." See, e.g., Bernard S. Jackson, *Law, Fact, and Narrative Coherence* (Legal Semiotics Monographs 1; Roby, Merseyside, U.K.: Deborah Charles, 1988); idem, "Narrative Theories and Legal Discourse," in Nash, *Narrative in Culture*, 23–50; Daniel A. Farber and Suzanna Sherry, "Telling Stories Out of School: An Essay on Legal Narratives," *Stanford Law Review* 45 (1993): 807–55; Lewis H. LaRue, *Constitutional Law as Fiction: Narrative in the Rhetoric of Authority* (University Park: Pennsylvania State University Press, 1995); Peter Brooks and Paul Gewirtz, eds., *Law's Stories, Narrative and Rhetoric in the Law* (New Haven: Yale University Press, 1996); Peter Brooks, "Narrativity of the Law," *Law and Literature* 14 (2002): 1–10.

11. These are the main ingredients of narrative according to the Aristotelian model. See Aristotle, *Aristotle's Poetics* (trans. J. Hutton; New York: W. W. Norton, 1982), 52–56.

one cannot usually point to narrative devices or to rhetorical ploys employed by the legislator.

These observations are valid not only in respect to modern laws, many of which do not "invite" a narrative reading, but also in respect to many ancient laws—those known to us from the law collections in the Pentateuch, as well as from other ancient Near Eastern law codes. The sixth commandment, "You shall not kill" (Exod 20:13), or the exhortation "Keep far from a false charge" (Exod 23:7),[12] or, equally, the section of the Eshnunna law "10 silas of grain is the hire of a winnower" (LE 8),[13] cannot serve as an object of narrative analysis. Although they contain the potential for narrative, since it is possible to reconstruct the background or event that precipitated the formulation of imperatives and of norms, and because stories could be invented to illustrate concretely their intention, in their current textual form this potential remains merely latent.

Unlike the laws mentioned here—of which other examples exist, known to biblical scholars as "apodictic laws"—most of the laws of the ancient Near East are constructed on the model of case law, more commonly known as "casuistic law."[14] This is the type of law that describes a hypothetical case, in which a certain problem is described, and to which the law provides a solution. For example: "When fire breaks out and catches in thorns so that the stacked grain or the standing grain or the field is consumed, he that kindled the fire shall make full restitution" (Exod 22:6). The law addresses here a realistic, familiar occurrence, presented in a minimalist narrative framework. It describes con-

---

12. English translations of biblical material follow the RSV.

13. The English translation of the Babylonian law is taken from Martha Roth, *Law Collections from Mesopotamia and Asia Minor* (SBLWAW 6; 2nd ed.; Atlanta: Society of Biblical Literature, 1997), 60.

14. In 1934 Albrecht Alt published his foundational study about the patterns of legal formulation in the Pentateuchal Laws, "Die Ursprünge des Israelitischen Rechts," in which he first coined the terms "casuistic law" and "apodictic law." The first pattern he characterized as a conditional clause (formulated in the third person and beginning with the particle כי or אם) that describes an event or state of affairs and elaborates their legal consequences; the second law is characterized as a definitive injunction or prohibition (like the three laws presented above). Albrecht Alt, "The Origins of Israelite Law," in *Essays on Old Testament History and Religion* (trans. R. A. Wilson; Garden City, N.Y.: Doubleday, 1967), 79–132. On the two patterns and their origins, see also Moshe Weinfeld, "The Origin of the Apodictic Law," VT 23 (1973): 63–75; John Bright, "The Apodictic Prohibition: Some Observations," JBL 92 (1973): 185–204; Jean Bottéro, *Mesopotamia: Writing, Reasoning, and the Gods* (trans. Z. Bahrani and M. Van De Mieroop; Chicago/London: University of Chicago Press, 1992), 170–79; Raymond Westbrook, "Biblical and Cuneiform Law Codes," in *Folk Law: Essays in the Theory and Practice of Lex Non Scripta* (ed. A. D. Renteln and A. Dundes; 2 vols.; Madison: University of Wisconsin Press 1995), 1:485–94.

cretely (if sparingly) a concatenation of events that involve transformation, conflict, development, and resolution. First, an event is described that results in damage to another person and changes the prevailing state of affairs; at the end an action is prescribed that is designed to restore equilibrium, as far as possible. Laws like this are in fact miniature stories, and therefore it is natural and appropriate to apply to them the interpretive method proposed here.[15]

What Is a Narrative Reading of a Law and How Is It Performed?

A narrative reading does not deal with the abstract content of the law: its norms, rules, fundamental principles, or policy prescriptions. A narrative reading focuses, rather, on the law's concrete elements—the situations, phenomena, characters, and events that it depicts, which together constitute its narrative content. Concentrating on these, and not on matters of abstract principle, reveals the human aspects of the law and illustrates how it acts as a mechanism that responds to human existence rather than imposing itself upon it.[16] Narrative reading, however, does not restrict itself to identifying the narrative content of the law. It examines how the legal text was composed, describing the textual means that the lawgiver employs in order to construct the details of the narrative; it investigates how we produce the meaning of

---

15. On the narrative nature of the casuistic laws, see Leonard L. Thompson, *Introducing Biblical Literature: A More Fantastic Country* (Englewood Cliffs, N.J.: Prentice-Hall, 1978), 145–59, esp. 147–48; Harry P. Nasuti, "Identity, Identification and Imitation: The Narrative Hermeneutics of Biblical Law," *Journal of Law and Religion* 4 (1986): 9–23, esp. 9; Jackson, *Law, Fact, and Narrative Coherence*, 97–98. My view, that the casuistic laws are mini-stories, differs from the view put forward by Moshe Simon-Shoshan, a scholar of the Mishnah. He argues that the laws are not stories, but at most texts possessing narrative characteristics, since they present hypothetical, unspecified cases (I am grateful to Moshe Simon-Shoshan for allowing me to consult his dissertation, "*Halachah Lema'aseh*: Narrative and Legal Discourse in the Mishnah" [diss., University of Pennsylvania, 2005], 18–71). The distinction between "narrative" and "story" is a common one (see Jackson, "Narrative Theories and Legal Discourse," 29), but I do not believe that it should be applied sweepingly to all of the casuistic laws. Some indeed should be characterized as no more than narrative texts, yet most merit consideration as stories in every respect.

16. I would like here to quote the personal remarks that Yohanan Muffs included in the introduction to his book about law and religion in ancient Israel, which I found particularly moving and which greatly influenced my own work: "I came to the study of law by a rather paradoxical road. I passionately disliked the prospective element in what was usually called law—the coercive, the anti-life, the limiting. Then suddenly, I realized that ancient legal documents were telling a story" (Yochanan Muffs, *Love and Joy: Law, Language and Religion in Ancient Israel* [New York: Jewish Theological Seminary of America, 1992], 1).

the text through reading and characterizes the communication process that is established between the lawgiver and his addressees[17]

Such a reading accords aesthetic value and profundity to the legal material, which may appear dry and technical on the surface. It engages the reader in the process of reading, creating involvement and identification and eliciting an emotional response—all this in respect to a text that was not authored for artistic purposes, that was not designed to entertain or to provide intellectual stimulation, but whose main goal (and some might say, only goal) is to legislate rights and duties, to determine what is allowed and what is prohibited, and to provide solutions on which human life, property, and welfare depend.

What Are the Premises and Interpretive Principles Guiding the Present Narrative Reading of the Laws of the Pentateuch?

When above I contrasted laws that invite a narrative reading with other laws to which such a reading would be inapplicable, I used the terms "casuistic" and "apodictic." However, determining which laws may be processed in the "narrative laboratory" and which may not does not follow from a formal-linguistic criterion, which is the key to distinguishing between these two formulaic patterns, but rather from a substantive criterion—the law's narrativity. In other words, I examine whether one can discern a narrative pattern in the law, minimal as it may be.[18] Is it possible to identify narrative elements within it? Does it use narrative techniques? As a result, in the corpus of laws to which I apply the narrative reading I also include laws that are not formulated along the classic casuistic pattern, as long as they present *cases* that allow them to be treated as miniature stories. Such, for example, is the Deuteronomic law, "If

---

17. A narrative reading of law deals with the same issues that are of concern in a reading of a narrative-literary text: (a) story—the narrated events; (b) text—the verbal representation of the "story"; (c) discourse—the process of producing the "text," a process of communication, in the course of which the "story" is conveyed as a message from sender to receiver. See Shlomith Rimmon-Kenan, *Narrative Fiction: Contemporary Poetics* (New Accents; London: Methuen, 1983), 1–5. Parenthetically, I will note that this sort of study responds to the challenge posed by Adele Berlin, in her comments about the possibility of using the tools of literary theory in application to the law: "Besides, modern literary theory has given us better tools to analyze narrative, whereas it is only beginning to give us tools to analyze law" (Adele Berlin, "Numinous Nomos: On the Relationship between Narrative and Law," in *"A Wise and Discerning Mind," Essays in Honor of Burke O. Long* [ed. S. M. Olyan and R. C. Culley; Brown Judaic Studies 324; Providence: Brown Judaic Studies, 2000], 26).

18. On a minimal narrative unit, a "minimal story," see Gerald Prince, *A Grammar of Stories: An Introduction* (De proprietatibus litterarum, Series maior 13; The Hague: Mouton, 1973), 31.

your brother, a Hebrew man, or a Hebrew woman, is sold to you, he shall serve you six years, and in the seventh year you shall let him go free from you" (Deut 15:12). Like a casuistic law, it describes the unfolding of an event and defines the norms that are derived from it, but unlike such laws it is not formulated in the third person; rather it addresses the addressee directly in second person.[19] Such too is the Priestly law, "any man of the people of Israel, or of the strangers that sojourn in Israel, who gives any of his children to *Molech* shall be put to death; the people of the land shall stone him with stones" (Lev 20:2). Like the casuistic laws, it begins with a (prohibited) action and ends with its outcome (punishment), but unlike those laws it does not use the prefatory conjunction כי or ואם but rather a relative clause introduced by אשר. Following the guidelines for a narrative reading, these laws too will be considered "casuistic"—or, in other words, "case laws."[20]

A final clarification: casuistic laws are composed of two parts that are sequentially and causally linked: (1) the first part describes an event or a state of affairs that presents some sort of problem, and (2) the second part presents or establishes its resolution.[21] The first descriptive part details the circumstances of the case and thus forms an independent narrative unit; it includes all the elements that constitute such a unit.[22] On the other hand, the second normative and prescriptive part is usually shorter and in any case does not form a separate and independent narrative unit. At the same time, because it also belongs to the narrative framework of the law (it is part of the narrative content without which the law would be incomplete), the narrative reading treats both parts together and together they form a common field for the identification of narrative devices. Having clarified the above two points, I shall

---

19. Such laws, which appear mostly in the Deuteronomic code, have been designated by Harry Gilmer as *"If-You* laws." See Harry W. Gilmer, *The If-You Form in Israelite Law* (SBLDS 15; Missoula, Mont.: Scholars Press, 1975).

20. The term "casuistic law" is used hereafter to describe any narrative law, both the classic form and mixed forms, as explained above. At the same time, it is important to note that not every casuistic law supports a narrative reading. When the law is laconic and lacks detail, so that its narrative content is too thin, such as "Whoever strikes his father or his mother shall be put to death" (Exod 21:15), it cannot serve as an object of narrative analysis. This law, as well as other laws using the participle form in the Book of the Covenant, which according to Alt's criteria are apodictic by virtue of their brief and decisive form, are in fact casuistic laws, since they do not enjoin or prohibit a future action but rather present an action or event and its legal outcome in the pattern of a narrative.

21. Since most of the casuistic laws are constructed as conditional sentences, they are composed of two parts: the *protasis* (the "if" part), which begins the conditional clause, and the *apodosis* (the "then" part), which ends it.

22. On narrative form and definition of a narrative unit, see Rimmon-Kenan, *Narrative Fiction*, 6–28.

now present four guidelines that define the framework for my inquiry into the laws of the Pentateuch:

1. My inquiry follows thematic clusters, each of which deals with a different aspect of narrativity. This thematic classification and subsequent organization of the study corpus allow us systematically to become cognizant of the broad diversity of narrative features that the laws display. These are sent into the "narrative laboratory," where they undergo a careful analysis that discloses their narrative characteristics. Conducting the narrative reading in this fashion reveals the legitimacy of the method and clarifies its contribution to an understanding of the laws. It goes without saying that when one is introducing a completely new interpretive approach, it is crucial to demonstrate that the method is both appropriate and advantageous.

2. My inquiry follows the classical division of the laws of the Pentateuch into codes or law collections: the laws of the Book of the Covenant (Exod 20:19–23:19) and the "small" Book of the Covenant (Exod 34:11–26); the Deuteronomic Code (Deuteronomy 12–26); and the Priestly laws (in Leviticus and Numbers). Presentation of the laws separately according to their contextual location, allows us to examine the stylistic and poetic differences that exist among the casuistic laws in each of the law collections. At the same time, the reading of the laws themselves is carried out synchronically, examining them as they appear in the text. I will therefore not discuss questions relating to the historical composition of the codes or the different textual strata that can be discerned in some of the laws, questions that such a separate investigation might indeed provoke.[23]

3. My present discussion does not pretend to examine all of the questions or topics raised by the laws (only occasionally does the discussion digress into other general or particular issues, when the textual inquiry requires it). Consequently, my treatment of the many commentaries and studies I consulted is quite selective. References to commentators and scholars of biblical law generally are limited to those who can contribute to the specific reading presented here, whether they support the proposed interpretation or not. I therefore do not refer to matters that do not advance our understanding of the narrative aspects of the laws, even if such matters could potentially enrich the discussion.

The present inquiry has one additional deficiency that deserves to be addressed in earnest, if somewhat apologetically. With the exception of one or two cases, I do not routinely consult the rabbinic literature of the mishnaic and talmudic periods. A study of biblical law ideally ought to turn to the Mish-

---

23. Similarly see Dale Patrick's comments, in the introduction to an edited volume on the pentateuchal laws: "Although all of us assume the diachronic analysis of the legal texts, the studies are generally synchronic in character" (Dale Patrick, ed., *Thinking Biblical Law* [*Semeia* 45; Atlanta: Scholars Press, 1989], 3).

nah and Talmud as the primary commentaries on the biblical legal corpus; a narrative reading of biblical law should to be expected to do so even more emphatically, since one of the central features of rabbinic literature is the way it combines the normative and narrative principles of *halakha* and *aggadah*.[24] Despite these justified expectations, I decided not to have recourse to the rabbinic literature for two reasons. Since the present study deals with all of the casuistic laws of the Torah it would be beyond its scope to encompass the vast treasure of commentary documented in the Mishnah and Talmud. A reading of the full breadth of the laws demands that one be practical in one's selection. Although the rabbis of the Mishnah and Talmud created a literary model that combines law and narrative, it constitutes a separate and independent literary stratum, constructed on and added to the foundational edifice of the Torah's laws. It is doubtful whether this stratum can contribute to a study that seeks to illuminate diverse aspects of narrativity as they are reflected in the legal texts themselves. For this reason, I have chosen to forgo the riches to be found in rabbinic literature.

4. The narrative reading of the laws of the Pentateuch includes comparative investigation into the other ancient Near Eastern law collections. The purpose of these comparisons, however, is not to illuminate the legal-normative aspects of the law (even when parallels can be found within the "foreign" laws), but rather to appreciate the nature and degree of the pentateuchal laws' narrativity when compared with Sumerian, Babylonian, Assyrian, and Hittite laws. A final comment: the investigation of literary devices will also lead us at times to inquire into the apodictic laws. This will permit us to discover additional artistic and rhetorical devices that the authors had at their disposal.

What Is Innovative about the Narrative Reading Compared to Former Research on the Laws of the Pentateuch, and What Is Its Chief Contribution?

One of the most researched areas of biblical law is the question of the interrelationship between the law and the surrounding narrative in which it is embedded. This topic has been examined from three main angles: the genre mixing of law and narrative in the Pentateuch;[25] the reflection of familiar narrative

---

24. The rabbinic attitude concerning the importance of narrative to interpreting and understanding the law is reflected in the famous story of the two Tannaitic scholars who came to a place where one expounded *aggadah*, while the other taught *halakha*. All of the local people came to hear the first teacher and ignored the second one (*b. Sotah* 40a).

25. See, e.g., Edward L. Greenstein, "Biblical Law," in *Back to the Sources: Reading the Classic Jewish Texts* (ed. Barry W. Holtz; New York: Summit Books, 1984), 83–103; Nasuti, "Narrative Hermeneutics of Biblical Law"; James W. Watts, *Reading Law: The Rhetorical*

or historical traditions in the laws;[26] and the appearance of legal elements in biblical prose and in other literary genres.[27] The narrative reading of the laws adds an additional dimension to this broad topic.

Methodologically, the proposed approach follows in the wake of other literary readings of the law collections, such as the detailed and meticulous "close readings" that examined the literary structure of the collections, the language of the laws, and their stylization.[28] I refer chiefly to the synchronic investigations of the Book of the Covenant and parts of the Priestly Code, which deviate from the standard classical methods of biblical criticism and elaborate an interpretive approach inspired by the literary character of the texts.[29] The interpretive approach underlying the present narrative reading is akin in spirit to some of the approaches embodied in these studies.

Shaping of the Pentateuch (Biblical Seminar 59; Sheffield: Sheffield Academic Press, 1999); Adele Berlin, "Numinous Nomos," 25–31; Simeon Chavel, "Law and Narrative in Four Oracular Novellae in the Pentateuch" (in Hebrew; diss., Hebrew University, Jerusalem, 2006).

26. Calum Carmichael, one of the most original scholars of biblical law, is one of the only scholars to address this issue. Although in quite a few cases Carmichael's arguments about the reflection of a specific narrative tradition in a certain law are unconvincing, this does not, in my opinion, detract from the legitimacy or correctness of the method in general. I note here only a few of his studies: Calum Carmichael, *Law and Narrative in the Bible: The Evidence of the Deuteronomic Laws and the Decalogue* (Ithaca, N.Y.: Cornell University Press, 1985); *The Spirit of Biblical Law* (The Spirit of the Laws; Athens: University of Georgia Press, 1996); *Illuminating Leviticus: A Study of Its Laws and Institutions in the Light of Biblical Narratives* (Baltimore: Johns Hopkins University Press, 2006).

27. See, e.g., Uriel Simon, "The Poor Man's Ewe-Lamb: An Example of a Juridical Parable," *Biblica* 48 (1967): 207–42; David Daube, *Studies in Biblical Law* (2nd ed.; New York: Ktav, 1969), 1–73; Charles Mabee, "Jacob and Laban: The Structure of Judicial Proceedings (Genesis 31, 25–42)," *VT* 30 (1980): 192–207; Assnat Bartor, "The 'Juridical Dialogue': A Literary-Judicial Pattern," *VT* 53 (2003): 445–64; Pamela Barmash, "The Narrative Quandary: Cases of Law in Literature," *VT* 54 (2004): 1–16.

28. Meir Weiss was the first to apply close reading ("the method of total interpretation," in his terms) to biblical narrative. See Meir Weiss, *The Bible from Within: The Method of Total Interpretation* (in Hebrew; Jerusalem: Mosad Bialik, 1962; an English version was published also by Magnes Press in 1984). See, in addition, Robert Alter, *The Art of Biblical Narrative* (New York: Basic Books, 1981); Meir Sternberg, *The Poetics of Biblical Narrative: Ideological Literature and the Drama of Reading* (Indiana Literary Biblical Series; Bloomington: Indiana University Press, 1985); Shimeon Bar-Efrat, *Narrative Art in the Bible* (trans. D. Shefer-Vanson in conjuction with the author; Sheffield: Almond, 1989).

29. Joe Sprinkle, *"The Book of the Covenant": A Literary Approach* (JSOTSup 174; Sheffield: JSOT Press, 1994); Baruch Schwartz, *The Holiness Legislation: Studies in the Priestly Code* (in Hebrew; Jerusalem: Magnes, 1999). In addition, concerning the literary function of biblical legal texts, see Hanna Liss, "Kanon und Fiktion: Zur literarischen Funktion Biblischer Rechtstexte," *Biblische Notizen* 121 (2004): 7–38.

Narrative reading has another affiliation. In recent years, as part of a new and welcome trend in biblical studies, some scholars have explored new avenues of research that represent a departure from the classical methods of biblical studies, and they have applied new interpretive methods to their object of inquiry. I will mention here two of the most important scholars of biblical law—Bernard S. Jackson and James W. Watts—who study the rhetoric and semiotics of biblical law.[30] Jackson's and Watts's studies examine the formal features of the laws, their rhetorical style, the way in which they are understood by readers, and the mode of their transmission to their audience. Among other things, Watts looks at the inherent connection between the tradition of the public reading aloud of the Torah's laws and the variety of their rhetorical devices. Jackson develops a "semio-narrative" method for reading the laws based on the semiotic theories of A. J. Greimas. Like the narrative readings, these studies, too, deal with the *how* and not with the *what*; they do not treat the legal-normative aspects of the law but deal, rather, with the essential role of the law as a means of constructing reality, and as a means of communication.

Narrative reading brings innovative contributions to each of the three methodological frameworks I have described; namely, close reading, semiotic, and rhetorical. It reveals an important and meaningful aspect of the relationship between law and narrative, one that has not received any serious attention until now. A few scholars have in fact pointed out the literary features of the laws. They have also thoroughly explored the connections between the laws and the surrounding stories and considered their location within the broader literary units in which they were embedded. But none has treated the laws themselves as an object of literary study as such.[31] The literary, rhetorical, and semiotic readings were developed from the outset to serve other ends within the framework of the historical-critical study of the law collections.[32] In

---

30. Bernard S. Jackson, "The Ceremonial and the Judicial: Biblical Law as Sign and Symbol," *JSOT* 30 (1984): 25–50; idem, *Studies in the Semiotics of Biblical Law* (JSOTSup 314; Sheffield: Sheffield Academic Press, 2000); idem, "Literal Meaning: Semantics and Narrative in Biblical Law and Modern Jurisprudence," *International Journal for the Semiotics of Law/Revue International de Sémiotique Juridique* 13 (2000): 433–57; James W. Watts, *Reading Law*; idem, *Ritual and Rhetoric in Leviticus: From Sacrifice to Scripture* (Cambridge: Cambridge University Press, 2007).

31. For the sake of accuracy I must note Chaya Halberstam's article, "The Art of Biblical Law," *Prooftexts* 27 (2007): 345–64, in which she examines the laws concerning the return of a lost object (Deut 22:1–3) in the contexts of her discussion of various aspects of the relation between law and narrative in the Bible.

32. Joe Sprinkle sought to demonstrate the internal and external integration of the Book of the Covenant; Baruch Schwartz attempted to use a literary close reading to delineate the unique outlook of the author of the Holiness Code, and the uniqueness of this

contrast, narrative reading is the only method to propose an exclusive legal-literary inquiry into the laws of the Pentateuch.

Many earlier studies have been devoted to the poetics of biblical narrative and poetry.[33] It is now time to deal thoroughly and systematically with the poetics of biblical law. This endeavor will lead to a deeper understanding of the laws and will present some of their other, unfamiliar aspects. These other facets of the law are not hidden from view; however, we who have been accustomed to employing only the principles of legal readings must follow different guidelines in order to discover them. Narrative reading, therefore, is not only a possible or worthwhile method of legal reading; it is an interpretive method that is important if we are to achieve a more complete understanding of the laws of the Pentateuch.

Discovering the poetic world of the authors and all that this notion signifies is the central innovation and chief contribution of narrative reading. But, as I illustrate in the following chapters, it also entails other rewards. Narrative reading is engaging, experiential, and emotionally stimulating; it is therefore also much more pleasurable than the standard method of legal reading. To my mind, these rewards are no less significant than its academic contribution.

OUTLINE OF THE BOOK

This book, which explains and exemplifies the narrative reading of biblical laws, contains five chapters. It begins with a brief chapter entitled "The Laws of the Pentateuch as 'Embedded Stories,'" which serves almost as an extension of the introduction. The first chapter proposes the adoption of a literary model that can illuminate the texture of the relationship between law and narrative in the Pentateuch; it explains the literary and poetic implications of choosing to situate the law collections within a narrative framework. My approach to the lawgivers as narrators is anchored in this model, which treats the laws as "embedded stories" within a "frame story."

The second chapter, "The Lawgiver as Narrator," examines the lawgivers' personalities as reflected in and deducible from each of the law collections.

---

distinct literary unit within the priestly literature; Watts looked at the rhetorical structure of the Pentateuch in general, and Jackson was interested in outlining the different stages of the historical development of the laws—the creation of a "diachronic semiotics."

33. I note here only a few of the many studies addressing this topic (in addition to those listed in n. 28 above): James L. Kugel, *The Idea of Biblical Poetry: Parallelism and Its History* (New Haven: Yale University Press, 1981); Adele Berlin, *Poetics and Interpretation of Biblical Narrative* (Bible and Literature Series 9; Sheffield: Almond, 1983); Robert Alter, *The Art of Biblical Poetry* (New York: Basic Books, 1985); Harold Fisch, *Poetry with a Purpose: Biblical Poetics and Interpretation* (Indiana Studies in Biblical Literature; Bloomington: Indiana University Press, 1988); Herbert C. Brichto, *Toward a Grammar of Biblical Poetics: Tales of the Prophets* (New York: Oxford University Press, 1992).

Recognition of their characteristics and the way in which they perceive their own role is achieved by examining the two criteria by which different types of narrator are commonly classified: the criterion of "participation" and the criterion of "perceptibility." The first is applied to examine whether and to what extent the lawgivers participate in the events described in the laws, and the reasons for this unique phenomenon; the second is applied to examine whether and to what extent the presence of the lawgivers in the laws is perceptible, that is, whether and to what extent they intervene in the "substance of the laws," reveal their attitude toward them, and how it affects the addressees and the readers of the laws.

The third chapter, "Representation of Speech: The Mimetic Illusion," focuses on one of the most typical narrative elements reflected in the laws—the direct representation of speech events. Not only do the lawgivers choose to present verbal events in which the characters participate, but they also quote them verbatim, as if they were the characters' own speech. Giving "voice" to speech creates an illusion of reality (one of the unique qualities of prose). The chapter presents a broad range of speech acts: words spoken by one character to another and words spoken internally (thoughts, desires, decisions), which are also conveyed as direct speech; also included are words displaying a unique form, "combined discourse," whose inclusion in the laws is both surprising and fascinating.

The fourth chapter "Representation of Interior Life: The Lawgiver as Psychologist," presents an unusual phenomenon, both with respect to the other ancient lawgivers and with respect to modern lawgivers—the biblical lawgivers' intensive preoccupation with the mental life of the characters. The many intrusions into the characters' minds and hearts, which serve to expose the background and motives for their behavior and their feelings toward other characters, demonstrate the meaning that the lawgivers attribute to the workings of the inner world, and their insights concerning how it affects external behavior. In many instances the presentation of psychological content is not vital or even useful from a legal perspective, and it belongs purely to the "plot" or narrative level of the laws.

The final chapter, entitled "Point of View," deals with an essential issue without which any textual analysis would be incomplete—the question of perspective. Are events narrated from the perspective of the narrator or from the perspective of one or more of the characters involved in the story? It seems that this question is relevant to the (narrative) laws too, since the lawgivers not infrequently present the substance of the laws not from their "objective" point of view but rather as mediated by the personal, subjective point of view of the character or characters taking part in the events. The chapter examines cases in which the lawgivers abandon the "neutral" presentation of events; it considers their motivations in doing so and the effect this has on the addressees and on the readers of the laws.

1

The Laws of the Pentateuch as "Embedded Stories"

"Once upon a time, in the Land of Canaan, there were a careless pit-owner, a rebellious son, and an inadvertent murderer. . . ." Anyone who is familiar with the laws of the Pentateuch that deal with these characters might wonder why they are presented within the format of a folk tale. And if I call to mind the character of Scheherazade from *One Thousand and One Nights*, my readers might be even more puzzled. But all will become clear when I explain how I propose to treat the law collections in the Pentateuch. Meanwhile, to confer a somewhat more dignified tone on my argument, I shall introduce two theoretical terms: "frame story" and "embedded stories," which should be kept in mind.

Harry Nasuti described the relationship between the laws and the narratives in the Pentateuch in one sentence: "Wherever one finds law in the Bible, one is in the presence of narrative as well."[1] This relationship includes three major elements: (1) The law collections (as well as individual laws) appear in the Pentateuch within a narrative frame; they are delivered at certain points along the time and plot axis of the main story. (2) Several laws mention historical events that occurred in the past, before the laws were given, or events that will occur in the future, following the outline of the main narrative. (3) A large proportion of all of the laws of the Pentateuch are constructed as "miniature stories." In the following chapters I will deal at length with the narrative laws; in this chapter I will briefly and somewhat schematically outline the two other elements.[2]

The choice by the biblical authors to locate the legal texts within a narrative frame rather than presenting them separately and independently (for instance, as the "Book of the Law" or the "Book of *Mishpatim*") stems primar-

---

1. Nasuti, "Narrative Hermeneutics of Biblical Law," 9.
2. I do not intend to cover the entire topic of the relationship between law and narrative in the Pentateuch or to present an exhaustive discussion of its various dimensions.

ily from their theological outlook.³ But this choice also has literary and poetic implications, on which I wish to focus.⁴ The narrative that begins in the book of Genesis and ends in the book of Kings is delivered by an unidentified narrator, a "voice" that enjoys no biographical existence beyond the act of narration.⁵ At certain junctures of the plot in the books of Exodus through Deuteronomy, the narrator describes events in which laws are transmitted: a dramatic and constitutive event such as the revelation at Mount Sinai, or less heroic events such as God's addresses to Moses in the Tent of Meeting. But the laws themselves are delivered not in the voice of the narrator but rather through the mouths of YHWH or Moses. In these instances the narrator entrusts the act of narration to two characters, and after the laws are pronounced, he takes up the narration again to continue to advance the main story line. This phenomenon is not unique to the biblical narrator; many other narrators use it (see, e.g., the narrator of *One Thousand and One Nights*), and in literary theory it is described along the following lines: every narrative text is composed of two levels—the first level, which contains the narration, and the second level, which contains the events and the characters. But when a certain character tells a story of his or her own, then the text contains three levels: the level of narration and two levels of story, one of which contains the narrator's story and the other the story of the character. The latter is called an "embedded story," and the story to which we return after the embedded story is over is the "frame story."⁶ This is how I propose to view the relationship between the laws and the narrative in which they appear. The laws are embedded stories; the mentions of historical events that appear in them from time to time open a window onto the frame

---

3. God made a covenant with the children of Israel and showed them favor, as the Pentateuch narrates. The many kindnesses created a contractual obligation toward God, which the people must fulfill by observing God's laws. This is the basic rationale underlying the narrative structure (see Greenstein, "Biblical Law").

4. It must be remembered that the integration of prose and law is not unique to the Pentateuch, but occurs also in other collections of ancient Near Eastern law: the Laws of Ur-Namma, Lipit-Ishtar, and Hammurabi (see Victor Hurowitz, *Inu Anum ṣirum: Literary Structures in the Non-Juridical Sections of Codex Hammurabi* [Occasional Publications of the Samuel Noah Kramer Fund 15; Philadelphia: University Museum, 1994]). The Pentateuch is innovative, not in its mixing of genres but in its creation of a *sui generis* literary genre, as Greenstein has written: a narrative prose that comprehends and governs the other genres (see Greenstein, "On the Genesis of Biblical Prose Narrative," *Prooftexts* 8 [1988]: 349–50; Berlin, "Numinous Nomos," 28–31).

5. See George W. Savran, "The Character as Narrator in Biblical Narrative," *Prooftexts* 5 (1985): 11.

6. See John Barth, "Tales within Tales within Tales," *Antaeus* 43 (1981): 45–63; Nilli Diengott, *Poetics of Narrative Fiction*, vol. 2 (in Hebrew; Tel Aviv: The Open University Press, 1988), 113–17.

story for the law's addressees and for the readers. The narrator demarcates the laws with opening and closing formulas, and the frame story both precedes and follows the laws.

One may suspect that my explanation of the relationship between the laws and the narrative in the Pentateuch is artificial, or, worse, inaccurate. First, the great majority of the verbal formulas that introduce the law collections or the individual laws are the very same formulas that the narrator employs when presenting direct speech. Thus,

> And the LORD said to Moses and Aaron, "This is the ordinance of the Passover ..." (Exod 12:43);
>
> And the LORD said to Moses, "Thus you shall say to the people of Israel ... Now these are the ordinances which you shall set before them" (Exod 20:22–21:1);
>
> And the LORD said to Moses, "Say to the people of Israel, If any one sins unwittingly ..." (Lev 4:1–2);
>
> Now the LORD said to Moses and to Aaron, "This is the statute of the law which the LORD has commanded ..." (Num 19:1–2)

In view of this resemblance, what I have considered a presentation of a narrative act by YHWH or by Moses, is no more than a direct quotation of their speech.[7] Moreover, from a literary point of view, there is no difference between the "laws" and YHWH's other instructions and commandments, which arise as a response to events during the wanderings in the wilderness, and which therefore belong to the main story. These too are delivered through direct speech. To be honest, neither does the proposed scheme conform to the literary structure of the Priestly passages that describe the "birth" of four laws[8]—laws that arose following judicial decisions, which were given ad hoc in regard to specific cases and received a broader validity, becoming binding norms for future conduct (a kind of biblical common law).[9] Each of these laws represents the climax of the story that describes how it was engendered, and therefore,

---

7. On biblical law as a type of direct speech, see Edward L. Greenstein, "Direct Discourse and Parallelism" (in Hebrew), *Studies in Bible and Biblical Exegesis (Presented to Uriel Simon)* 5 (2000): 34–35.

8. The stories of the blasphemer (Lev 24:10–23); the second Passover (Num 9:1–14); the man who collected firewood on the Sabbath (15:32–36); and the daughters of Zelophehad (27:1–11).

9. One calls to mind another text, not from the Pentateuch, that describes the creation of a law. This is David's order to distribute the loot taken from Amalek equally among all the warriors—those who fought and those who did not fight—an order that became "a statute and an ordinance for Israel to this day" (1 Sam 30:25). Compare God's commandment to Moses regarding the distribution of booty (Num 31:27–30).

like the story itself, it belongs to the main plot line and cannot be considered an "embedded story."

The artificiality of this construct is even more conspicuous in the case of the Deuteronomic laws. These laws are delivered in the context of Moses' speech—a uniform utterance in literary terms that does not contain multiple narrative levels. And when the speaker simultaneously wields the orator's wand and the lawgiver's staff, it is difficult to treat his laws (or any other part of his speech) as "embedded stories."[10] Further, the law collections contain not only the casuistic narrative laws but also many laws that do not have any narrative elements whatsoever. Can these also be considered "embedded stories"?

Nevertheless, in spite of these obstacles, I still propose to employ the model of "frame story and embedded stories," because it is useful for understanding the texture of the relationships between law and narrative in the Pentateuch. Let me justify my thesis. According to the proposed model, the law and the narrative simultaneously maintain two types of relationship: subordination and independence. The narrative level on which the laws are found is subordinated to the narrative level on which the main story is located, but the narrative level of the laws exists at a separate and therefore independent level. The coexistence of both types of relationship, which are seemingly in conflict, underscores the mutuality that governs the relationship—the dependence of each type on the other.

The laws play a central role in advancing the main story, as they constitute a necessary condition for the realization of the divine plan. The laws themselves, even if we ignore their content, motivate the story plot, since the continued survival of the nation is dependent on receiving and observing them.[11] If we glance for a moment at *One Thousand and One Nights*, we find that this work too includes embedded stories that motivate and activate the frame story, because the life of Scheherazade is dependent on her act of narration—delivering stories whose only purpose is to secure the addressee's attention. And just as the reader in *One Thousand and One Nights* monitors the effects that Scheherazade's stories have on the sultan, so also does the reader of the biblical narrative scrutinize how the acceptance and (non-)observance of the laws affect the destiny of the children of Israel.[12] So much for the dependence of the

---

10. On Moses' status as a narrating protagonist see Robert Polzin, *Moses and the Deuteronomist: Deuteronomy, Joshua, Judges* (A Literary Study of the Deuteronomistic History 1; New York: Seabury, 1980), 25ff.; Watts, *Reading Law*, 123.

11. On the different functions fulfilled by embedded stories in relation to the frame story, see Barth, "Tales within Tales," 56–57; Rimmon-Kenan, *Narrative Fiction*, 92–94.

12. The analogy to *One Thousand and One Nights* is, of course, a contrastive analogy: whereas the role of the laws is to ensure the survival of their addressees, Scheherazade's stories are meant to preserve her life as the narrator.

frame story on the embedded laws. On the other hand, the references in many of the laws to "historical" events from the past, and to future events, such as,

> ... for in six days the LORD made heaven and earth ... and rested the seventh day. (Exod 20:11)
>
> When the LORD your God cuts off before you the nations whom you go in to dispossess.... (Deut 12:29),

illustrate the various effects that the main story has on the content of the laws; they indicate that the laws respond to the plot, are motivated by it, and serve its aims.[13]

> ... for you were strangers in the land of Egypt. (Exod 22:21, 23:9)
>
> I am the LORD your God, who have separated you from the peoples. (Lev 20:24)
>
> I made the people of Israel dwell in booths when I brought them out of the land of Egypt. (Lev 23:43)
>
> For I will cast out nations before you, and enlarge your borders. (Exod 34:24)
>
> When you come into the land of Canaan, which I give you for a possession.... (Lev 14:34)
>
> When the LORD your God enlarges your territory.... (Deut 12:20)

Moreover, many allusions to past events create an analogy between the law and parts of the main story, inasmuch as the legal norms are presented as the emulation of God's deeds—*imitatio dei*. Thus, for example, the Sabbath commandment is based on God's resting after six days of creation; the commandment to care for the sojourner and the slave stems from YHWH's treatment of the children of Israel when they were enslaved in Egypt; the commandment to distinguish between the pure and impure is rooted in the distinction between the people of Israel and other nations. Such analogies turn the laws in which they appear into "miniature mirrors" of parts of the main narrative,[14] and thus contribute to strengthening the connection that already exists between them.[15]

---

13. On the influence of the major narratives of the creation and the exodus on biblical law, see Greenstein, "Biblical Law."

14. This technique is known as *mise en abyme* (see Rimmon-Kenan, *Narrative Fiction*, 93). For an in-depth discussion of *mise en abyme* see in Lucien Dällenbach, *The Mirror in the Text* (trans. J. Whiteley with E. Hughes; Chicago: University of Chicago Press, 1989). See in addition David A. Bosworth, *The Story within a Story in Biblical Hebrew Narrative* (CBQ Monograph Series 45; Washington, D.C.: Catholic Biblical Association of America, 2008).

15. Calum Carmichael has shown a great number of analogies between the laws and narrative passages—some explicit, but mainly implicit. The various (not always convincing) examples appear in Carmichael, *Law and Narrative in the Bible*; *The Spirit of Biblical Law*;

We are left with one final aspect to discuss. This is the effect of the "frame story and embedded stories" model on one's approach to reading the text as a whole. As mentioned above, the narrator of the frame story is anonymous, and so too are the addressees. On the other hand, the narrative communication regarding the laws takes place among familiar characters—YHWH, Moses, and the children of Israel, the protagonists of the main story. In light of the mutual dependence between the narrative and the laws, determining the identity of the laws' addressees affects the attitude of the reader toward the events and the characters in the main story. Thus the embedded laws serve as an "interpretive guide" to the frame story.[16]

Must an understanding of the relationship between the laws and narratives of the Pentateuch be achieved only by means of the model discussed above? Not necessarily. It is possible to appreciate the interrelationships between them without it. But this model is convenient and effective, because it helps us bear in mind simultaneously the relationships of subordination and dependence between the laws and the narrative, as well as their separateness and independence. And it also has another function, which is important at present only to me and my readers. It instills in our awareness the approach that will accompany us throughout this book—the treatment of the lawgivers (also) as storytellers.

In the next chapter we will become acquainted with their narrating personalities. Not the characters of YHWH and of Moses as they are depicted in the main story, based on the information provided by the narrator, but the character of the lawgivers that emerges from the laws themselves, their content and manner of presentation, and from the lawgivers' engagement with and attitude toward their message—all this will give us a notion of their narrating personality.[17]

---

and *Illuminating Leviticus*. According to the author, the arrangement of the laws within the collections is influenced also by their order of appearance in the narrative passage. I note that the order of the laws within the law collections (including transitions from apodictic to casuistic laws, and vice versa) can be treated also as a narrative continuum (or as several narrative continuums), chiefly because of the associative principle of arrangement employed by redactors. In the present study, I do not discuss this aspect of the law collections.

16. See Nasuti, "Narrative Hermeneutics of Biblical Law," 19.

17. On the characterization of the biblical lawgiver by means of his laws, see Watts, *Reading Law*, 92–93.

2

The Lawgiver as Narrator

The attempt to characterize the legislating-narrating personality of the biblical lawgivers is a fine tightrope walk that requires striking a balance between the concrete and the abstract. While it sometimes seems appropriate to take into account the self-proclaimed identity of the speaker, that is, to characterize the figures of YHWH and Moses as lawgivers, it is more often the case that the biographical identity of the speakers is of little material significance. In such cases I characterize the personality of the "lawgiver-narrator" as an abstraction of those two concrete figures. Whether the speaker's personal identity is relevant or not depends first and foremost on *his* standpoint—when he exposes his identity one must take it into consideration, otherwise one may ignore it.

When the lawgiver takes a vehement stance against the persecution of widows and orphans and says,

> and my wrath will burn, and I will kill you with the sword, and your wives shall become widows and your children fatherless (Exod 22:24)

we will consider the significance of the fact that it is YHWH who speaks. And when he states,

> The LORD your God will raise up for you a prophet like me from among you, from your brethren—him you shall heed (Deut 18:15)

we will take account of Moses' personal engagement. But when the lawgiver chooses the meaningful word "misfortune" (אסון), to speak of the fatal injury of a pregnant woman (Exod 21:22–23), or when he glosses an odd foreign term in the law,

> You shall not wear a mingled stuff [שעטנז] wool and linen together (Deut 22:11)

or presents a summary statement:

> This is the law pertaining to beast and bird and every living creature that moves through the waters and every creature that swarms upon the earth (Lev 11:46),

then we will not focus on the personal identity of YHWH or Moses, but will rather apply ourselves to understanding the attributes of "the lawgiver of the Book of the Covenant" (Exod 20:19–23:19), "the Deuteronomic lawgiver," or "the Priestly lawgiver." Each of these characters, as evidenced in the individual corpus of laws, displays a unique personality as lawgiver-narrator.[1]

The brief examples just presented encompass the two criteria I employ to characterize the lawgivers. The first two examples demonstrate the lawgivers' *participation* in the events: the lawgiver YHWH responds emotionally ("and my wrath will burn"), punishes the transgressor severely, and declares that the sanction will be carried out personally ("I will kill you with the sword"). The lawgiver Moses, who is also the first prophet, self-referentially alludes to future prophets who will follow his way ("a prophet like me"). He participates in the law that describes how the institution of prophecy came into being.

The first criterion by means of which I consider the legislating-narrating personality of lawgivers is their very presence in the events described in the laws, the extent of their participation, and its nature and causes.[2] This feature is unknown in other ancient Near Eastern law collections. The other three examples present lawgivers' *interventions* in the legal material. A lawgiver who employs emotionally charged language to describe an event is not merely presenting facts but is taking a position. By doing so, he exposes his persona. He also exposes his own presence when he interprets or clarifies a "difficult" word or concludes the law with a summary statement that contributes nothing substantial to its contents. The *perceptibility* of the lawgiver, that is, the abundance or the paucity of signs indicating his engagement or intervention, the type of signs and their meanings—is the second criterion that will serve us in investigating the lawgiver's personality.[3] As we shall see, both the lawgivers' participation and their perceptibility are important factors that shape the law's addressees' (and our) understanding of, and attitudes toward, the laws' contents.

---

1. There is a mutual relationship between the substance of the laws and the character who renders them: the lawgiver influences the laws and their mode of presentation, and they reciprocally reflect his legislative personality. This is the reason that we must occupy ourselves with three characters and not two (even though one character represents two of the law collections). The different natures of the law collections require us to make a distinction between three legislative personalities.

2. On "participation" as a criterion for characterizing different types of narrators, see Genette, *Narrative Discourse*, 244–45.

3. For the textual markers that attest to the narrator's different degrees of perceptibility, see Chatman, *Story and Discourse*, 219–52; Rimmon-Kenan, *Narrative Fiction*, 96–100.

Participation

The delivery of the laws is an event involving an encounter between the lawgiver and the laws' addressees. He speaks (either himself, or through a messenger) and they listen. Sometimes a different kind of encounter transpires. The two parties meet on another plane of existence, within the framework of the events described in the laws; the lawgiver and the addressees (and sometimes only the addressees) take part in the events along with the other characters. We will familiarize ourselves with each lawgiver's mode of participation in the laws and see how he invites the participation of his addressees. We will also attempt to understand the significance of this participation. However, we will not always be able to determine why we find it in certain laws and not in others. Unfortunately, I have not been able to discern any regularity that governs the phenomenon. As this is surely not the only unresolved riddle in the law corpus, this issue will be set aside for the time being.

The Book of the Covenant

The lawgiver of the Book of the Covenant (Exod 20:19–23:19) participates only marginally in the events recounted in the laws. Nor does he invite the addressees to participate to a very great extent. Neither lawgiver nor addressee takes part in the stories describing serious bodily injuries (21:18–21); they are also left out of the narrative scenes depicting hazards such as the goring ox, an open pit (21:28–36), or damage to agricultural crops (22:5–6). The lawgiver's position as exterior to the events is apparent in the way he refers to YHWH—namely, to himself—in the third person. This mode of reference is employed, for instance, in the laws of safekeeping and of borrowing by defining the oath of the safekeeper (which exonerates him from responsibility for the loss of the animal in his charge) as *"an oath by the LORD"* (22:11) and not *"my oath,"* as one might have expected.[4]

On six occasions, however, the lawgiver deviates from this practice and involves himself or his addressee in the law's events. These cases can be easily identified: when the lawgiver participates he refers to himself in the first person, and when he draws the addressee into participation, he addresses him directly, in the second person. Thus, for example, the lawgiver locates the addressee on the same plane of reality with the Hebrew slave by saying, "When *you buy a Hebrew slave* . . ." (21:2). This coexistence is temporary, however, for the addressee is just as quickly omitted from the picture and replaced by "the

---

4. Cf. the law of the altar Exod 20:23–26 and other ritual instructions that are formulated as apodictic laws (e.g., 22:29–31; 23:14–15, 18).

master" ("If his master gives him a wife . . ." [v. 4]).[5] In the law concerning injury to a pregnant woman (21:22–25) too, the addressee is integrated into the action (rather artificially, it must be admitted), for the sanction established in the secondary law is addressed to him: "then *you shall give* life for life, eye for eye" (21:23–25). But who is the addressee? Is it the man who harmed the woman and her fetus, that is, the man who is subject to punishment (as in the main law "the one who hurt her shall be fined" [v. 22b])?[6] Or is the addressee the judge who is instructed to punish the injurer according to the principle of *talion*, namely, the institution authorized to execute the punishment?[7] Or is it the entire Israelite congregation, that is, a collective addressee whose identity shifts depending on the topic treated by the law?[8] Opinions differ on this matter. More importantly, though, it is difficult to discern why the lawgiver suddenly addresses him and turns him into an active participant during the unfolding of events.[9]

---

5. The standard view is that the second person opening is a reworking of an original third person opening (as typical of the casuistic laws). See Alfred Jepsen, *Untersuchungen zum Bundesbuch* [Beiträge zum Wissenschaft vom Alten und Neuen Testament 3.5; Stuttgart: Kohlhammer, 1927], 56; Alt, "Origins," 93–94; Sara Japhet, "The Relationship between the Legal Corpora in the Pentateuch in Light of Manumission Laws," *Scripta Hierosolymitana* 31 [1986]: 70–74). According to Shalom M. Paul, the opening of the law is in fact original (see *Studies in the Book of the Covenant in the Light of Cuneiform and Biblical Law* [SVT 18; Leiden: Brill, 1970], 46 n. 7). It seems to me that he is correct, although not necessarily for the reasons he states. The notion that the direct address is not original is based on its "linguistic strangeness"—within the law itself, within its close textual environment, and within all the other casuistic laws in the Book of the Covenant. Indisputably, the "pure" casuistic model is quantitatively dominant, yet the examination of the laws in their totality shows that they contain stylistic diversity and different linguistic formulations so that it would be incorrect to treat one type of formulation or another as "strange." As far as I am concerned, the alternation of grammatical person in itself cannot be used as proof of textual stratification. More importantly, even if we suppose that an original opening was reworked, this would not answer the question of why the lawgiver chose to open the law with a direct address to the addressee. In my opinion, previous answers given to this question are unsatisfactory (see, e.g., Anthony Phillips, "The Laws of Slavery: Exodus 21:2–11," *JSOT* 30 [1984]: 52; Benno Jacob, *The Second Book of the Bible: Exodus* [trans. W. Jacob; Hoboken, N.J.: Ktav, 1992], 612).

6. See, e.g., Cornelis Houtman, *Exodus*, vol. 3 (Historical Commentary on the Old Testament; Leuven: Peeters, 2000), 170.

7. See, e.g., Umberto Cassuto, *A Commentary on the Book of Exodus* (trans. I. Abrahams; Jerusalem: Magnes Press, 1967), 275; Jacob, *Exodus*, 659.

8. See Sprinkle, *Book of the Covenant*, 95.

9. It is broadly agreed that vv. 23b-25 (or at least vv. 24–25) are not original but were appended to the law at a later stage (the way the talionic formulas were added to the case of the blasphemer [Lev 24:19–20] and the law of the false accuser [Deut 19:19–21]). See, e.g., Daube, *Studies in Biblical Law*, 106; Dale Patrick, *Old Testament Law* (Atlanta: John Knox,

The addressee is made a full participant in the laws that require relieving the distress of animals:

> ⁴If *you* meet *your* enemy's ox or his ass going astray, *you* shall bring it back to him. ⁵If *you* see the ass of one who hates *you* lying under its burden, *you* shall refrain from leaving him with it, *you* shall help him to lift it up. (23:4–5)

Unlike the previous two cases, here it is easy to explain why the lawgiver makes the addressee the law's protagonist. Both laws deal with ethical norms (not with "pure" legal norms) and therefore invite a human, emotional tone, which is achieved by using the direct address; they address the heart, the protagonist's conscience.¹⁰ But is this explanation really enough? Do not other casuistic laws in the Book of the Covenant (that are concerned with interpersonal relationships) also describe dramatic events that engage human emotions and conscience? Do the vicissitudes in the life of a young-woman-turned-slave not call for a direct address to her father or her master, inviting them to participate in the events? Furthermore, in some laws the lawgiver invites the addressee (and himself) to participate in events that do not concern ethics. On the contrary, they deal with the core of criminal law—the felony of homicide. I therefore turn to examine the "experiencing self" of the lawgiver and the addressee, as reflected in the law of homicide.¹¹

> ¹²Whoever strikes a man so that he dies shall be put to death. ¹³But if he did not lie in wait for him, but God let him fall into his hand, then I will appoint for you a place to which he may flee. ¹⁴But if a man willfully attacks another to kill him treacherously, you shall take him from my altar, that he may die. (21:12–14)

1985), 76; Nahum Sarna, *Exodus-Shemot: The Traditional Hebrew Text with the New JPS Translation* (JPS Torah Commentary; Philadelphia: Jewish Publication Society, 1991), 126; Bernard Jackson, *Wisdom-Laws: A Study of the Mishpatim of Exodus 21:1–22:16* (Oxford: Oxford University Press, 2006), 207–8. This view is convincing in and of itself (especially because of the incongruity between the talionic formula and the circumstances described), but it does not provide an answer to the question of the use of the second person. I find the explanations offered hitherto to justify the sudden second person address unconvincing (see a thorough discussion in Jackson, *Wisdom-Laws*, 227–33).

10. See Patrick, *Old Testament Law*, 89. Harry Gilmer has grouped the laws of providing help to animals in a category of "humanitarian laws." All (casuistic and apodictic laws in the three law collections) contain the direct address, which he has dubbed "the humanitarian if-you formulation" (Gilmer, *If-You Form*, 46–56).

11. The "experiencing self" is a concept that points to the double identity of narrator and addressee when they are both part of the narrative. Both the "narrating self" and the "listening self" are joined by the "self" who experiences the narrated events (see Diengott, *Poetics of Narrative Fiction*, 120–21, 138–40).

This legal unit is composed of separate laws that were combined together.[12] It opens with a law that employs the grammatical participle form, reflecting a legal outlook that makes no distinction among different degrees of homicide and which disregards the circumstances leading to the death. Neither the lawgiver nor the addressee participates in this law. It then proceeds with two casuistic laws that distinguish between intentional killing and inadvertent killing, in which both lawgiver and addressee do participate.

The law as a whole describes three episodes. Three characters participate in the first: the assailant; the man who dies as a result of the latter's blows;[13] and an additional, unidentified character whose role is to execute the death sentence.[14] The second episode involves four characters: the man who "did not lie in wait"; God; the lawgiver who is exposed through the phrase "*I* will appoint";[15] and the addressee, whose presence is indicated in the direct address "for *you*." The deceased receives no mention, and if not for the first episode it would not be apparent that the law deals with homicide; after all, the protagonist did not perform any action ("he *did not* lie in wait"), and we are not told what happened as a result of the divine intervention. The third episode, too, involves four characters: the slayer; the slain; the lawgiver, who reveals himself

---

12. According to the standard view, v. 12 belongs to an ancient law collection (to which the laws in 21:15–17 and 22:18–19 also belong), and vv. 13–14 were added to it later (see, e.g., Patrick, *Old Testament Laws*, 73). On the law's evolution into its current form, see Gershon Brin, *Studies in Biblical Law: From the Hebrew Bible to the Dead Sea Scrolls* (trans. Jonathan Chipman; JSOTSup 176; Sheffield: Sheffield Academic Press, 1994), 32–33. For a different approach arguing that vv. 13–14 are dependent on the Deuteronomic law of homicide, see Yair Zakovitch, "The Book of the Covenant Interprets the Book of the Covenant: The 'Boomerang Phenomenon,'" (in Hebrew), in *Texts, Temples, and Traditions: A Tribute to Menahem Haran* (ed. Michael V. Fox et al.; Winona Lake, Ind.: Eisenbrauns, 1996), 62; Moshe Anbar, "L'influence Deutéronomique sur le Code de L'Alliance; le cas d'Exodus 21:12–17," *Zeitschrift für Altorientalische und Biblische Rechtsgeschichte* 5 (1999): 165–66.

13. The phrase "to strike a man so that he dies" refers not only to death caused by a blow but to different incidents in which a death is caused (see Paul, *Book of the Covenant*, 61). Compare LH 207, *šumma ina maḫāṣišu imtūt* ("If he should die from his beating"), and HL 3–4, *tāku LÚ . . . walaḫzi kuiški naš aki* ("[If] anyone strikes a free [man] or woman so that he dies"). All Akkadian transliterations of the ancient Near Eastern laws and their translation into English are taken (with minor modifications) from Roth, *Law Collections*; the transliteration of the Hittite laws and their translation are taken (with minor modifications) from Harry A. Hoffner Jr., *The Laws of the Hittites: A Critical Edition* (Documenta et monumenta Orientis antiqui 23; Leiden: Brill, 1997).

14. The expression מות יומת does not make explicit who is to execute the murderer—whether a judicial authority, some other governing body, a local authority, or perhaps the blood avenger. See Sprinkle, *Book of the Covenant*, 84; Jackson, *Wisdom-Laws*, 131–32.

15. The Peshitta reflects a version in which the lawgiver does not participate in the events, "*you* will appoint." The Masoretic Text should be preferred.

by mentioning "*my* altar"; and the addressee, who is drawn in as a participant via the command "*you* shall take him."

Unlike v. 12, which formulates a categorical and unequivocal principle, vv. 13–14 describe a situation in which social interests come into conflict and a decision is required to determine whose interest will win out. The understanding that under certain circumstances taking the life of the slayer cannot be justified conflicts with the familial duty/right to avenge the blood of the slain;[16] at the same time, the duty to execute the killer conflicts with the requirement to preserve the sanctity of the altar and not to trespass on its precincts. It is in such cases that the lawgiver sees fit to participate. Since he himself is the source of the binding norms, only he, by means of his own participation, can indicate a solution that will decide between the conflicting values. In order to implement the solution, he invites the addressee to participate, first passively and then actively.

According to the lawgiver, it would seem (or so he would have it appear) that, if not for his active participation, the first case (v. 13) would remain unresolved. For he not only describes, decides, or ordains the solution; he actually creates it, establishes it himself.[17] What is the precise nature, in practical terms, of this solution? It is hard to tell, because the lawgiver employs the vague term "place," which makes it hard to determine where this protective precinct might be located. It could refer to a cult site (e.g., Gen 12:6; 13:3; Deut 12:5; Isa 26:12), or perhaps to a settlement, a city, or a city of refuge (as is explicitly stated in the corresponding laws, Num 34:9–34; Deut 4:41–43; 19:1–13]).[18] Unlike the

---

16. The law does not treat the blood avenger explicitly (as in the corresponding laws [Deut 19:1–3; Num 35:9–34]), but his presence is inferred from the need to flee (from him). All three laws attest to a desire to constrain the custom of blood vengeance as part of the process of subordinating tribal-familial law to public law. The first constraint is reflected in the creation of a protective precinct, which is meant to prevent the possibility of carrying out the custom. A second constraint is reflected in the apportioning of roles to the blood avenger, so that he acts as a representative of a judicial body, rather than as a representative of a domestic tribal unit: the executioner (Deut 19:12; Num 35:19, 21) and the prosecutor (v. 24).

17. לשׂים means to establish (see *BDB*, s.v. שׂום, 963b). Is it possible to say that the lawgiver takes part not only in the provision of the solution but also in creating the problem, for it is he, God, who is responsible for the lethal action? The answer is no. The lawgiver describes a divine intervention but does not attribute it to himself.

18. Some scholars support the former interpretation (see, e.g., S. R. Driver, *The Book of Exodus: In the Revised Version* [1911; repr., Cambridge: Cambridge University Press, 1953], 215–16; Paul, *Book of the Covenant*, 62–63; Sarna, *Exodus*, 121–22), and others support the latter (see, e.g., Moshe Greenberg, "The Biblical Concept of Asylum," *JBL* 78 [1959]: 125–32; Martin Noth, *Exodus: A Commentary* [trans. J. S. Bowden; OTL; London: SCM, 1962], 180; Sprinkle, *Book of the Covenant*, 83–84); Pamela Barmash, *Homicide in the Biblical World* (Cambridge/New York: Cambridge University Press, 2005), 78.

lawgiver, who is active, the addressee participates passively. He does not take action himself, nor is he enjoined to act, but he is only told that the solution is formulated for his sake—that it serves the general interest.[19]

In the second case (v. 14), the roles are reversed. The active participant becomes passive and the passive participant is given an actual role. The lawgiver seemingly does not participate at all in the events that follow the murder, for the words "*my altar*" are merely a place designation. But this phrasing (rather than the neutral phrase "the altar") conveys something else—the presence of the "Divine self" in the event. This presence is undoubtedly important, because it motivates the series of events: the slayer flees[20] to the altar to enjoy the immunity and protection provided to those who take shelter in God. But this is not the chief reason why the lawgiver stresses his presence. The "Divine self" is present in order to reflect the reversal that occurs the moment the slayer arrives: instead of being manipulated by the slayer to obtain protection, God puts his "lawgiver-self" into action, commanding that the offender be taken away to die.

The addressee plays a central role in executing justice (which was delayed because of the slayer's flight): he is required to take the slayer out of the holy precinct and kill him. The addressee might be the general public or the representative of a judicial body or some other institution authorized to administer the death penalty. In any event, the lawgiver is convinced that the addressee's participation is necessary, otherwise he could have established that the killer be put to death by the "Divine self."[21] Is this last comment farfetched? As we shall see, the "Divine self" can sometimes be extremely lethal. Let us look into the laws protecting the rights of the weak.

> [21]You shall not wrong a stranger or oppress him, for you were strangers in the land of Egypt. [22]You shall not afflict any widow or orphan. [23]If you do afflict them, and they cry out to me, I will surely hear their cry; [24]and my wrath will burn,

---

19. In this case the addressee is undoubtedly the entire public (it is not possible to attribute the expression "for you" to the murderer, because the lawgiver refers to him in the third person). The notion that the protective precinct serves the common good is clearly reflected in Deut 19:10.

20. As opposed to the Masoretic Text, which does not describe fleeing to an altar, the Septuagint reflects a phrase "and he goes for refuge," which echoes the phrase "to which he may flee." It is thus stressed that the law deals with two types of flight: one is legitimate, under the auspices of the law, and the other is illegitimate, requiring the law's intervention to prevent it.

21. Jacob Milgrom notes that the murderer's survival, despite his contact with the altar, reflects a later stage in the Holiness doctrine. In its earlier phases, any contact with a sacred object was lethal (see Milgrom, "Sancta Contagion and Altar/City Asylum," in *Congress Volume: Vienna 1980* [ed. J. A. Emerton; SVT 32; Leiden: Brill, 1981], 297).

and I will kill you with the sword, and your wives shall become widows and your children fatherless. ²⁵If you lend money to any of my people with you who is poor, you shall not be to him as a creditor, and you shall not exact interest from him. ²⁶If ever you take your neighbor's garment in pledge, you shall restore it to him before the sun goes down; ²⁷for that is his only covering, it is his mantle for his body; in what else shall he sleep? And if he cries to me, I will hear, for I am compassionate. (22:21–27)

The "pseudo-casuistic" formulation of vv. 23–24, a conditional sentence presenting the transgression in the "if" clause and the sanction in the next, provides an entry into the discussion of the lawgiver's unusual mode of participation here. I treat these verses as if they were a casuistic law describing the violation of the commandment "You shall not afflict a widow or orphan."[22]

To present a commandment together with a description of its violation is highly realistic. The unfortunate fact that not everyone has respect for the law is brought to the fore. At the same time, this mode of presentation obscures and diminishes the categorical and absolute nature of the commandment; it therefore also diminishes the authority of the one who issues the commandment. The lawgiver recognizes human weakness; he chooses to give it expression, but his extreme reaction to the violation of the commandment may also be a reaction to the blatant affront to his authority.[23]

The two verses present three events: *wrongdoing, crying out,* and *punishment*. Each of the characters—the addressee-afflicter, the orphan/widow (whom I shall refer to in shorthand as "the weak"), and YHWH the lawgiver—participates in two of the three events. Thus, a chain of events emerges in which one character influences the actions or the fate of the next character and so on: the addressee afflicts the weak; the weak cry out to YHWH, who

---

22. Both verses constitute an expanded motive clause attached to the apodictic law in v. 22. On the classification of this motive clause, see Rifat Sonsino, *Motive Clauses in Hebrew Law: Biblical Forms and Near Eastern Parallels* (SBLDS 45; Chico, Calif.: Scholars Press, 1980), 114.

23. This is the only example in the Book of the Covenant in which an apodictic law is established, immediately to be followed by the possibility that it might be violated. This is also a rare juxtaposition in the other law collections (see, e.g., Lev 17:15–16; 19:6–8; and compare Deut 15:7–9). Cases where the violation of an injunction is a punishable sin should be distinguished from cases in which the lawgiver establishes a binding norm but failure to perform it is not considered a sin but rather a permissible option, even if undesirable (see, e.g., Exod 13:13; 21:11; Deut 25:7–10). For these examples and others, see Gershon Brin, "The Formula 'If He Shall Not (Do)' and the Problem of Sanctions in Biblical Law," in *Pomegranates and Golden Bells, Studies in Biblical, Jewish, and Near Eastern Ritual, Law, and Literature in Honor of Jacob Milgrom* (ed. David P. Wright, David Noel Freedman, Avi Hurvitz; Winona Lake, Ind.: Eisenbrauns, 1995), 341–62.

comes to their aid; YHWH punishes the addressee. This chain of events does not come to end, but more on this later.

The dual "self" of the lawgiver is reflected in the events of crying out and punishment. One, the "lawgiver self," describes the cry for help, while the other, to whom the cry is addressed, who hears it and responds to it, is the "Divine self" who is revealed as a sort of judicial body that delivers justice to the victim.[24] The addressee's punishment is decided by the "lawgiver self," but put into practice by the "Divine self." The lawgiver's participation in the events involves different modes which complement each other: the mode of divine compassion toward the weak and the mode of divine vengeance against the afflicter (see, e.g., Ps 72:4). In the event of crying out, he responds immediately (the sense of urgency flows from the three consecutive verbs and the use of the absolute infinitive שמע אשמע, צעק יצעק, ענה תענה), while in the punishment stage he refers to future events.

However, the forcefulness of his response imparts a unique character to his participation here. The "Divine self" reveals a vindictive and impulsive aspect, which is at odds with the rational and even-keeled "lawgiver self," and the lawgiver does not conceal this. He makes it clear that his reaction, that is, the harsh sanction against the addressee, arises from anger. Is this anger occasioned only by the severity of the offense and the injustice of afflicting the weak? Or does the outcry of the weak, defenseless person in need of aid provoke his wrath? Or is there perhaps another reason for the anger that provokes such an unusually severe reaction? So it would seem. His anger is a response not only to the addressee's conduct toward the weak, but also to his attitude toward him, the lawgiver; the violation of an explicit commandment is a rude insult to his authority.

Indeed, the lawgiver's anger leads him to administer the death penalty by himself—an unusual reaction by any standard.[25] However, his elaboration of the blatant implications of the punishment in a direct address ("and your wives

---

24. The victims' outcry to YHWH and his response (or lack thereof) appear, for instance, in Gen 4:10; Exod 2:23; Deut 15:9; Hab 1:2; and Job 19:7. According to Hans Jochen Boecker, the outcry reflects an actual custom where the victim of an injustice turned for redress to whoever was authorized to carry out justice, namely, the king, as described, for example, in 2 Kgs 6:16; 8:3 (see Hans J. Boecker, *Law and the Administration of Justice in the Old Testament and Ancient East* [trans. J. Moise; London: SPCK, 1980], 50–52).

25. This case, in which the legal sanction is affected by the lawgiver's passions, is a unique occurrence in the Book of the Covenant, as is the declaration "I will kill you with the sword." They have no parallels in Deuteronomic legislation. On the other hand, in three laws in the Holiness Code the lawgiver declares himself to be the executor of the punishment of "cutting off" (Lev 17:9–10; 20:2–6; 23:29–30); in the first two laws the declaration follows a statement professing his hostility to anyone who violates the instructions of the law: "I will set my face against that person" (see Jacob Milgrom, *Leviticus 17–22: A New*

shall become widows and your children fatherless") intensifies the severity of his reaction. This could be seen as a rhetorical choice designed to warn against forbidden behavior, for the personal implication is terrifying and threatening. Yet this choice is problematic, because the lawgiver here advocates an approach to which he himself is opposed. The rationale for the punishment seems to be the talionic principle, with which he is in agreement, but its specific elaboration reflects a distorted extrapolation of this principle.[26] The wrongdoer who inflicted injury but did not kill will die, while his family, who is guiltless, will be punished by becoming potential victims of affliction. In his anger the lawgiver inscribes a vicious circle of afflicted and afflicters. The passion-driven "Divine self" seems to have taken over the rational "lawgiver self." A lawgiver so emotionally overwhelmed that he is swept into a vortex of human relationships that he must sort out is at risk of taking an unbalanced view of things and applying poor judgment.

In the two following laws—the law of lending to the poor and the law of the deposit (vv. 25–27)—the lawgiver turns to the addressee seven times, engaging him in a particularly active and intensive form of participation. On the other hand, and in contrast to the previous law, his participation is of a more minor and certainly a more moderate nature. He immediately gives himself away with the words "my people," but this is not enough to indicate an active participation. He merely presents the weak as being cloaked by his solicitude, evoking a positive disposition in the addressee, as well as fear of taking advantage of the disadvantaged's situation.[27]

Participation in a more tangible sense is found in the concluding verse of the law of deposit: "And if he cries to me, I will hear, for I am compassionate." The scenario described is identical to v. 23b, but it is not clear why it occurs in the present context. It is therefore also not clear why the lawgiver chooses to participate here. Does the lawgiver suggest that the command (to return the garment before sundown) will be disregarded at the very same time he articulates it? Apparently not. First, he does not preface the outcry by stating that the commandment has been transgressed, such as: "if you do not return it to him. . . ." Second, the wording והיה כי יצעק אלי ושמעתי ("And if he cries to me, I will hear") unlike the previous phrase כי אם צעק יצעק אלי שמע אשמע צעקתו

Translation with Introduction and Commentary [AB3A; New York: Doubleday, 2000], 1471, 1733).

26. The lawgiver's threat reflects a certain variety of vicarious punishment, which is indeed acceptable in ancient Near Eastern law collections but is foreign to biblical law.

27. On the concept of "belonging" and divine protection, see Brevard S. Childs, *The Book of Exodus* (OTL; Philadelphia: Westminster, 1974), 479; Jacob, *Exodus*, 706. For another meaning of the expression "my people," see Sarna, *Exodus*, 139.

("and they cry out to me, I will surely hear their cry" [22:22])[28] conveys a lack of urgency on the part of the aggrieved party and only a moderate response by the lawgiver (which we saw above is not in line with his reaction to a blatant violation of an explicit commandment). Third, since the lawgiver does not punish the addressee, who is in possession of the deposit, he appears not to find fault in his behavior. This suggests that the outcry is not occasioned by a particular event or by the addressee's conduct[29] but rather conveys the indigent's general complaint about his bitter fate, for even if he receives the garment in time, his situation is still dire.[30]

The general character of the complaint may explain the nature of the lawgiver's participation. The "Divine self" is not asked to provide immediate redress. Only if the indigent cries out to him, so he promises, will he treat him compassionately. Unlike the previous law, where the behavior of the addressee provoked the wrath of the lawgiver and required both levels of his active participation, in the present law he is seemingly confident that the addressee will perform his obligation, so that his presence is not crucial.

I now have only to address the nature of the motive clause: "for I am compassionate" (v. 27b). Unlike the motive clause at the beginning of the

---

28. The absolute infinitive is used in the Book of the Covenant in two types of cases: (1) in the protasis of secondary laws, in order to illustrate the difference/contrast between the situations described therein and those described in the primary laws (e.g., ואם אמר [22:11a, 12a]); ואם גנב יגנב ... אם טרף יטרף [22:3a]; אם המצא תמצא בידו הגנבה [21:5a]; יאמר העבד (2) in the apodosis, for emphasis (e.g., מות יומת in the participial laws; נקם ינקם [21:20b]; ענוש יענש [21:22]; סקול יסקל [21:28]). The question then arises, why does the lawgiver make use of it in the protasis of the law of deposit (אם חבל תחבל), which is not a secondary law, but rather a separate and independent law? This is because its role is identical to the role it fulfills in the protasis of a secondary law. My conclusion depends on the possibility of pointing out reciprocal relations between the law of lending and the law of the deposit, such that the expression חבל תחבל will illustrate the contrast between the two situations. In the law of lending two injunctions are given: "you shall not be to him as a creditor, and you shall not exact interest from him." The first forbids the lender to press for return of the loan, and the second forbids lending with interest. Now, the action described in the law of deposit, that is, the possession of a garment as security against repayment of a debt, is a form of pressure on the debtor. While the law permits this, the person who seizes another person's garment as a pledge is in fact acting like a creditor. By using the absolute infinitive the lawgiver illustrates the tension between the two situations and stresses his ambivalence toward the norms that he himself has set down.

On the uses of this stylistic form in the Book of the Covenant see Reuven Yaron, "Stylistic Conceits II: The Absolute Infinitive in Biblical Law," in Wright et al., *Pomegranates and Golden Bells*, 449–60.

29. Compare the situation described in the parallel law: "lest he cry *against you* to the LORD, and *it be sin in you*" (Deut 24:15b).

30. See Jacob, *Exodus*, 708.

verse (which I will discuss at length in the next chapter), the lawgiver's self-characterization[31] is not meant to supply the rationale for the legal arrangement but rather to clarify his own mode of participating in the events.[32] His responsiveness to the outcry (and of course the poor man's choice to cry out to him) is explained as one of his unique qualities. Whereas in the previous law the particular style of participation was occasioned by an impulse, in the present law participation is motivated by God's basic and permanent attribute.[33]

A few words in summary: the participation of the lawgiver in the Book of the Covenant is sparse (he also rarely invites the addressee to participate). Sometimes it is active, at other times passive; it can be practical, creative, or only aimed at instilling hope for the future. The participating "self" wears different personae, but it always aims to provide a solution to a problem. What can we learn about its character? How does it affect us? I will return to these questions after examining the modes of participation manifested by the colleagues of the lawgiver of the Book of the Covenant.

THE LAWS OF DEUTERONOMY

Contrary to expectation, the participation of the Deuteronomic lawgiver (in the events described in his laws) is not the focus of my discussion (for my reasons, see below). Rather, I address two other issues, each of which bears the distinguishing marks of this lawgiver: the intensive and varied modes of *integration of the addressee*, and the repeated reference to *the act of legislation*. In truth, it is the lawgiver's own preference that has dictated my choice not to address his own participation in events, since he takes care to stay outside the narrative scenes of the laws.[34] Even when mentioning events in which

---

31. In James Watts's terms "emotional self-characterization" (*Reading Law*, 101).

32. Also in the motive clause in the law concerning the justice and morality of the judicial process—"for I will not acquit the wicked" (23:7)—the self-characterization of the lawgiver is not meant to present the rationale of the legal norm (as opposed, for instance, to the motive clause in the following verse: "for a bribe blinds the officials . . ."), but contains rather a veiled threat of punishment. On "threatening" motive clauses, whose purpose is to persuade one not to violate the legal ordinance, see Sonsino, *Motive Clauses*, 113–14.

33. This attribute is associated in the Bible only with YHWH, and whenever it appears, with the exception of the current verse, it is associated with mercifulness. Another difference between the present verse and other verses is that only here do we find a self-characterization, whereas in the others the characterization is given by a third party: prophet, poet, or leader.

34. In at least one instance it appears that the lawgiver's remote positioning has influenced the way in which events are presented by one of the characters. In the law of going to war, the priest, like the lawgiver, describes the events "from the outside," as someone who is not part of the "collective" and does not participate in the action (20:3–4).

he certainly did participate he does not employ the pronoun "we" but rather "you" (see, e.g., 16:1, 3; 23:5; 24:9).[35] Only twice, in the context of the law of the centralization of the cult (12:5–8) and the law of the prophet (18:15–18), does he deviate from this convention and position himself among the other actors, his addressees, in the context of the event or the situation that he describes. In both cases the addressees are part of the main story (they belong to the first level of the narrative). The lawgiver introduces them into the law for various purposes, while drawing comparisons between the familiar reality and the events that are the subject of the law (the second level of the narrative). Thereby, his approach is different from that of the lawgiver in the Book of the Covenant, who also participates in only a small number of events but, when doing so, takes an active part in the narratives whose origin is intrinsic to the laws.

The Addressee's Participation—Here, There, and Everywhere

The questions I raised earlier (which I left unanswered)—Why does the lawgiver in the Book of the Covenant involve his addressee as a participant in only six cases? Why in these six and not others?—do not arise in reference to the Deuteronomic law's addressee, since the lawgiver involves him intensively, turning him into the unrivaled protagonist of the laws. This is easy to show by demonstrating the inverse. The addressee *does not* participate in only five (!) laws (the inheritance of the firstborn [21:15–17]; a false accusation of a woman by her husband [22:13–19]; sexual congress with a virgin who was not betrothed [vv. 28–29]; exemption from recruitment to the army [24:5]; and the law of levirate marriage [25:5–10]), but he is present, participating or otherwise involved in the events, in all the rest. His constant presence, receiving linguistic expression in direct second person addresses, establishes a firm bond, indeed a relationship, between him and the lawgiver. Although the lawgiver does not participate in the events, he maintains a constant presence through these direct addresses, for each such address reflects an "I–You" relationship. Furthermore (and here we enter the picture), the direct addresses serve rhetorically to implicate the external addressees, the readers, in the laws' narrative scenes. The lawgiver addresses us by "piggybacking" on the internal addressee, and thus maintains an "I–You" relationship with us as well. Accordingly, all

---

35. The lawgiver's avoidance of the (anticipated) use of the first person is especially conspicuous in light of its intensive use in other sections of Moses' oration (especially in the historical surveys). For this style of formulation as one of the means of establishing Deuteronomy's legal fiction, see Yair Hoffman, "'Pseudoepigraphic Constraints' in the Book of Deuteronomy" (in Hebrew), *Shnaton* 5–6 (1981–82): 48–50.

of us, just like the original listeners, may consider ourselves protagonists of the laws.

I divide the broad range of cases in which the addressee participates into three categories and present them in reverse order of magnitude: beginning with partial participation of a declarative-conceptual nature, to partial participation of a practical kind, and finally full participation. The first category comprises the seven instances in which the lawgiver involves the addressee only by means of the motive clauses that conclude the laws: the law of the broken-necked heifer (21:1–9);[36] the rebellious son (vv. 18–21); the secondary law concerning charges of shameful conduct (22:20–21); the law of adultery (v. 22); the law concerning marriage and divorce (24:1–4); kidnapping (v. 7); and finally, the law of corporal punishment (25:1–3).[37] His participation in these laws is not immanent—he does not take part in the events themselves and is not required to uphold any kind of legal norm. After the rite of expiation has been completed to the satisfaction of God and the community; after the last stone has been pelted at the rebellious son or daughter, the pair of adulterers, or the kidnapper; and when the saga of the "latter and former husbands" comes to a close, the addressee suddenly "shows up" at the margins of the laws and is cast by the lawgiver in a grand role. It is he who is responsible for the fulfillment of broad social goals, namely, to preserve the moral level of the community and to maintain its members' standards of conduct (to purge evil, to purge the guilt of innocent blood, to do what is right in the sight of the LORD, not to bring guilt upon the land).

Now let me define the addressee's participation in the law of corporal punishment. Since this law is a bit tricky, I present it in full.

> ¹If there is a dispute between men, and they come into court, and the judges decide between them, acquitting the innocent and condemning the guilty, ²then if the guilty man deserves to be beaten, the judge shall cause him to lie down and be beaten in his presence with a number of stripes in proportion to his offense. ³Forty stripes may be given him, but not more; lest, if one should go on to beat him with more stripes than these, *your* brother be degraded in *your* sight. (25:1–3)

As in other laws, the addressee's participation is reflected here only in the motive clause, and not before. According to vv. 1–2, only three characters are in attendance in the judicial process: the innocent, the guilty, and the judges. But the phrase לעיניך ("in your sight"), used by the lawgiver in the

---

36. The presence of the addressee is indicated also by means of the phrases that use possessive pronouns "the LORD your God gives you to possess"; "your elders and your judges."

37. The law of corporal punishment poses an exception to the other laws and therefore will be treated separately.

motive clause, clearly indicates that the addressee witnesses the punishment's execution.[38] Hence, the concluding clause, which only explains why the degree of punishment must be restricted, casts a new light on the events. Suddenly we are made aware that the addressee is present during the judicial process, or at least at its conclusion, and we ask ourselves, to what end?

Executing the punishment in the addressee's presence, in public, is designed to achieve one of the goals of punishment—deterrence. The transgressor will be deterred because the trauma of physical pain is added to the shame of his public disgrace; and the public will be deterred, because the picture of the crouching man and his body—contorted from the blows delivered to his back—will be "branded" in its memory. The lawgiver's rationale for meting out punishment proportionally, preventing it from turning into an act of vengeance and humiliation against the transgressor (who is therefore no longer called "guilty" but "your brother"), thus also provides a platform for enacting the part of the addressee in the creation of one of the central purposes of punishment.

Turning from the addressee's meaningful, albeit passive, participation in the punitive procedures, I now examine his active participation, in instances where the lawgiver grants him a role in the judicial process—execution of the punishments. The lawgiver equips the addressee with information of different levels of specification to enable him to fulfill this role. In the law of the woman who seized a man's genitals he defines the type of punishment for him: "you shall cut off her hand" (25:12). In the law concerning sexual congress with a betrothed virgin, besides defining the type of punishment, he ordains the mode and venue of its execution: "you shall bring them both out to the gate of that city, and you shall stone them to death with stones" (22:24). In the law prohibiting leaving a hanging man overnight, a guideline and reservation about treatment of the corpse accompanies the general instruction about the mode of execution: "you hang him on a tree, his body shall not remain all night upon the tree but you shall bury him the same day" (21:22–23). Only in the law of the false accuser does the lawgiver refrain from defining the type of punishment in advance. Nevertheless, he establishes the principle of *talion*, which governs the punishment: "you shall do to him as he had meant to do to his brother" (19:19–21).[39]

---

38. The expressions לעיני and בעיני should be distinguished. While the first relates concretely to what the eyes perceive (see, e.g., Deut 4:34; 2 Sam 12:11), the second is metaphorical and refers to understanding or thought (see, e.g., Gen 19:19; Num 13:33). See *BDB*, s.v. עין, 3c, 744b ("in the view, opinion of"); 5, 745a ("in full view of").

39. On the integration of two *talio* formulas in the present law (the כאשר formula and the נפש בנפש formula), see Jackson, *Wisdom-Laws*, 199–201. It is interesting to pay attention to the instruction "your eye shall not pity," which precedes the second formula and

In summary: it can be said that in all the instances of participation presented up to this point the addressee is depicted as a positive figure. He himself does not transgress the law; he punishes the sinner, maintains community standards of conduct, and contributes to the fulfillment of broader social goals. It is no exaggeration to say that he functions as the lawgiver's right-hand man.

This homogeneous and idealized picture changes when we examine the third category. Here we are confronted with a complex reality in which the addressee is staged in a broad range of situations that have either a positive or negative impact on his life and on the life of others. He participates in dramatic, fateful events alongside everyday routine scenarios. In some cases he is the chief protagonist and in others he is only a supporting character in the exploits of other protagonists. This variety of roles can be found in the many laws formulated in the "if you" pattern (which might be better called "when you," but I will adhere to the standard jargon). Although they differ from one another in substance, they are all characterized by the addressee's full participation.[40]

---

appears also in three other laws dealing with: (a) a relative who entices to idolatry (13:9); (b) homicide (19:13); and (c) a woman who seizes a man's genitals (25:12). The purpose of the instruction is to eliminate any aversion to executing the punishment; an aversion stemming from its type—mutilation—or because of the close relationship to the person who is punished. In this respect it is difficult to understand why it refers to the punishment of a murderer and a false accuser, since neither their identity nor the graveness of their deed is likely to arouse the sympathy of the public.

I shall set aside for future consideration whether the instruction appears in conjunction with punishments that reflect the principle of *talion* (in three of the four cases, but not in the law of enticement to idolatry), since it was once an integral part of the *talio* formula, as reflected in the law of the false accuser. In the two other laws (homicide and seizing the genitals) the lawgiver is content to use it, but elliptically refrains from using the entire *talio* formula (see the discussion in Jackson, *Wisdom-Laws*, 237). This issue is taken up again in chapter 4.

40. The following is the full list of relevant laws: the law of secular slaughter (12:20–28), Canaanite worship (vv. 29–31), enticement to idolatry (13:1–5, 6–11, 12–18), the law of the pauper (15:7–11), the male and female slave (vv. 12–18), idolatry (17:2–7), the supreme court (vv. 8–13), the law of the king (vv. 14–20; apart from the opening verses and the direct address that presents YHWH's words [v. 16], the rest of the verses that set down the duties and prohibitions incumbent on the king are formulated in the third person), the prohibition of magic (18:9–14), the law of the prophet (vv. 15–22), homicide (19:1–13; three linguistic patterns are involved in this law. For the different approaches to the redaction of the law see A. D. H. Mayes, *Deuteronomy: Based on the Revised Standard Version* [NCBC; 2nd ed.; Grand Rapids: Eerdmans, 1981], 284–88; Alexander Rofé, *Introduction to the Book of Deuteronomy* [in Hebrew; Jerusalem: Academon, 1988], 86–109; Brin, *Studies in Biblical Law*, 36–37), the laws of warfare (20:1–9, 10–18, 19–20; 21:10–14), sending away the mother bird (22:6–7), building a parapet (v. 8), the purity of the camp (23:10–15), making a vow (vv. 22–24), appropriating agricultural produce (vv. 25–26); deposit (24:10–13), gleaning (vv. 19–22).

Among the different theories regarding the provenance of legal "if-you" formulations, I found Harry Gilmer's the most appealing.[41] From the fact that these formulas do not appear in other ancient Near Eastern law collections, he deduces "that they have borrowed from an area of life other than that of law codes."[42] Following Erhard Gerstenberger's view of the source of apodictic instructions, Gilmer suggests that these too "originate in the family ethos—in the instructions of parents to children."[43] I have decided therefore to bring these formulas "back home," if you will, into the bosom of the family. I treat the participation of the addressee in the "if-you" laws as models of familial relationships, interactions that typify the father–son relationship (which is also a metaphor for the teacher–pupil relationship). Lest this be seen as a "childish" interpretive maneuver, I stress how this interpretation in fact underscores the educational, pedagogic, and sermonizing nature of the Deuteronomic law collection.

I have discovered four patterns of relationships in the laws:

1. "*The needy son.*" The addressee encounters a problem he is unable to resolve, and the supportive and beneficial lawgiver provides him with a solution. This type of relationship is reflected in the law of secular slaughter (12:20–28), the supreme court (17:8–11), the prophet (18:15–22), and the law of going to war (20:1–9).

2. "*The son who has been subject to a bad influence.*" The addressee is subjected to the bad influence of negative characters and the lawgiver advises and warns him not to fall into their traps. This pattern is reflected in the law concerning Canaanite worship (12:29–31), enticement to idolatry (13:1–5, 6–11), and the prohibition against magic (18:9–14).

3. "*The powerful son.*" The fortunate addressee is admonished by the lawgiver, who is aware of the weakness of his character, not to use his power to his advantage but instead to act beneficently toward those who are weaker than he. This type of relationship is apparent in the laws of the pauper (15:7–11), the male and female slave (vv. 12–18), the captive woman (21:10–14), deposit (24:10–13), and the laws of gleaning (vv. 19–22).

4. "*The mature and independent son.*" The addressee is the independent master of his own life, but the wise and experienced lawgiver still proffers advice on how to improve his lot. This pattern is reflected in a great number of laws. Some deal with unusual events: the city enticed to idolatry (13:13–19); idolatry (17:2–7); the king (vv. 14–15); the cities of refuge (19:1–3, 7–10);

---

41. See Gilmer, *If-You Form*, 99–111.
42. Ibid., 102.
43. Erhard Gerstenberger, "Covenant and Commandment," *JBL* 84 (1965): 38–51; Gilmer, *The If-You Form*, 103–4.

and capture and siege of a city (20:10–20). Other laws describe natural and routine events: sending away the mother bird (22:6–7); building a parapet (v. 8); the sanctity of the camp (23:10–15); appropriating agricultural produce (23:25–26).

I illustrate these patterns of relationship—one father and four types of sons—in several laws.[44]

The Law of the Prophet

> [15]The LORD your God will raise up for you a prophet like me from among you, from your brethren—him you shall heed—[16]just as you desired of the LORD your God at Horeb on the day of the assembly, when you said, 'Let me not hear again the voice of the LORD my God, or see this great fire any more, lest I die.' ... [20]But the prophet who presumes to speak a word in my name which I have not commanded him to speak, or who speaks in the name of other gods, that same prophet shall die.' [21]And if you say in your heart, 'How may we know the word which the LORD has not spoken?'—[22]when a prophet speaks in the name of the LORD, if the word does not come to pass or come true, that is a word which the LORD has not spoken; the prophet has spoken it presumptuously, you need not be afraid of him. (18:15–22)

The lawgiver presents two difficulties that the protagonist is obliged to confront. The first is an existential issue. The protagonist has a need to communicate with God but fears direct communication. Since all other vehicles of communication are illegitimate (the mantic and magical vehicles spelled out in vv. 9–14), he is offered an alternative medium of communication. The institution of prophecy arises as a response to the protagonist's conflict, and this is also how it is explained: "your God will raise up *for you* a prophet." But the solution appears to be incomplete, and the protagonist runs into another difficulty—not a frequent one, but one that could on occasion sabotage his relationship with God. Among the legitimate agents of communication lurk impostors whose relationship with God is only a pretense, and the protagonist fails to identify them. They too come "from among his [people]" and he is liable to err and believe that they act in the name of God. The lawgiver again comes to the addressee's rescue and allows him to reveal the truth and uncover the falsehood, providing him with the test of unfulfilled prophecy: "if the word does not come to pass or come true, that is a word which the LORD

---

44. An analogy could be made, of course, between the lawgiver's and addressee's relationship and the relationship between the speaker and the addressee in the book of Proverbs (father/teacher and son/pupil). On the connection between Deuteronomy and wisdom literature, see Moshe Weinfeld, *Deuteronomy and the Deuteronomic School* (1972; repr., Winona Lake, Ind.: Eisenbrauns, 1992), 51–58, 171–78.

has not spoken." Yet it is doubtful if this test can fulfill its own promise; it is questionable whether it can provide an answer to the human failure to distinguish truth from falsehood.[45] The protagonist is therefore left in a quandary with the recognition that he inhabits a world in which different forces and contradictory messages are at large, which he is not always equipped correctly to appraise.

The encounter with people who wish to entice him to idolatry—a prophet or dreamer, a relative or close friend—presents the protagonist with knotty dilemmas.

> [1]If a prophet arises among you, or a dreamer of dreams, and gives you a sign or a wonder, [2]and the sign or wonder which he tells you comes to pass, and if he says, 'Let us go after other gods,' which you have not known, 'and let us serve them,' [3]you shall not listen to the words of that prophet or to that dreamer of dreams; for the LORD your God is testing you, to know whether you love the LORD your God with all your heart and with all your soul. [4]You shall walk after the LORD your God and fear him, and keep his commandments and obey his voice, and you shall serve him and cleave to him. [5]But that prophet or that dreamer of dreams shall be put to death, because he has taught rebellion against the LORD your God. . . . So you shall purge the evil from the midst of you. (13:1–5)
>
> [6]If your brother, the son of your mother, or your son, or your daughter, or the wife of your bosom, or your friend who is as your own soul, entices you secretly, saying, 'Let us go and serve other gods,' . . . [8]you shall not yield to him or listen to him, nor shall your eye pity him, nor shall you spare him, nor shall you conceal him; [9]but you shall kill him;[46] your hand shall be first against him to put him to death, and afterwards the hand of all the people. [10]You shall stone him to death with stones, because he sought to draw you away from the LORD your God. . . . [11]And all Israel shall hear, and fear, and never again do any such wickedness as this among you. (13:6–11)

The protagonist knows that all these are attempts to lead him astray—he is aware of the inherently dangerous nature of the messages, but in both cases circumstances thwart his ability to cope with the detrimental influence. The lawgiver is ready to rescue him. In the first law he must cope with two difficulties: the identity of the enticer—a figure who would appear to be beyond suspicion—poses a challenge to his faith. But instead of shoring up his resistance

---

45. See, e.g., S. R. Driver, *A Critical and Exegetical Commentary on Deuteronomy* (ICC; 3rd ed.; Edinburgh: T&T Clark, 1902), 230; Jeffrey H. Tigay, *Deuteronomy-Devarim: The Traditional Hebrew Text with the New JPS Translation* (The JPS Torah Commentary; Philadelphia: Jewish Publication Society, 1996), 177–78.

46. The version reflected in the Septuagint "you shall surely report concerning him" (כי הגד תגידנו) should be preferred to the Masoretic version כי הרג תהרגנו. The reason will be explained below.

to the unsavory messages of someone he perceives to be a messenger of God, he is forced to cope with an even more troublesome difficulty than before. Contrary to expectation, the verbal messages gain support from a prophetic sign and wonder—an external and public event. Therefore, to counteract the damaging potential of this double deception—at the level of sensory perception and at the level of faith—the lawgiver promptly reveals to him that this is part of a divine test: "to know whether you love the LORD your God."

The revelation extricates the protagonist from danger and allows him to overcome the threat of being averted from the straight path. He is no longer a passive character subject to a bad sphere of influence, but an active protagonist who returns to a proper mode of life, that is, to the worship of YHWH.[47] The perfection of faith that now suffuses the protagonist primes him to fulfill his destiny, namely, "to purge the evil from his midst."

In the second law, the protagonist is not portrayed as the victim of a single public, dramatic event. The attempt to divert him from the straight path occurs at home, and, like other misdemeanors in families, it is a secret. Although it is not explicitly stated, one can assume that the scenario recounts not a single event but rather a series of recurring events. At the heart of the protagonist's own milieu, from which he draws strength and confidence, someone seeks to puncture his faith.[48] The lawgiver lists the identities of the enticers in hierarchical order, reflecting the extent of their influence over the protagonist. First is "your brother, the son of your mother,"[49] the figure who occupies a status and degree of influence within the family identical to that of the protagonist; next "your son, or your daughter," the family members who will impact the character of the nuclear family in the next generation; third "the wife of your bosom,"[50] his partner, who, alongside him, is responsible for preserving family values;[51] and fourth, "your friend who is as your own soul," belonging to an

---

47. The nature of worship of YHWH is described with six different verbs—"to walk after [him]"; "to fear [him]"; "to keep [his commandments]"; "to obey [his voice]"; "to serve [him]"; "to cleave to [him]" (v. 4)—and they are joined to the verb "to love" (appearing in the previous verse). This is the broadest range of verbs that the Deuteronomist uses to describe the nature of worship of YHWH (cf. 6:13; 8:6; 10:12–13, 20; 11:13, 22; 30:20).

48. The view that a person is most endangered by those close to him is voiced by the prophet Micah (Mic 7:5–6).

49. The version reflected in the Septuagint and in the Samaritan Pentateuch also includes a half brother "your father or mother's son."

50. The lawgiver uses an intimate term and not the neutral term "your wife," in order to stress that in the context of intimate relationships one's power of resistance may weaken (see Judg 14:15–17; 16:4–17).

51. In a strictly hierarchical ordering, from major to minor influence, it would seem that the wife should have been mentioned before the children since her powers of influence

external sphere, and whose influence is therefore weaker, but toward whom the protagonist feels a psychological affinity.[52]

The lawgiver teaches the protagonist how to cope with enticement: first, inwardly, he must set his mind against the enticements and the enticer; then he must expose the deed in public; and finally he is required to take part actively in punishing the enticer. The process includes four phases, each of which the lawgiver describes with two verbs, as if to tool the protagonist for his task: first he must place a wedge between him and the enticer ("you shall not yield to him or listen to him"); later, recognizing the danger he and his words embody, he must overcome his natural feelings of sympathy toward him ("nor shall your eye pity him, nor shall you spare him");[53] the inward recognition and acceptance of the enticer's fate allows the protagonist to expose the affair in public ("nor shall you conceal him; you shall surely report concerning him");[54] at the end he will personally administer death to the enticer ("your hand shall be first against him to put him to death . . ."). The protagonist's ability to cope successfully with the danger that lurked at his doorstep allows the lawgiver to entrust him with the office of executioner.[55]

The Law of the Pauper and the Law of the Male and Female Slaves

In the law of the pauper (15:7–11) and the law of the male and female slave (vv. 12–18), we encounter a protagonist and an "other" of a different type, both of whom of course are treated differently by the lawgiver.

> [7]If there is among you a poor man, one of your brethren, in any of your towns within your land . . . you shall not harden your heart or shut your hand against your poor brother, [8]but you shall open your hand to him, and lend him sufficient for his need, whatever it may be. [9]Take heed lest there be a base thought in your

---

are greater. See, for example, the influence attributed to Sarah (Gen 16:6), to Achsah (Josh 15:18; Judg 1:14), to Jezebel (1 Kgs 21:25), and to Athaliah (2 Kgs 8:18).

52. Recall Jonathan's affection for David (1 Sam 18:1, 3).

53. Compare the pitiless attitude of the parents, almost a zeal for putting their own son who prophesied falsely to death, as reflected in the words of Zechariah: "and his father and mother who bore him shall pierce him through when he prophesies" (Zech 13:3). Even the description of a "private" execution, which does not flow from a judicial decision, reflects an unusual outlook (cf. the law of the rebellious son [Deut 21:18–21]).

54. This is the version reflected in the Septuagint. This version is preferable in my opinion because it forms a parallelism (vv. 8c + 9a) that is added to the previous two parallelisms (v. 8a + 8b) and the subsequent repetitive structure (vv. 9b + c + 10a).

55. The personal and public dimensions, reflected in the mode of executing the enticer, are embodied in the two motive clauses. The first is addressed to the protagonist: "because he sought to draw you away from the LORD . . ." and the second to the public: "And all Israel shall hear, and fear, and never again do any such wickedness."

heart . . . and your eye be hostile to your poor brother, and you give him nothing, and he cry to the LORD against you, and it be sin in you. ¹⁰You shall give to him freely, and your heart shall not be grudging when you give to him; because for this the LORD your God will bless you in all your work and in all that you undertake. ¹¹. . . therefore I command you, You shall open wide your hand to your brother, to the needy and to the poor in the land. (15:7–11)

¹²If your brother, a Hebrew man, or a Hebrew woman, is sold to you, he shall serve you six years, and in the seventh year you shall let him go free from you. ¹³And when you let him go free from you, you shall not let him go empty-handed; ¹⁴you shall furnish him liberally out of your flock, out of your threshing floor, and out of your wine press; as the LORD your God has blessed you, you shall give to him. ¹⁵You shall remember that you were a slave in the land of Egypt, and the LORD your God redeemed you. . . . ¹⁶But if he says to you, 'I will not go out from you,' because he loves you and your household, since he fares well with you, ¹⁷then you shall take an awl, and thrust it through his ear into the door, and he shall be your bondman for ever. . . . ¹⁸It shall not seem hard to you, when you let him go free from you; for at half the cost of a hired servant he has served you six years. So the LORD your God will bless you in all that you do. (15:12–18)

Fate has smiled on this protagonist—he is powerful—and the lawgiver must formalize his relationships with those weaker than he and dependent on him. Aware of the protagonist's human failings, the lawgiver promptly converts a relationship that might be wrongfully exploited into a bond between benefactor and beneficiary. This is already apparent at the beginning of the first law. Designating the pauper as his brother who lives in his midst, in his towns, and in his country signals to the protagonist that he cannot remain an outsider in the face of pauperism, but that it is his personal duty to offer help.[56] This duty, from which the lawgiver allows the protagonist no possibility of escape, is spelled out with a profusion of dos and don'ts that clearly convey what is an unworthy attitude toward the poor, and what are the beneficent acts that the protagonist must undertake. This thorough elaboration is reflected also in the two motive clauses, which complement each other and address the protagonist's contemptible attempt to shirk responsibility as the fallow year approaches (vv. 9b, 10b). The first clause contains a threat of retribution, while the second promises a positive reward. With the metaphorical iterations of the word "hand," the lawgiver creates a circle of giving. First comes the prohibition "to shut the hand against the poor" (a metaphorical term for rejection, or refusal to give); next is the imperative "to open the hand to him" (a metaphorical phrase for giving); finally there is the promise that he will succeed "in every putting forth of his hand"—the benefactor ends up as a beneficiary.

---

56. The concluding sentence reiterates the element of possession. This is conspicuous in the Hebrew, לאחיך, לעניך, ולאבינך (lit., "to your brother, to your needy and to your poor").

In the law of the male and female slave the protagonist's status changes from beneficiary to benefactor (and vice versa). For six years he enjoys the fruit of the slaves' labor; afterwards he is munificent with them and sets them free with full hands; finally, in return for his positive deeds, God is beneficent to him (v. 18b).[57] The dual status of the protagonist as benefactor and beneficiary is reflected in the secondary law (vv. 16–17). He is beneficent with the slave who does not want to go free (כי טוב לו עמך) and he is a beneficiary of the slave's future labor (והיה לך עבד עולם). The inequality of the social order and the dependence of the weak on the strong never appeared more advantageous.

We turn now to the mature and independent protagonist, examining the portrayal through the prism of two laws that are radically different. The ceremonial law of the king is of national import, whereas the law of building a parapet addresses a personal and quotidian matter.

The Law of the King

> [14]When you come to the land which the LORD your God gives you, and you possess it and dwell in it, and then say, 'I will set a king over me, like all the nations that are round about me'; [15]you may indeed set as king over you him whom the LORD your God will choose. One from among your brethren you shall set as king over you; you may not put a foreigner over you, who is not your brother. [16]Only he must not multiply horses for himself, or cause the people to return to Egypt in order to multiply horses.... [17]And he shall not multiply wives for himself, lest his heart turn away; nor shall he greatly multiply for himself silver and gold. [18]And when he sits on the throne of his kingdom, he shall write for himself in a book a copy of this law. (17:14–20)

Here the protagonist is portrayed as an independent and assertive figure who initiates action. He expresses his desire decisively and this desire is fulfilled, word for word. The protagonist says: "I will set a king over me like all the nations that are round about me," and the lawgiver, who chooses a non-confrontational approach, responds affirmatively. His speech begins responsively, without challenge or reservation: "you may indeed set as king over you," although the second part of the protagonist's wish is certainly unsavory to him. The lawgiver refrains from an incisive negative response such as: "you shall not

---

57. The positive reward promised to the protagonist is joined to two additional justification clauses that are supposed to allow him to reconcile himself with the hardship of making such a generous release grant (vv. 15, 18b). The first offers a historical perspective, and the second reflects an aspect of economic profitability. I will address the essence of the protagonist's hardship, and the lawgiver's various responses to it (in the current and previous law) in chapter 4.

set a king over you like all the nations round about you." Instead, he deals gently with the protagonist and little by little disarms him of his desire to conform to his surroundings.

The immediate affirmative response is "corrected" by the addition of two cumulative conditions: "him whom the LORD your God will choose" and "One from among your brethren." But neither of these conditions explicitly negates the protagonist's desire (since the Israelite king, even if chosen by God, might imitate the ways of foreign kings). The challenge to his attitude is played out only later, indirectly, in the prohibitions that restrict the king's prerogatives as well as the imposition of duties on him, both of which seem to signal the distinctiveness of the Israelite king vis-à-vis other monarchs in the region (vv. 16–20).[58] In fact, even the way in which these two cumulative conditions are formulated seems to indicate that the lawgiver is chary of spoiling the protagonist's sense of control. Although the right to elect a king is taken out of his hands and put in YHWH's charge, the lawgiver upholds this illusion, and the coda: "*you* shall set a king over you," precisely reflects his original wish: "*I* will set a king over me."

How then should the lawgiver's final statement, which summarizes the direct address to the protagonist, be regarded? This statement contains no new stipulation or information, and in contradistinction to the lawgiver's usually refined language, oddly contains two consecutive negatives: "you *may not* put a foreigner over you, who *is not* your brother." However, what appears as a flat-out prohibition actually sets two positive elements into relief. First, the king is one of the protagonist's own, "flesh of his flesh"; second, the prohibition has his well-being in mind—it is to his advantage. It seems to be saying "for your own good, don't place a foreign king over you who is not one of your brethren" (see, e.g., Deut 7:22). Thus, clear legal restrictions are established without diminishing the protagonist's sense of independence.

The Law of Building a Parapet

Many accidents occur in the residential environment, at or near home. Sometimes they are caused by carelessness, lack of forethought, or a belief in one's own immunity to accident. This is the case in the next law to be treated. It begins with a common action, continues with lack of forethought, perhaps

---

58. For similar instructions that appear in books of guidance for kings in the ancient Near East and the Hellenistic world, see Wilfred G. Lambert, *Babylonian Wisdom Literature* (Oxford: Clarendon, 1960), 110–15; Moshe Weinfeld, "The Temple Scroll or 'The Law of the King,'" in *Normative and Sectarian Judaism in the Second Temple Period* (Library of Second Temple Studies; London: T&T Clark, 2005), 170–79; *ANET*, 414–20.

indifference, and almost ends with heavy disaster. Why almost? Because the lawgiver guides the protagonist and forewarns him of the danger.

> When you build a new house, you shall make a parapet for your roof, that you may not bring the guilt of blood upon your house [lit., that you may not put blood in your house], if any one fall from it. (22:8)

The law is formulated in a unique way. It begins with a casuistic "if-you" address that seems to anticipate a protasis and an apodosis, but the legal norm is actually given in the first part, while the second part contains only a motive clause. In true casuistic garb the verse might have looked like this:

> When you build a new house, and if you do not make a parapet for your roof, and any one fall from it, you shall bring the guilt of blood upon your house

Indeed this is the precise form of other laws that deal with negligence or disregard of safety. Thus, for example, the law of the pit:

> [33]When a man leaves a pit open, or when a man digs a pit and does not cover it, and an ox or an ass falls into it, [34]the owner of the pit shall make it good. (Exod 21:33–34)

LH 55:

> *šumma awīlum atappašu ana šiqītim ipte aḫšu iddīma eqel itēšu mê uštābil šeʾam kīma itēšu imaddad*
>
> If a man opens his branch of the canal for irrigation and negligently allows the water to carry away his neighbor's field, he shall measure and deliver grain in accordance with his neighbor's yield.

LH 229, which is quite similar to the law in question:

> *šumma itinnum ana awīlim bītam īpušma šipiršu la udanninma bīt īpušu imqutma bēl bītim uštamīt itinnum šû iddâk*
>
> If a builder constructs a house for a man but does not make his work sound, and the house that he constructs collapses and causes the death of the householder, that builder shall be killed.

These three laws display a threefold structure: an opening describing a negligent action, followed by the damage it caused, and finally the punishment. They are all retrospective laws, whereas the Deuteronomic law under discussion is a prospective-preventative law. It therefore does not describe a negligent action that causes harm nor does it contain a sanction, but rather only a legal norm (supported by a justification).

There is another difference between the three laws above and the law of building a parapet. In the other laws the negligent person is liable for damage because the site for which the negligent person is responsible and where the *negligent act* occurred is connected to the site where the *damage* occurred, and which belongs to the damaged party (the law of the pit deals with the linkage between public space, where animals are permitted to roam about, and the pit, which belongs to the negligent party; the law of flooding the field deals with the relation between the negligent party's water conduit and the neighboring field; and the law of the builder deals with the relation between the house under construction, for which the builder is in charge, and the built house in which the damage occurred). In the law of building the parapet, on the other hand, both spaces (which are in fact one space) are owned and controlled by the protagonist. The law invades private, autonomous space, and establishes rules, lest the protagonist, in the course of building his new home, focus only on functionality and aesthetics and fail to display diligence concerning matters of safety.

I am now left to examine the motive clause, which I translate here literally: "that you may not put blood in your house" (ולא תשים דמים בביתך). Are these words meant to instill fear of the guilt and punishment awaiting the protagonist if a person falls off his roof? This common notion is evidently reflected in the nonliteral translation: "that you may not bring the guilt of blood upon your house."[59] I believe otherwise. The lawgiver is not asking the protagonist to imagine his guilt or punishment. If so, he would have explicitly said: ולא יהיה לך דמים (cf. Exod 22:2–3); or ולא תשים דמים בך יהיה (cf. Lev 20:9); ולא יהיה עליך דמים (cf. Deut 19:10); ולא יהיה דמך על ראשך (cf. Judg 9:24); ולא יהיה דמך על עליך דמים (2 Sam 1:16). In all the cited formulations the (guilty) person is the object of blood-guilt, and sometimes this includes his father's house (2 Sam 3:29; 1 Kgs 2:31–33). Only here, "the house"—a term designating the actual residential space, not the head of the household or its members—is the object of the blood.

The lawgiver appeals to the protagonist's common sense but does not threaten him with sanctions. He warns against being the cause of bloodshed in his home, lest his home become, through his own doing, a house with the danger of blood hanging over it. The starkly imagined contrast between a new house symbolizing ongoing life, and a "blood house" signifying the taking of life, should persuade the protagonist (a responsible person by nature) to build a parapet on the roof.

To sum up: the foregoing discussion was focused on the actual life and needs of addressee-protagonist. Transforming the addressee into a character

---

59. See Sonsino, *Motive Clauses*, 114.

who regularly participates intensively and variously in the laws has literary and rhetorical implications (that are inconsequential from a legal standpoint). The first such implication concerns the way in which the "I–you" relationships that exist in actual reality (the laws being the product of "face to face" legislation) are imported into the laws themselves textually. The permanent participation of the addressee, even without the lawgiver's participation, solidifies the relationship between the two parties; law becomes an additional medium for managing this relationship. Next, the intensive and diverse modes of participation, signaled by the addressee's range of roles, and personal, familial, and social representations, demonstrate the lawgiver's perception of his addressee. Moreover, they attest to the multifaceted nature of the lawgiver's relationship with the addressee—whether he is educating, guiding, supervising, admonishing, or sometimes even threatening.

I Am Your Lawgiver

Various sections of Moses' oration contain statements that demand the utter obedience of the children of Israel to the laws and commandments.[60] These statements prepare them for what is to come—the transmission of the law. Two such statements appear at the beginning and at the end of the law collection, each serving as a formal declaration of the binding validity of the laws:[61]

> you shall be careful to do all the statutes and the ordinances which I set before you this day. These are the statutes and ordinances which you shall be careful to do. (11:32–12:1)
> ... Keep all the commandment which I command you this day. (27:1)

Nevertheless, these two declarations are not sufficient. Seven times, in five different laws, the lawgiver integrates similar utterances, with reference to a specific norm, to a group of norms, or to an entire law. In other words, seven times the lawgiver sees fit to reiterate the binding validity of the commandments. Is this necessary? Do the laws require additional validation? Evidently not. It is not the laws, therefore, that he seeks to validate but rather his own authority. It is not the laws that require formal approval but the character legislating them.

Let us look for a moment at two instructions contained in the law of the centralization of the cult:

---

60. See, e.g., Deut 4:2, 40; 6:6; 7:11; 8:11; 10:13.

61. These statements and similar ones are labeled by biblical scholars "the promulgation formula." See Simon J. De Vries, "The Development of the Deuteronomic Promulgation Formula," *Biblica* 55 (1974): 301–16.

> ... and thither you shall bring your burnt offerings and your sacrifices, your tithes and the offering that you present, your votive offerings, your freewill offerings, and the firstlings of your herd and of your flock. (12:6)
>
> ... thither you shall bring all that I command you: your burnt offerings and your sacrifices, your tithes and the offering that you present, and all your votive offerings which you vow to the LORD. (12:11)

In the first verse the lawgiver states the commandment, and in the second verse, which repeats the earlier commandment with a few slight variations, he adds a personal comment, noting the (well-known) fact that it is *he* who commands—"all that I command you." If this comment were removed, nothing substantive would be lost. These first person statements, which appear another six times in the law collection (12:14, 28, 32; 13:18; 15:5; 19:9) will be the next topic of discussion. I refer to this feature as *the lawgiver's repeated reference to the art of legislating*.

In the following statements (the first one appears at the end of the law of profane slaughter, and the second one at the end of the law of remission of debts), together with the injunction to uphold the legal norms that were just uttered, the lawgiver's statement reverberates: the law is his personal creation, the product of his legislative action.

> Be careful to heed all these words which I command you. (12:28)
>
> ... if only you will obey the voice of the LORD your God, being careful to do all this commandment which I command you this day. (15:5)

Another ancient legislator's approach to the act of legislation comes to mind in this context. In the epilogue of his eponymous law collection, King Hammurabi declares several times that the laws are his own creative labor, that he has inscribed his precious and just pronouncements upon his stela (*awātīya šūqurātim ina narîya aštur[ma]* [xlvii 59–78]; *awāt mīšarim ša ina narîya ašturu* [xlviii 59–94]). However, the language of the laws themselves contains no such declarations, for the simple reason that the figure of the lawgiver is never really present in them.

The key to understanding the Deuteronomic lawgiver's recurring allusions to the art of legislation is not therefore to be found by analogy to the ancient legislators, or to the moderns, but rather in the realm of narrative. The reference to the act of creating the laws, which exposes and highlights the figure responsible for legislating them, is analogous, I suggest, to the way in which the narrator involves the reader in the narrative craft, in its creative process. Such a narrator does not limit him/herself to presenting the story but rather reflexively refers to him/herself by making comments in the first person, as the author behind the story. Seymour Chatman calls this type of narrator "*self-conscious.*"[62] As we shall see presently, the lawgiver, who not only points to himself as the one who is responsible for the laws but also involves the addressees in the creative process, in matters of legislative discretion, is a "self-conscious lawgiver."[63]

Prior to that discussion, however, I will comment briefly on the expression "*this day,*" which appears in some of the statements.[64] The phrase "all this commandment which I command you this day" (19:9) describes "*the epic situation*" of the legislative act and includes four components: what has been legislated, who is the legislator, for whom, and when.[65] The element of time appears twice: it is intimated once in the use of the verb "to command" in the particle form (מצוך), indicating that the act is occurring in the present moment of the utterance,[66] and a second time more explicitly, by employing a temporal phrase. Despite its redundancy, this addition emphasizes that at this very moment in the context of the direct interaction between the parties something important and crucial is happening—the act of legislation. Obviously, the lawgiver's indication of his present time and that of his audience grants the situation greater authenticity and thus contributes to the establishment of Deuteronomy's fictional premise.[67] The certainty implied in relying

---

62. Chatman, *Story and Discourse,* 228. The classic example of "self-conscious narration" is the novel by Laurence Sterne, *The Life and Opinions of Tristram Shandy, Gentleman* (1767), which deals, among other things, with the experience of writing. The novel is woven through with direct addresses to the reader that share with him or her the process of writing and even deliberations over what is written.

63. Chatman deals with the "self-conscious narrator" as part of his discussion of the narrator's "perceptibility," which, it will be recalled, is an additional criterion for characterizing different types of narrators (Chatman, *Story and Discourse,* 196ff.). Although the latter part of this chapter will examine the degree of perceptibility of each of the lawgivers, I prefer to address the comments that deal with the art of legislation in the context of the criterion of "participation," first and foremost because of the lawgiver's use of the first person, the identifying mark of participation.

64. According to the Masoretic Text, the expression appears in three of the seven statements (13:18; 15:5; 19:9) and, in the version reflected in the Septuagint, in three others (12:11, 14, 32).

65. The "epic situation" is the apparently "real" plane in which the story is told out loud or written. It is realized in adjectives of place and time in which the narrative or the writing take place, including the storyteller or writer's thoughts and actions at the time of telling or writing. See Yosef Ewen, "Writer, Narrator, and Implied Author" (in Hebrew), *Hasifrut* 18–19 (1974): 153.

66. On the use of the participle to indicate the present, see Jan Joosten, "The Predicative Participle in Biblical Hebrew," *Zeitschrift für Althebräistik* 2 (1989): 128–59; idem, "Do the Finite Verbal Forms in Biblical Hebrew Express Aspect?" *JANES* 29 (2002): 53–54, 56.

67. See Hoffman, "Pseudoepigraphic Constraints," 48–49. On the intensive use of the expression "this day" in Deuteronomy, its meaning, and the relations between "Moses' day"

on things in the present, whose truth may be clearly seen, led to a situation in which the phrase היום or היום הזה became a kind of "magical" language that would assure certainty.[68]

In five laws—the pauper, the male and female slave, the law of homicide, the rights of the weak, and gleaning—the lawgiver opens a window onto the legislative process and reveals to the addressee the reasoning that guided him in the creation of the norms. He does so by adding his personal statements (with which we are familiar by now) to the motive clauses.

> For the poor will never cease out of the land; therefore I command you, You shall open wide your hand to your brother. (15:11)
>
> You shall remember that you were a slave in the land of Egypt ... therefore I command you this today. (15:15)
>
> ... though the man did not deserve to die, since he was not at enmity with his neighbor in time past. Therefore I command you, You shall set apart three cities. (19:6–7)
>
> but you shall remember that you were a slave in Egypt ... therefore I command you to do this. (24:18)
>
> You shall remember that you were a slave ... therefore I command you to do this. (24:22)

The recurrence of the formula *"therefore I command you"* sufficiently illustrates the feature under discussion. But so as not to underestimate its value—for the motive clause in itself reveals the legislative reasoning even without a personal note by the legislator—let me mark one interesting fact. Each of the laws (except for the law to protect the rights of the weak, which is an apodictic law [24:17–18]) has an additional motive clause (and sometimes more than one) to which the lawgiver does *not* append a personal statement. It is as though he has made a distinction, perhaps an artificial one, between the justification of the logic and propriety of a certain legal norm, and his own motivation to legislate—why *he* has decided to command the (proper) norm. But examination of the additional motive clauses indicates that such a distinction might not be at all artificial, since they all give pride of place to the addressee's interests, or in other words, they justify the norm especially for his sake. In the law of the pauper, the lawgiver announces to him that refraining from giving is

---

and the "Deuteronomist's day," see De Vries, "Promulgation Formula," 301–2; Polzin, *Moses and the Deuteronomist*, 32. On the "reader's day," see Jacob Licht, "The Biblical Claim of Establishment" (in Hebrew), *Shnaton* 3–4 (1980–81): 106.

68. Gershon Brin, *The Concept of Time in the Bible and the Dead Sea Scrolls* (Studies on the Texts of the Desert of Judah 39; Leiden/Boston: Brill, 2001), 184–85.

not profitable, because this might subject him to the judgment of the tribunal in heaven. Generous giving, on the other hand, will bring him blessings:

> ... and he cry to the LORD against you, and it be sin in you; ... because for this the LORD your God will bless you in all your work. (15:9b, 10b)

In the law of the male and female slave as well, the lawgiver provides the addressee with two utilitarian justifications (the second one, which appears in the previous law, appears also in the laws of gleaning [24:19b]),

> for at half the cost of a hired servant he has served you six years. So the LORD your God will bless you in all that you do. (24:18b)

In the law of homicide, the addressee has a clear interest to allow the inadvertent slayer to arrive at the city of refuge safely, or else the guilt of bloodshed will be upon him (19:10b).

In contrast to these examples, the motive clauses to which the lawgiver adds a personal statement reflect another plane of reasoning, based either on a broader, social or historical perspective, or on principles of legal justice. In the law of the pauper, the personal statement refers to the perpetual nature of poverty; in the law of the male and female slave and the laws of gleaning, it points to the social lesson learned from the emancipation from Egypt; and in the law of homicide, it draws on a legal outlook that finds no justification in putting to death an inadvertent killer. Such reasons, the lawgiver points out, are the type of reason to which *he* gives weight.

One might think of additional reasons that the lawgiver chooses to make his point through these cases in particular. The motive clause in the law of the pauper ("For the poor will never cease out of the land") contradicts his earlier statement in the law of the seventh fallow year: "But there will be no poor among you for the LORD will bless you in the land" (15:4).[69] Having changed his mind and abandoned the utopian vision in favor of a more realistic view, he chooses to explain that reality has forced him to do so; reality has dictated legislation. As for the motive clause in the law of the male and female slave ("You shall remember that you were a slave"), this may be seen as referring not to the general obligation to release them after six years of bondage, but rather to the concomitant requirement to make them a grant of property. This particular norm is one of the central innovations of the Deuteronomic lawgiver (to which the word "this" refers ["therefore I command you this today"]). By virtue of its novelty, the lawgiver is not content merely to mention the his-

---

69. According to A. D. H. Mayes, this verse is a late addition. For the original form of the law and the rationale for the addition, see Mayes, *Deuteronomy*, 24.

torical analogy (which was already alluded to indirectly before, in the phrase "you shall not let him go empty-handed"),[70] but rather states explicitly that this norm was founded on a historical event.[71]

In concluding my discussion of the Deuteronomic lawgiver's reference to the art of legislation, I refer to these remarks of Jean-Pierre Sonnet:

> Moses not only speaks but constantly says that he speaks, calling his audience's attention to the content and the formality of his own speech. In an almost obsessive fashion, Moses reminds his audience of his speaking to them, beseeching his addressees to heed, and eventually observe, the "words" or "commandments" he is uttering and enjoining upon them.[72]

Time after time, subsumed within the demand to uphold the laws ("the promulgation formula"), the lawgiver points to his own activity with such a degree of emphasis that he seems to be bent not only on declaring the binding validity of the laws but also on bolstering his own authority. The personal statements that foreground his own voice obscure the lines between his definition as a conduit and mediator (who delivers the divine laws and perhaps illuminates them or interprets them), and his own independent status as a lawgiver.[73] Clearly he has a powerful need to validate his authority "*today.*"

As we shall see presently, the issue of validity and authority is of great concern also to the Priestly lawgiver (or more precisely the lawgiver of the Holiness Code). This seems to be his reason for seeking an effective way of obscuring the "fact" that the laws were delivered to the addressee by a human mediator.

---

70. See Exod 3:21–22. Another expression, familiar to us from the story of the exodus: "with rigor/harshness" (Exod 1:13–14), appears in the Priestly law (Lev 25:43). On the connection between the slave laws and the story of the exodus, see Daube, *Studies in Biblical Law*, 49–50 (see in addition Greenstein, "Biblical Law," 96–98).

71. The proposed explanation is merely "food for thought" for there is no rule by which the Deuteronomic lawgiver adds motives or clarifications when altering or renovating the law (in relation to the Book of the Covenant). This is the place to add a clarification of my own. In addressing "the promulgation formula" in the context of the laws, I do not pretend to offer an "authoritative" answer as to why it is embedded in certain laws and not in others. But even lacking the ability to point out any consistency or method in this regard, the phenomenon should be considered a key to characterizing the lawgiver, as I do here.

72. Jean-Pierre Sonnet, *The Book within the Book: Writing in Deuteronomy* (Biblical Interpretation Series 14; Leiden: Brill, 1997), 258 (see in addition pp. 14–15).

73. See Polzin, *Moses and the Deuteronomist*, 47–65.

The Book of Holiness

On account of the broad scope of the Priestly legislation I have chosen to focus on the Holiness Code (Leviticus 17–26) and only on the participation of the lawgiver (disregarding the participation of the addressee). Since in a great number of laws the lawgiver's modes of participation are similar to those of his predecessors. Sometimes he participates in the events described in the laws;[74] sometimes he indicates his participation in the events of the main narrative;[75] and in some cases he refers to the art of legislation.[76] I will address briefly the mode of participation that distinguishes him from the others (and which is in fact one of the distinguishing features of the Holiness Code).

The feature in question is the lawgiver's permanent presence in the laws, reflected in the numerous instances in which he identifies and characterizes himself, through the use of formulas and refrains such as "I am the Lord," "I am the Lord your God," "for I am the Lord am holy," "I am the Lord who sanctify you," and other variants.[77] These formulas appear before and after particular instructions, in the opening and closing verses of sections of the code, of chapters and of more extensive units. Seemingly unnecessary, because

---

74. The lawgiver himself executes punishments (see 17:10; 20:3, 5–6; 23:30); he also plays a part in the rituals (see, e.g., 19:12a, 30; 21:23b; 22:2b; 23:2b).

75. The lawgiver notes actions performed for the benefit of the addressees and other actions that will be performed for their anticipated benefit in the future. In some cases he identifies himself only through these actions (see, e.g., 19:36; 20:24; 22:33; 25:38); in another part they supply the legal instructions with their conceptual base, according to the principle of *imitatio dei* (e.g., 20:26; 23:43). In one case, the action forms the legal infrastructure of the commandment (25:42, 55), and the future actions are a precondition for the existence of certain instructions (see, e.g., 18:3; 20:22–24; 23:10; 25:2. Cf. Deut 12:29–30; 18:9, 12).

76. The lawgiver repeats time and again that the laws are his own—"my statutes," "my ordinances," "my commandments" (see, e.g., 18:4–5; 20:22; 22:31; 25:18)—sometimes in order to stress the contrast between these norms and those of the neighboring nations (e.g., 18:3; 20:23).

The laws set down in Leviticus 17 contain more detailed references to the art of legislation: the lawgiver refers to the act of lawmaking twice and reveals the reasons behind legislation three times. But since some of his statements are addressed to the addressees and another part is addressed only to Moses ("This is to the end that the people of Israel may bring their sacrifices which they slay in the open field" [vv. 5–7]; "Therefore I have said to the people of Israel" [vv. 12a, 14b]), it is difficult to say whether he exposes the entire scope of his reasoning to them as well (see vv. 11–12, 14). On the distinction between the statements addressed to the children of Israel and those addressed to Moses, and on "concealment" of reasoning from the addressees, see Schwartz, *Holiness Legislation*, 37–41; Milgrom, *Leviticus 17–22*, 1458, 1472, 1483.

77. See, e.g., 18:2, 4–5, 30; 19:2–4, 10, 12, 36–37; 20:7–8, 24, 26; 21:8, 12, 15, 23; 22:2–3, 8–9; 23:22, 43; 24:22; 25:55.

the identity and the properties of the lawgiver are common knowledge, these declarations are impressed upon the listener or reader's mind and impose the recognition that YHWH is the source and cause of all the laws.

It goes without saying that the identity of the speaker who gives the commandments grants them a binding force, and this indeed is one of the functions of the "*self-identification*" formulas—validation.[78] Yet it appears that the lawgiver is attempting to say something more through these formulas. He repeats them again and again not only to establish the status of the laws relating to the addressees (in other words as "promulgation formulas") but also to present the relationship *between himself* and the laws, and *between himself* and the addressees via the laws. "The laws are I," he reiterates, and therefore I am embossing them with my signature. By means of this signature, which embodies my identity, my personality, my actions, I reveal myself to you again and again. Every law, every commandment confirms my existence. The presentation of the symbiotic relationship between the divine lawgiver and his laws is an effective way to impress upon the minds of the addressees the recognition of the source of law. As noted earlier, it may also obscure the fact that they are conveyed to them by a human mediator.

What has emerged from the discussion of "participation" (the general phenomenon, regardless of the different forms and degrees of participation employed by each lawgiver)? In a word, *a relationship*. The participation of the lawgiver and of the addressees is the concrete embodiment of their relationship, for which the law (among other means) is a vehicle. The lawgivers are not content merely to have established an overt relationship through the act of transmitting the laws "face to face," but rather embroider the laws themselves with signs of this relationship as a natural extension of its real-life manifestations. The interaction reflected in the laws cements the ties that already exist between lawgivers and addressees, but, no less important, it tightens the link between the laws and the narrative framework in which they are embedded. Only someone familiar with the overarching narrative understands who "I"

---

78. This can be seen as having a validating-motivating function, because the fact that the one who gives the commandments is YHWH provides reason enough without the need for further justification. For this reason, the "self-identification" formulas are the most common motive clauses in the Holiness Code (see Sonsino, *Motive Clauses*, 110). According to Jacob Milgrom, the formulas "I am the Lord [your God]" should be regarded as ellipses for "I the Lord [your God] have spoken," equivalent to the prophetic formula, "says the Lord" (נאם ה'). Both formulas are meant to validate the content spoken/commanded by the speaker (*Leviticus 17–22*, 1518). See in addition David W. Halivni, *Midrash, Mishnah, and Gemara: The Jewish Predilection for Justified Law* (Cambridge, Mass.: Harvard University Press, 1986), 9–15.

and "you" are and what the relationship is that has developed between them through the instrumentality of the laws.

The phenomenon of "participation" is unparalleled in other ancient Near Eastern law collections, and to underscore its uniqueness let us recall again a lawgiver who is present within his law collection. The Laws of Hammurabi appear between two prose sections; the prologue outlines the god's charges to Hammurabi, and the epilogue claims fulfillment of these charges. The laws demonstrate the king's skill and wisdom.[79] In both the prologue and the epilogue Hammurabi declares his great concern that his subjects not be oppressed or wronged by persons in powerful positions; for that purpose he has inscribed his precious laws.

In one section in the epilogue ("the Wronged Man passage") he illustrates his care for the weak,[80]

> *awīlum ḫablum ša awatam irraššû ana maḫar ṣalmiya šar mīšarim lillikma narî šaṭram lištassīma awâtiya šūqurātim lišmēma narî awatam likallimšu dīnšu līmur libbašu linappišma.* (xlviii 3–19)
>
> May the wronged man who has a law case come before the statue of me, the king of justice, and may he read aloud my inscribed stela, and thus may he hear my precious pronouncements, and may my stela produce the law case for him; may he perceive his case; may he ease his heart, and [saying thus]....

There is a conspicuous difference between that episode and the episodes described, for instance, in the laws commanding safeguarding the rights of the weak (Exod 22:21–27). Hammurabi, referring to his most typical addressee, does not urge him to bring his lawsuit before him for legal remedy but rather to his stela where he can find rescue only through prayer and by offering blessings to the king. The wronged man is to be awed by the king's wisdom and compassion.[81] Even if this passage has a legal purpose (rather than a propagandist one), that is to say, Hammurabi has set up his stela so that anyone who has been wronged may read it and learn the law applicable to his case,[82] still it has no legal force. Unlike the biblical lawgiver, who hears the cry of the weak and rushes to their succor, the monarchic lawgiver *ša kīma abim wālidim ana nišī* ("who is like a true father to the people") does not offer a true remedy.

---

79. See Hurowitz, *Inu Anum ṣirum*, 45–61.

80. The Akkadian text and its English translation are taken from Martha Roth, "Hammurabi's Wronged Man," *JAOS* 122 (2002): 38–39.

81. See ibid., 39, 44–45.

82. See G. R. Driver and John C. Miles, *The Babylonian Laws*, vol. 1, *Legal Commentary* (Oxford: Clarendon, 1952), 41.

Perceptibility

Does the lawgiver respond to the content of the laws—the cases he describes and the norms he establishes—or does he merely present them? Do the laws contain any overt signs indicating (the obvious) existence of the speaking authority, or is his presence not at all felt? The answers are sometimes yes, sometimes no. We all recall the motive clauses that the lawgiver employs to voice his attitude toward the norms he himself has established, which reveal his legal understanding and his religious, national, social, or moral point of view. Undoubtedly this is a clear sign of the lawgiver's views in respect to the laws' contents.[83] But there also exist other signs that indicate his engagement/intervention. These signs attest to his understanding of his own role as lawgiver and consequently affect the way the laws' addressees and readers perceive, process, and relate to their contents. In view of the abundance of examples (in each of the law collections), I treat only a few here.

The Book of the Covenant

I begin with the laws of slavery in the Book of the Covenant because few laws are their equal in illustrating the distinct modes of rendering—that of "the covert and imperceptible lawgiver," and that of "the perceptible and intrusive lawgiver."

The law of the Hebrew slave (Exod 21:2-6) presents a series of events and establishes the legal arrangements that ensue from them. The lawgiver

---

83. In modern legislation generally no such comments will appear within the laws themselves, but rather in their explanatory sections; that is where the justifications for the legal norms are presented by the legislators. On motive clauses, see Berend Gemser, "The Importance of the Motive Clause in the Old Testament Law," in *Congress Volume: Copenhagen 1953* (SVT 1; Leiden: Brill, 1953), 50–66; Sonsino, *Motive Clauses*. Here it should be noted that among the Laws of Hammurabi and the Middle Assyrian Laws there are some motivated laws, but this is a minor phenomenon in comparison with the laws of the Pentateuch, which are replete with motive clauses (for the list of laws, see Sonsino, ibid., 155. To my mind this list is too expansive and includes laws that do not contain motives but rather other types of comments. I shall address these when I discuss the perceptibility of the Priestly lawgiver). In most cases (e.g., LH 107, 136, 194, 232) the motive that appears after the preposition *aššum* ("because") uses identical or similar words to repeat the main substance of the law and adds nothing significant to what has already been said (see Sonsino, 156–59; Martha Roth, "The Because Clause: Punishment Rationalization in Mesopotamian Laws," in *Veenhof Anniversary Volume: Studies Presented to K. R. Veenhof on the Occasion of his Sixty-Fifth Birthday* [ed. W. H. van Soldt; Leiden: Nederlands Instituut voor het Nabije Oosten, 2001], 407–12); and in other cases (e.g., LH 137, 162-163) the reason for the legal ordinance must be "extracted" from the text because it is formulated asyndetically (see Sonsino, 159–66).

describes the events vibrantly, moving from one narrative scene to the next, while the cast of participating characters changes from scene to scene (first we encounter the addressee-master and the slave; later the master, the slave, and his wife; next the master, the slave, the woman he gave him, their sons and daughters; and finally the slave and his master). The lawgiver even gives voice to the slave, but he himself is imperceptible. Matters speak for themselves, he appears to be saying.

In the law of the female slave (21:7–11) the approach is different, as the lawgiver guides us along toward a comprehension of contents and meanings. He reveals his own outlook and knowledge, emphasizes and glosses his words, all for the benefit of the addressees.

His presence is made perceptible from the opening verse: "When a man sells his daughter as a slave, she shall not go out as the male slaves do" (and four additional times in later verses). The lawgiver establishes the legal norm concerning the female slave in comparison to that of the male slave. He does not communicate what transpires later—that the woman has been purchased not simply to be a slave but for marriage/concubinage/breeding—but opens the law with a clear cross-reference to the previous law.[84]

Reference to an event or norm existing outside the reality described in the law is made here by "someone," who actually treats the specific events described in the law as part of a broader context—"someone" who attempts, for example, to impress upon the minds of the addressees the gender or institutional distinction of his own making. He therefore does not limit himself to presenting the facts and establishing the consequent norms (even if they inherently bespeak the difference between the female slave and the male slave). Rather, he directs his addressees to view them as analogous to a different case in order to sharpen or clarify the point, or to eliminate any doubt.

The second alternative in the law is this:

> If he designates her for his son, he shall deal with her as with a daughter [in accordance with the custom regarding freeborn daughters-in-law]. (21:9)

This case contains another analogy, which obviously reveals the presence of whoever is making the analogy. Here too the lawgiver compares the concrete case under discussion with a situation that is extraneous to the framework of the law and refers his addressees to the system of norms that is familiar to them both. Embedded within a statement that establishes the woman's status– in fact shifting her status from slave girl to free woman—is an instance of the lawgiver's distinct presence, as if he says to his addressees: "I know that

---

84. Joe Sprinkle illustrates this nicely, translating the verse as follows: "If, on the other hand, someone sells his daughter . . ." (*Book of the Covenant*, 51).

you know what the applicable norms are; therefore I see no reason to spell them out."[85]

Now let us focus on the most conspicuous sign of the lawgiver's perceptibility—the motive clause,[86]

> If she does not please her master, who has designated her for himself, then he shall let her be redeemed; he shall have no right to sell her to a foreign people, *since he has dealt faithlessly with her*. (21:8)

To justify why the master has no right to sell the woman in the slave market, the lawgiver employs the verb בגד, which bears a double meaning: a technical legal one and a broader ethical one. Legally, this term denotes the intention to violate the purchase contract, which designated her for sexual purposes only. The lawgiver thus conveys his (legal) position that agreements must be honored.[87] And as the woman, and not her father, is here the object of the verb בגד (בבגדו בה), the lawgiver is also articulating an ethical stance by suggesting that

---

85. In the law concerning the seduction of a virgin, the lawgiver follows a similar tack and directs the addressees to an "external" source, mentioning a familiar custom ("he shall pay money equivalent to the marriage present for virgins [Exod 22:17b]). In the laws of the goring ox, on the other hand, the lawgiver refers to the arrangement set down earlier in the law itself ("If it gores a man's son or daughter, he shall be dealt with according to this same rule" [21:31]). Nonetheless, it is commonly assumed that this verse is polemical and is in contrast to the principle of vicarious punishment, which is part of the norm in other ancient Near Eastern law collections (see Daube, *Studies in Biblical Law*, 167; Cassuto, *Book of Exodus*, 194–95); that is to say, the "internal" reference is actually oriented to the "outside." In Priestly legislation there are frequent references to rites described earlier, with use of the formula "according to the ordinance" (כמשפט; see, e.g., Lev 5:10 and 9:16, which refer respectively to Lev 6:2–6 and 4:3–17). The application of a familiar normative system to the case presented by the law occurs, for example, in LH 141. According to the secondary law, if a woman has disparaged her husband or caused damage to the domestic economy but he still chooses not to divorce her, he is permitted to marry another woman and his first wife *kīma amtim ina bīt mutīša uššab* ("[she] shall reside in her husband's house as a slave woman"). This example is important to the matter at hand for two reasons: first, it shows that the "shorthand cross-references," as Michael Fishbane calls them (see *Biblical Interpretation in Ancient Israel* [Oxford: Clarendon, 1985], 209), are a common scribal technique in ancient Near Eastern laws; but, more important, the example teaches us that it is not necessary to see these references as secondary interpolations, as Fishbane believes (pp. 210–11). We may rather treat them as clear signs of the lawgiver's perceptibility.

86. Motive clauses appear in ten additional laws in the Book of the Covenant (Exod 20:25b, 26b; 21:21b; 21:26b, 27b; 22:21b; 22:27a; 23:7b; 23:8b; 23:9b; 23:12b; 23:15b).

87. For the use of the verb בגד in respect to the violation of an agreement or covenant, see, e.g., Hos 6:7. Shalom M. Paul sees a parallel with the Akkadian verb *nabalkutu* (root b-k-t), which means to break an agreement (*Book of the Covenant*, 54).

selling her is an act of unfairness toward *her* (even though she is not a party to the agreement).[88]

Verse 8 requires further examination, however, because the intervention of the lawgiver is not limited to the motive clause. This verse contains an "extra" sentence. Rather than surmise that the lawgiver was careless in formulating the law, I prefer to see in the textual superfluity another sign of his intervention.

What is the relation between the two statements "then he shall *let her be redeemed*" and "he shall *have no right to sell her* to a foreign people"? The first instructs the master to allow her to be redeemed by family members,[89] and the second establishes that he has no right to sell her to someone who is not a member of her nuclear or extended family.[90] And it seems that the first excludes the second; that is, the obligation to permit redemption renders superfluous the statement that he has no right to perform the *contrary action*, namely, selling into slavery.[91] If so, what purpose does this statement serve (insofar as it contributes nothing in the practical sense)?

---

88. Rashi and Nahmanides stress the injustice caused to the girl, who has been twice betrayed—by her father who sold her, and by her master who did not designate her for himself or for his son.

89. See, e.g., Noth, *Exodus*, 179; Sprinkle, *Book of the Covenant*, 53 n. 1; Houtman, *Exodus*, 128; Jackson, *Wisdom-Laws*, 92–93. The law does not indicate the identity of the person who redeems, because there is no need to state the obvious. According to the rules of family law, it is the father, or another relative, who has the right/obligation to redeem a family member; and according to contract law, not fulfilling a basic condition of a sale agreement may lead to its annulment and to reversion to the original state, that is, returning the young woman to her family. Therefore the explanation that she can be redeemed by anyone of Israelite origin (see, e.g., Phillips, "Laws of Slavery," 59–60) is incorrect.

90. I prefer to interpret the expression "foreign people" as Israelites from outside the nuclear family (as do Rashi and Nahmanides; see also Sprinkle, *Book of the Covenant*). The word "people" is used here in an archaic significance, preserving its original meaning "kin" (see Cassuto, *Exodus*, 268; Sarna, *Exodus*, 121). For the other meaning—a person of a foreign nation—see Phillips, "Laws of Slavery," 59–60; Raymond Westbrook, "The Female Slave," in *Gender and Law in the Hebrew Bible and the Ancient Near East* (ed. V. H. Matthews, et al.; JSOTSup 262; Sheffield: Sheffield Academic Press, 1998), 220.

91. Only if her family cannot or does not want to redeem her does the second statement have a practical meaning, because in this case, although she was not redeemed, the master still has no right to sell her to a third party. Such a situation could transpire in reality, but it does not seem as though the lawgiver had this in mind, for otherwise he would have noted explicitly: "and if she is not redeemed then he shall have no right. . . ." According to Westbrook, to understand the purpose of the prohibition it should be pointed out that alienability is not the opposite of redeemability; the woman can always be exercised against a subsequent purchase and than she can become redeemable (Westbrook, "Female Slave," 220). I do not believe that the lawgiver had the scenario of redemption by a third party in

In presenting the second side of the same coin, the lawgiver might be attempting to clarify or emphasize the (practical) imperative, and this is certainly a type of intervention. But the unique way in which the statement is formulated—not as a direct prohibition ("he shall not sell her to a foreign people") but as a declaration of a lack of right—indicates that the answer to the question above is not so trivial. The statement is oriented not to the practical aspect of the law but rather to its conceptual aspect, to the "spirit" of the law.

Similar to the double meaning of the verb בגד, the verb משל also has two meanings—one legal and specific and the other broader. The first is the equivalent of the Akkadian *šalāṭu* and the Aramaic שלט, which in the legal context means "to lay claim to"; hence, לא ימשל, like *la išalliṭ*, means "to have no right."[92] But these verbs have another meaning, "to have/to exercise control over"; it is through this meaning that the lawgiver seeks to convey the "spirit of the law." The master, this statement underscores, cannot exercise unlimited control over the woman and her fate, because unlike an ordinary slave, she is not considered his property.[93]

The final intervention of the lawgiver is reflected in the law's concluding statement: "she shall go out for nothing, without payment of money" (21:11). The law ends on a parallelism. Is the reiteration entailed by the parallelism to be understood as an intervention by the lawgiver, or is it merely a rhetorical flourish? After all, parallelism is a standard aesthetic vehicle in every genre of biblical discourse. But when the parallelism can be understood to serve *a particular purpose*, it is not only a rhetorical ornament but can and should be regarded as a meaningful expression of the lawgiver's intervention.

---

mind. The prohibition (in Westbrook's terms) and the duty apply to the master simultaneously, during the time that the woman is in his possession.

92. See Yochanan Muffs, *Studies in the Aramaic Legal Papyri from Elephantine* (Leiden: Brill, 1969), 178; Paul, *Book of the Covenant*, 54.

93. It should not be ruled out that the law might be polemicizing against a common practice, as reflected, for example, in Nuzi *mārtūtu u kallatūtu* contracts. In these documents a woman bought for the purpose of marriage may be sold to another person or transferred to another husband with no restriction (see Paul, *Book of the Covenant*, 52–53). In this context an interesting fact should be noted. The law contains four sentences that are couched in the negative: "she shall *not* go out as the male slaves do" (v. 7); he shall have *no* right to sell her" (v. 8); "he shall *not* diminish her food, her clothing, or her marital rights" (v. 10); "And if he does *not* do these three things for her" (v. 11). The *ketib* version should be added here: "he has *not* designated her" (v. 8). This "surplus" creates a sense that the law wishes to respond to familiar norms that have no application, to standard customs that he opposes, or to a potential conduct of the master of which he disapproves, such as diminishing the woman's rights if he marries another (cf. LH 148 and LL 28; in these laws the duty to continue and provide for the needs of the first woman who was rejected is formulated in the affirmative).

The parallelism here plays a role that can be understood by analogy to the two earlier instructions that appear in the opening verses of the law of the male slave and of the female slave: "he shall go out free, for nothing" and "she shall not go out as the male slaves do." Both slaves go out "for nothing," but since the statement that the female does not go out under identical conditions is similarly broad and lacking specification, it might be construed as though it also governs the identical norm, namely, going out for nothing. The lawgiver anticipates this uncertainty, and in order to remove any doubt he adds the phrase "without payment of money." The parallelism, therefore, serves a semantic purpose; it has a clarifying function.[94]

I wish to call attention to one other clarifying comment by the lawgiver, although I do not fully understand its rationale. In the two laws pertaining to an ox that gored a man or another ox to death (21:28–32, 35–36), a distinction is made between an ox that gores for the first time and an ox that has habitually gored in the past (vv. 29, 36). The latter is described in a locution that combines two terms: the adjective נגח ("gorer") and the temporal marker מתמל שלשם (from "aforetime" [lit., "from yesterday and three days ago"]). The first term is undoubtedly sufficient to describe the ox's character, especially when accompanied by the following information, that "its owner has been warned" (v. 29) or that its character "is known" (v. 36). And indeed, in the parallel laws LE 54 and LH 251, a goring ox is defined as *alpum nakkāpū* ("a gorer" as distinct from *alpum ikkip* "an ox [that once] gored"), and it is also noted that the authorities notify its owner that it is a known gorer (*bābtum ana bēlīšu ušēdī*). Neither contains a phrase like מתמל שלשום. As noted above, I cannot explain why the lawgiver felt it necessary to clarify the meaning of the term נִגָּח twice.[95] Perhaps this simply reflects a common literary convention, since other ancient Near Eastern law collections also contain explanatory comments now and again.[96]

---

94. Jackson proposes viewing this as "a post-D addition, designed to stress that the אמה makes no payment, in the light of D's apparent understanding of the expression חנם as referring to a payment from the master" (*Wisdom-Laws*, 92 n. 73). It is difficult to accept this view, because this expression does not appear in the Deuteronomic law, and the expression used to determine that the slave (male and female) will receive a "release grant" is ריקם ("you shall not let him go empty-handed"). It is more logical, in my opinion, that the Deuteronomic lawgiver, in seeking to prevent a misunderstanding, chose a different expression from that of the Book of the Covenant.

95. Perhaps in the time when the text was written and read without vocalization, the scribe wanted to make sure that the sequence *ngh* was read *naggaḥ* and not *nogeaḥ*. The addition of the phrase disambiguates the ambiguous Hebrew form. The rabbinic sages specified the meaning of the clarifying phrase and claimed that it refers to an ox that has gored three times (*Mekilta*, Nezikin, section 10).

96. See, e.g., LH 29, *šumma mārūšu ṣeḥerma ilik abīšu alākam la ile'i* ("If his son is too

I conclude the discussion of the lawgiver's perceptibility in the Book of the Covenant by examining the law of injury to a pregnant woman. It reveals signs of intervention unlike those discussed above.

> ²²When men strive together, and hurt a woman with child, so that there is a miscarriage [Hebrew has plural form], and yet no harm follows, the one who hurt her shall be fined, according as the woman's husband shall lay upon him; and he shall pay as the judges determine. ²³If any harm follows, then you shall give life for life. (Exod 21:22–25)

What happened on the day a pregnant woman went out and whether by chance or by design found herself caught in a brawl? What do the two alternatives presented by the law really describe? Some surmise, as I do, that the woman was beaten or knocked over by one (or more) of the quarreling parties and that she miscarried as a result, or else the blow was lethal and caused her death (or maybe just severe bodily harm).[97] Others believe that the woman emerged unharmed and that only her pregnancy was lost—the fetus [Hebrew has plural] was still in the embryonic phase or had a recognizable human form.[98] The optimistic reading holds that the injury was not so severe and that the fetus survived, even if premature, or alternately, it was a violent blow that caused the miscarriage. In any event, the woman's person was not injured in any way.[99]

---

young [i.e.,] he is unable to perform his father's service obligation"); LH 37, *tuppašu iḫḫeppe u ina kaspīšu ītelli eqlum kirûm u bītum ana bēlīšu itâr* ("his deed shall be invalidated [i.e.,] he shall forfeit his silver, the field orchard or house shall revert to its owner").

97. This view is compatible with the parallel laws LL d-f; LH 209–214; MAL A 50–52; it is reflected in the Vulgate and *Targum Onqelos*; in rabbinic literature (*Mekhilta*, *Nezikin*, section 8); in *Antiquities* 4.278 (*Josephus in Nine Volumes*, vol. 4, *Antiquities* [trans. H. St. J. Thackeray; Loeb Classical Library; Cambridge, Mass.: Harvard University Press, 1962–65]). This is also the common position of traditional commentators (e.g., Rashi, Rashbam, and Ibn Ezra), and it is supported by no small number of modern commentators (e.g., Samuel E. Loewenstamm, "Exodus 21: 22–25," *VT* 27 [1977]: 352–60; Paul, *Book of the Covenant*, 72; Sarna, *Exodus*, 125; Sprinkle, *Book of the Covenant*, 89, 92–93).

98. This description finds support in HL 17–18. The sanction for causing the miscarriage is a function of the term of pregnancy; that is, it corresponds to the maturity of the fetus that was lost. Such a distinction is reflected also in the Septuagint and Vetus Latina; and in Philo's *On the Special Laws* 3.108–09 (*Philo*, vol. 7 [trans. F. H. Colson; Loeb Classical Library; Cambridge, Mass.: Harvard University Press, 1950]. For an extensive discussion of the so-called minority tradition, see Stanley Isser, "Two Traditions: The Law of Exodus 21:22–23 Revisited," *CBQ* 52 (1990): 30–45.

99. See Bernard S. Jackson, "The Problem of Exodus 21: 22–5 (Ius Talionis)," in *Essays in Jewish and Comparative Legal History* (Studies in Judaism in Late Antiquity; Leiden: Brill, 1975), 94–96; idem, *Wisdom-Laws*, 214–20.

The uncertainty regarding the reconstruction of the scenario (which is just one of many controversies over the meaning and application of the law's sanctions, which happily do not concern us here) arises because the lawgiver chose to describe the outcome of the injury by means of an unusual term, אסון, which does not appear anywhere else in the legal corpus.[100]

We may regard this expression as a technical legal term for deadly injury, or as a medical term describing a serious injury that leads to corporeal damage.[101] I argue, however, that the enlistment of such an unusual expression stems from the lawgiver's desire to reveal his personal sentiment toward such a dramatic event as the death of a pregnant woman.[102] This is why he does not employ "objective" language (like the phrase used in the law of bodily injury, "and the man does not die" [21:18]),[103] but prefers an idiom that is intellectually and emotionally charged. The word אסון (which I prefer to translate as "calamity" rather than "harm"), occurs only three times elsewhere in the Bible, all in the cycle of Joseph stories (Gen 42:4, 38; 44:29), expressing Jacob's fear of what might happen to his beloved son, Benjamin.[104] The emotionally laden word betrays the speaker's feelings with respect to the situation at hand

---

100. According to Westbrook, this term relates not to the outcome of the injury, that is, the type of damage incurred, but to the question of who is responsible for the damage. It is a legal term meaning an unknown perpetrator, so in the main law the perpetrator is known whereas in the secondary law he is unknown (Raymond Westbrook, "Lex Talionis and Exodus 21, 22–25," *RB* 93 [1986]: 55–57).

101. See Sprinkle, *Book of the Covenant*, 92–93. William H. C. Propp believes that the term refers to any injury or corporeal damage caused to mother or child (see *Exodus 19–40: A New Translation with Introduction and Commentary* [AB 2A; New York: Doubleday, 2006], 225). Loewenstamm suggests that the use of the term in this context reflects a "particular Hebrew dialect" ("Exodus 21: 22–25," 358).

102. Generally (as we have already seen), the lawgiver explicitly reveals his views in "motive clauses" relating to the apodosis. Here the (implicit) exposure occurs in the protasis.

103. In the parallel laws (LL e; LH 210, 212, 214; MAL A 50) the woman's death is described by regular phrases: *tukum-b[i b]a-ug* ("If she dies"); *šumma sinništum ši imtūt* ("If that woman should die"); *šumma amtum ši imtūt* ("If that slave woman should die"); *šumma sinniltu šīt mētat* ("And if that woman dies"). The Vulgate and *Targum Onqelos* also use "objective" language: *sed ipsa vixerit* ("but she remains alive"); *sin autem mor seius fuerit subsecuta* ("if however her death follows"); ולא יהא מותא; ואם מותא יהא.

104. Jackson argues that the term's usage to express Jacob's fear for the safety of his son supports his (Jackson's) view that the word refers to the death of the fetus. Although Benjamin is not a fetus, a different term is used to refer to the death of a child, who does not have the same legal personality as an adult (*Wisdom-Laws*, 216–17). Westbrook's view is totally different, saying that Jacob is afraid of a disaster for which nobody can be blamed ("Exodus 21, 22–25," 57). I find it implausible to relate Jacob's deep feelings to a legal question of culpability/responsibility. He is afraid of the disaster itself and is not concerned with the legal problem that no one can be blamed for it.

(its first use is part of Jacob's interior speech). To find a word so laden with emotional nuance in a legal text might be contrary to expectation. But our awareness of the lawgiver's engagement in the substance of the laws leads us to believe that the word reflects the way he sees the events, his shock and sorrow at the death of a woman in her condition (perhaps touched by the profound feelings of her relatives in view of their loss). By expressing his subjective attitude, the lawgiver lends an emotional depth to the events.

It remains now to clarify one more puzzline point. The role of the phrase "If any harm follows" in the secondary law is clear. This is the substrate of fact upon which the legal sanction is based. But what is the role of the *negative phrase* "and yet no harm follows" appearing in the main law? The legal arrangement (monetary compensation for the husband) takes into account only the harm that was incurred in practice (the loss of the fetus) and naturally does not reflect what did not occur (death/injury of the woman). Why, then, does the lawgiver find it necessary to note a fact that is irrelevant to the formulation of the legal sanction? In other words, what reason can there be for the appearance of a phrase that has no value from a legal point of view?[105] I suggest a purely literary reason, that is, the role the lawgiver designates for this phrase in the process of reading the law. The phrase foreshadows the serious event that is to be presented next, "If any harm follows," and allows the reader to become aware of this eventuality gradually. The reader processes the information—no harm followed, at present, one says to oneself, but it could happen. Did it occur? The negative phrase arouses curiosity and creates a tension that accompanies the reader until the (suspended) presentation of the more dramatic event. This phrase keeps the mind occupied and prompts the reader to orient oneself to an event that is not (yet) presented in the text. The lawgiver, of course, was not familiar with theories concerning the dynamic character of the reading process, which stress the reciprocal relations between text and reader.[106] Nonetheless, owing to this intervention, which "leads" us from one event to another, the lawgiver renders the reading of the law into a dynamic process.[107]

---

105. Even according to the interpretation that the main law describes a premature birth and not a miscarriage (Jackson's view), the sentence is irrelevant from a legal standpoint, because the sanction is based on the positive determination ויצאו ילדיה, that is, "they were born." Only if the law has in mind the immaturity of the fetus (i.e., "the minority tradition") does it have a legal value, because the sanction is derived directly from this fact.

106. See Rimmon-Kenan, *Narrative Fiction*, 117–29.

107. On the role of the sentence "and the man does not die," in the reading process of the law of bodily injury (21:18–19), see Assnat Bartor, "Reading Law as Narrative: A Study in the Casuistic Laws of the Pentateuch" (in Hebrew), *Igud, Selected Essays in Jewish Studies*, vol. 1 (ed. B. Schwartz et al.; Jerusalem: World Union of Jewish Studies, 2008), 62–67.

In conclusion, a few short summary remarks. Some of the lawgiver's interventions in the Book of the Covenant stand out, while other, less obvious ones are hidden within the "functional" language of the law. The lawgiver reasons, explains, presents his position, refers to other norms, expands the scope of the argument, and broadens the point of view, all for the sake of objectives that go beyond the presentation of (relevant) facts and the establishment of legal norms. It is interesting to note, and also somewhat surprising, that the practically minded lawgiver, whose style is terse and measured, does not shy away from generating textual superfluity (from a legal standpoint) in a great number of laws. Yet in this respect he is still not as bold as the Deuteronomic lawgiver.

The Laws of Deuteronomy

The signs of the lawgiver's engagement in the Book of the Covenant, be it a word, an idiom, or a single phrase, must frequently be "extracted" from the legal instructions within which they are so seamlessly embedded. In the Deuteronomic Code the reverse is true. In a great many laws, it is the legal elements, rather, that must be extracted from the hortatory speeches.[108] In addition, the lawgiver's engagement with the content of the laws is very intensive (note the frequent use of motive clauses, sometimes several times within the same law). All this is presented openly, explicitly, in perfect congruity with the lawgiver's own declarations, and with the narrator's preamble to the book of Deuteronomy:

> Beyond the Jordan, in the land of Moab, Moses undertook to explain this law. (1:5)
>
> And the LORD commanded me at that time to teach you statutes and ordinances. (4:14)[109]

These verses indicate that Moses' role does not end with the establishment of norms, but that he must guarantee their transmission and see that they are instilled, taught, and explicated so that the addressees understand the nature of the laws, recognize their righteousness,[110] and are persuaded to uphold them.

---

108. Much has been written about the oratory preaching style of the Deuteronomic lawgiver; see, e.g., George Thomas Manley, *The Book of the Law: Studies in the Date of Deuteronomy* (London: Tyndale, 1957), 24–27; Norbert Lohfink, *Das Hauptgebot: Eine Untersuchung literarischer Einleitungsfragen zu Dtn. 5–11* (Analecta Biblica 20; Rome: Pontificio Instituto Biblico, 1963), 90–97; Weinfeld, *Deuteronomy and the Deuteronomic School*, 171–78.

109. See also 4:1, 5; 5:28; 6:1.

110. See 4:8. It is plausible that the phrase "statutes and ordinances so righteous" is the equivalent of the Akkadian *dīnāt mīšarim*.

THE LAWGIVER AS NARRATOR

To fulfill this role the lawgiver developed a "mode of intervention" that eschewed objective delivery of the bare substance of the laws in favor of a diverse use of clarification, emphasis, and persuasion. His systematic intervention engendered laws that combined two levels of discourse—the legal and the notational. The first level contains the legal norms, along with the relevant facts underlying them, while the second, no less important, level includes a variety of utterances that reflect the additional role assumed by the lawgiver and his constant engagement with the substance of the laws. The great many comments in which he speaks his mind create "*textual superfluity*," and the innumerable repetitive structures he employs create an "*informational redundancy*,"[111] which is untypical of legal texts. Yet, in this instance they are in the service of his needs and those of his addressees.

A note concerning rhetoric is in order here. The means of repetition employed in the laws are no different from those employed in other biblical literary genres. The laws too reflect literary-artistic conventions, and in this respect their authors did not innovate using any unique literary techniques. However, the intensive use of these literary means and their impact on how we process the laws' contents indicate not only that their function is aesthetic but that they reflect the lawgiver's evident desire to enact "annotated laws." In light of this remark we now begin to acquaint ourselves with the lawgiver's modes of engagement through his use of repetitive structures. Only a small number of examples among many are presented here, but they are sufficient to illustrate how the "system" works.

Quite often it is difficult to discern what "actual" purpose the repetition serves. See, for instance, the superfluous statement in the law of adultery and in the law of kidnapping.

> If a man is found lying with the wife of another man, both of them shall die, *the man who lay with the woman, and the woman*. (22:22)
>
> If a man is found stealing one of his brethren, *the people of Israel* . . . (24:7)

Clearly there is no need to specify who the "both" are who are destined to die; no one would err in thinking that one of them is the betrayed husband. It is also unnecessary to point out who the "brethren" are, since it is inconceivable that the law is addressing a kidnapping "within the family." The lawgiver nevertheless does intervene, for emphases that have a "merely" rhetorical function are also valuable to him.[112]

---

111. This term was coined by Meir Sternberg in reference to the repetitive patterns in biblical narrative (see *Poetics of Biblical Narrative*, 365–440). On repetitive structures in the laws of the Pentateuch, see Watts, *Reading Law*, 68–74.

112. However, there might be a legal purpose for the emphasis in the law of adultery.

A different motivation is apparent in the lawgiver's intervention in the law of the broken-necked heifer (21:1-9). When a slain body is found in the open country and it is not known who the killer is, a rite of expiation must be immediately performed. To inform the addressees of the proper procedure, the lawgiver provides all the necessary details, even those that do not appear to be useful.

> ³and the elders of the city which is nearest to the slain man shall take <u>a heifer which has never been worked</u> *and which has not pulled in the yoke.* ⁴And the elders of that city shall bring the heifer down to <u>a valley with running water, which is neither plowed</u> *nor sown,* and shall break the heifer's neck <u>there</u> *in the valley.* (21:3-4)

In the first part, each underlined phrase contains the complete relevant information—which heifer should be chosen, what valley to lead it to, where its neck should be broken. However, the lawgiver is not content to impart just the essential information but adds clarifying comments (indicated in italics) that reflect an indirect dialogue with his addressees. Although his instructions are clear and precise, still, if questions arise—Which heifer has never been worked? Which valley has not been plowed? Where is "there"?—they will be answered respectively: a heifer that has not pulled a yoke; a perennial stream that is not sown; in the valley.[113] The lawgiver seems to anticipate and preempt potential questions. If someone were to argue that he appears simply to have employed a common artful convention of parallelism (synonymous or complementary), I would reply that this is true, but his is a dynamic usage that transforms a familiar repetitive structure into a vehicle for communication.

Frequently the lawgiver sets down duties and prohibitions within a frame that juxtaposes a general and a particular statement. In some cases the general statement is sufficient to define the boundaries of the commandment, while the particulars are of no real use. In other cases it is precisely the details that are essential, because the general statement is not feasible. At any rate, the law-

---

One might argue that the woman should be spared, because she was overpowered by the man, who knew that he was lying with a married woman. Or one could argue the opposite: the woman knows she belongs to her husband, and so she is more at fault and should be punished more severely. The lawgiver dismisses such argumentation, or excuse making, in advance by insisting that both parties to the adulterous act be put to death.

113. The reason for a heifer that has not worked, a free-flowing stream, and so on, is that things can be holy when they remain close to the condition in which God made them; being close to their created state, they properly belong to God; see Edward L. Greenstein, "The Torah as She is Read," in *Essays on Biblical Method and Translation* (ed. Edward L. Greenstein; Brown Judaic Studies 92; Atlanta: Scholars Press, 1989), 49.

giver does not dispose of the superfluous phrases, since he considers the blend of concrete and abstract to have value. Let me illustrate it.

Two of the central segments of the dietary laws (14:3–21) open with general statements: "You shall not eat any abominable thing" (v. 3); "You may eat all clean birds" (v. 11). Neither statement provides any practical inference, so the lawgiver enumerates in a list which animals and fowl may or may not be eaten (vv. 4–8, 12–18). Why, then, is it not enough just to furnish the lists that define the dietary regulations? Apparently, the lawgiver does not wish to forgo the general declarative statement of the law's rationale—the substantive distinction between impure and pure.[114]

The permission to take spoils from a conquered city exhibits an inverse relationship between the general and concrete statement.

> but the women and the little ones, the cattle, and everything else in the city, all its spoil, you shall take as booty for yourselves; and you shall enjoy the spoil of your enemies, which the LORD your God has given you. (20:14)

The permission granted is sweeping and unrestricted, as is shown by the double use of the word כל ("all"). Accordingly, the three examples enumerated in the beginning of the verse are unnecessary. Though it is understandable why the lawgiver should wish to provide illustrations, as this reinforces comprehension, would it not have been more sensible to begin with the general statement of permission to enjoy the spoils, and only then to offer examples?[115] Possibly, but in this instance the superfluous wording does not arise from a desire to provide illustrations; the reason for the internal order of the wording would seem to be different. Since the lawgiver wants to emphasize that the addressee is here given carte blanche to enjoy the spoils, he chooses to start with a restricted list of the items, and then to intensify it with two sweeping statements.[116] The lawgiver allows the addressee gradually to absorb the mean-

---

114. The law that prohibits magic (18:9–11) exhibits a similar repetitive structure. It begins with a general, declarative, "non-applied" commandment that articulates the rationale of the law, and later details the prohibited behaviors themselves. In terms of the function it fulfills, this type of parallelism is similar to the structure that Adele Berlin has called "the particularizing parallelism." The detail or details that appear in the second colon provide specification for the information in the first colon (e.g., "The voice of the LORD breaks the cedars, the LORD breaks the cedars of Lebanon" [Ps 29:5]). See Adele Berlin, "Shared Rhetorical Features in Biblical and Sumerian Literature," *JANES* 10 (1978): 35–42.

115. See, e.g., the repetitive structure in LE 36, which is meant to illustrate that no proof exists that the house (in which the lost property was deposited) had been broken into: *bītum la pališ sippu la ḫališ aptum la nashat* ("without evidence that the house has been broken into, the doorjamb scraped, the window forced").

116. This form of parallelism is similar to the structure in which one colon intensifies

ing of this great windfall and feel thrilled at its boundless promise (the final motive clause stresses the enjoyment that is held in store).

One of the most effective figures of repetition commonly employed by the lawgiver, exhibiting his tendency to facilitate understanding and internalization of the norms, is a grammatical construction that presents the legal norm in a binary contrasting pattern. This construction has two chief variants: the legal norm appears both in the affirmative and in the negative, describing the performance of an action and simultaneously the nonperformance of the opposite action (e.g., "you shall save alive nothing that breathes, but you shall utterly destroy them" [20:16b-17a]); or when two different norms, one permitted and the other forbidden, are presented side by side (e.g., "You shall eat no leavened bread with it; seven days you shall eat it with unleavened bread" [16:3a]). The combination of the command and the prohibition and their interdependence are mutually illuminating. Presenting the legal norm by means of a contrasting analogy enables the addressee to understand better the lawgiver's assertions. I therefore label this literary device a *clarifying contrast*.[117]

Unlike the victory celebrations and reveling in the spoils that begin once a distant city has been captured (20:15), another type of din and clamor follows the belligerent acts that must be taken against an Israelite city, whose inhabitants have enticed others to idolatry.

---

the information or the argument communicated in the first colon, which Robert Alter has called a "structure of intensification" (e.g., "Look, answer me LORD my God, give light to my eyes..." [Ps 13:4]—the looking is heightened in the second verset into giving light to the eyes). See Alter, *Art of Biblical Poetry*, 62–84.

117. Many of the clarifying contrasts are phrased in the form of a parallelism commonly used in biblical poetry, known as "negative parallelism." See Moshe Held, "The Action-Result (Factitive-Passive) Sequence of Identical Verbs in Biblical Hebrew and Ugaritic," *JBL* 84 (1965): 275, 282 n. 71; Kugel, *Idea of Biblical Poetry*, 14; Adele Berlin, *The Dynamics of Biblical Parallelism* (Bloomington: Indiana University Press, 1985), 56–57; Chaim Cohen, "The Phenomenon of Negative Parallelism and Its Implications for the Study of Biblical Poetry" (in Hebrew), *Beer-sheva* 3 (1988): 69–107. Clarifying contrasts also appear in other ancient Near Eastern law collections. See, e.g., LH 44, *aḫšu iddima eqlam la iptete* ("he is negligent and does not open the field"); LH 61, *eqlam ina zaqāpim la igmurma niditam īzib* ("[he] does not complete the planting of the field, but leaves an uncultivated area"); LH 133b, [*pa*]*garša la iṣṣurma ana bīt šanîm īterub* ("[she] does not keep herself chaste but enters another's house"); LE 12–13, 28 *imāt ūl iballuṭ* ("[he/she] shall die, he/she will not live"). Reuven Yaron and Raymond Westbrook differ in regard to the function of this last contrast. Yaron, who calls it a "negated antonym parallelism," believes that it has a rhetorical function and is meant only to emphasize the statement ("Stylistic Conceits: The Negated Antonym," *JANES* 22 [1993]: 141–48). Westbrook attributes legal significance to it—it decrees that the transgressor should be executed without granting the right of pardon (Raymond Westbrook, "A Matter of Life and Death," *JANES* 25 [1997]: 61–70).

> ¹²If you hear in one of your cities . . . ¹³that certain base fellows have gone out among you and have drawn away the inhabitants of the city . . . ¹⁵you shall surely put the inhabitants of that city to the sword, destroying it utterly, all who are in it and its cattle, with the edge of the sword. ¹⁶You shall gather all its spoil into the midst of its open square, and burn the city and all its spoil with fire, as a whole burnt offering to the LORD your God; it shall be a heap for ever, it shall not be built again. (13:12–18)

The cries of those slain by sword; the wails of slaughtered livestock; the sound of spoils gathered into the city square; and the crackling of the fire consuming the houses and the property of their inhabitants—these are the noises produced by the devastating acts taken against the idolatrous city. But once these acts are concluded, all other activity in the city will cease. This is the broad contrastive structure the law presents—the din and clamor of intensive effort, as opposed to the perpetual, absolute silence and cessation of activity implied in the image "it shall be a heap for ever, it shall not be built again." Even this final sentence exhibits a contrastive pattern—a double utterance, first phrased in the affirmative, then in the negative—clearly illustrating the fate of the city. In this ominous phrase one may hear the silence and see the nothingness of desolation.

I conclude my discussion of repetitive patterns with a selection of clarifying contrasts that appear in less dramatic laws, dealing with mundane scenarios in the protagonist's life. The first is the law of sending off the mother bird.

> ⁶If you chance to come upon a bird's nest, in any tree or on the ground, with young ones or eggs and the mother sitting upon the young or upon the eggs, you shall not take the mother with the young; ⁷you shall let the mother go, but the young you may take to yourself; that it may go well with you, and that you may live long. (22:6–7)

The normative section begins with a prohibition that is not sufficiently lucid: "you shall not take the mother with the young." Is it forbidden to take the bird and the young ones together but permitted to take each separately? Or perhaps it is forbidden to take the young ones but it is all right to take the mother? The picture becomes clearer later in the commandment where the necessary specification of the legal norm is provided: "you shall let the mother go, but the young you may take to yourself." Why does the lawgiver choose to begin with a negative statement, which not only lacks all legal significance (apart from its declarative value), but also is not without ambiguity? At the very least he might have started with the practical commandment and expanded it through the clarifying contrast, to emphasize the main statement. The pattern employed seems, nonetheless, to serve the spirit of the law. The law limits the power of the protagonist (to obtain the bird and its offspring). It restrains the natural impulse to appropriate everything that is available and up for grabs. The lawgiver, therefore, begins with a prohibition and not with permission, establishing a boundary from the very outset.

The following laws too, which address the appropriation of agricultural produce, deal with boundary setting and establishing norms of decency toward other persons. But here the contrastive pattern is presented in reverse order—first with the affirmative statement (the permission) and later with negative wording (the prohibition). We shall presently understand why.

> [24]When you go into your neighbor's vineyard, you may eat your fill of grapes, as many as you wish, but you shall not put any in your vessel. [25]When you go into your neighbor's standing grain, you may pluck the ears with your hand, but you shall not put a sickle to your neighbor's standing grain. (23:24–25)

The lawgiver sets down the permissions before the prohibition because he has an understanding of human nature. The most effective way to restrain the protagonist's impulse to take whatever he can from the abundant crops—to guard him from temptation or from violating the implicit trust placed in him when no one else is in the field—is to preempt and respond to his immediate need, namely, his appetite or desire. The lawgiver therefore allows him to eat his fill without restraint—"as many as he wishes." When the protagonist is sated and satisfied, it is easier for him to accept the prohibition and to internalize the boundary that strikes a balance between his own needs and the needs of others.

In the laws concerning the welfare of indigents the contrastive pattern is inverted again.

> [10]When you make your neighbor a loan of any sort, *you shall not* go into his house to fetch his pledge. [11]*You shall* stand outside, and the man to whom you make the loan shall bring the pledge out to you. [12]And if he is a poor man, *you shall not* sleep in his pledge; [13]when the sun goes down, *you shall* restore to him the pledge ... [14]*You shall not* oppress a hired servant who is poor and needy ... [15]*you shall* give him his hire on the day he earns it, before the sun goes ... lest he cry against you to the LORD, and it be sin in you. (24:10–15)[118]

Each law first describes the improper behavior and only afterwards, in the concluding clause, sets forth the proper conduct, which is the binding legal norm. Although the negated command adds nothing substantive to the legal norm, it adds much to its comprehensibility and assimilability, as it addresses itself to the sensibility of the addressee. In view of his understanding of human nature, the lawgiver employs the negated command as a rhetorical device, to clarify that the protagonist is not meant to behave according to his bad,

---

118. See similar contrastive structures in the laws of gleaning (24:19–22).

albeit natural, inclination. It is a lawgiver's response toward anticipated human behavior, aiming to help the addressee internalize norms, which transparently reflect a high level of socioethical commitment.[119]

Other "lawgiver's responses" can be recognized in texts that extend regulations already prescribed in the law to additional objects or subjects. The "analogical extensions" (as Michael Fishbane calls them) [120]exist in three laws: the law of the male and female slave; the capture of cities; and the return of lost property. All of them employ the phrase "you shall do likewise" (כן תעשה).[121]

> And to your bondwoman you shall do likewise. (15:17b)
>
> Thus you shall do to all the cities which are very far from you. (20:15)
>
> And so you shall do with his ass; so you shall do with his garment; so you shall do with any lost thing of your brother's, which he loses and you find; you may not withhold your help. (22:3)

Instead of taking the additional elements into account in advance, as an integral element of the legal arrangement, the lawgiver presents them as an *afterthought*. He seems to have reexamined his statements, realized that the legal arrangement is partial and insufficient (or poorly worded), and to have made up his mind to add elements that should have been initially included: that a Hebrew bondwoman may be made a permanent slave by submitting to the ear-piercing ceremony (15:16–17a);[122] that when the people attack distant cities an offer of peace must be made, and only if this offer is declined are the inhabitants to be treated with severity (20:10–14); that lost property must be returned to its owner, and that when the owner's identity is unknown, the finder must safeguard it until the owner is found (22:1–2).[123]

---

119. In the law prohibiting the delay of wages there are two additional clarifying contrasts that are not reflected in the English translation: ביומו תתן שכרו ולא תבוא עליו השמש (v. 15a) and ולא יקרא עליך אל ה' והיה בך חטא (v. 15b).

120. See Fishbane, *Biblical Interpretation*, 183.

121. Analogical extensions also appear in the Book of the Covenant in the law of firstborn and in the law of the fallow year (Exod 22:29; 23:11).

122. The juxtaposition of the comment with the piercing ceremony implies that it is referring back to it (see, e.g., Driver, *Deuteronomy*, 184). Rashi, Rashbam, and Ibn Ezra, who state that "the woman is not pierced," associated the extension with the seventh year's release grant.

123. The proposed interpretation of the analogical extensions as "afterthoughts" and as "lawgiver's responses" departs from the standard scholarly interpretation (although the two approaches have much in common). It is widely agreed that the analogical extensions reflect legislative additions to existing legal regulations, aiming to adjust the fixed legal rules to different or new circumstances or conceptions, and the decision whether a specific analogical extension is primary or secondary (which is itself interpolated into the original law

Characterizing the extensions as "afterthoughts" is only a partial explanation of the lawgiver's intervention here, because the question remains why he (presents himself as someone who) must reexamine his words? The answer relates to the implicit dialogue that he is conducting with his addressees. He considers the legal arrangements from their point of view, and in anticipation of questions that might occur to them he provides clarifying extensions. These are indeed "lawgiver's responses"—responses to the needs of the addressees.

In the law of the male and female slave, the question might arise whether the piercing ceremony applies to the female slave, since, with the exception of the opening phrase of the law ("If your brother, a Hebrew man, or a Hebrew woman, is sold to you . . ." [15:12a]), all its remaining instructions are couched in the masculine form. Such a question does not arise in regard to the application of "the release arrangement," which appears in proximity to the opening phrases. But the textual distance of the piercing ceremony may provoke doubt with respect to its sphere of application. The extension is designed to remove this doubt (although according to the rules of legal formulation the opening sentence governs all of the legal arrangements established by the law, unless otherwise specified). The rules of subduing and capturing a city contain no reference to the city's geographical location or the identity of its inhabitants. A question might therefore arise whether these rules are valid in regard to any city against which war is waged. The lawgiver provides the answer.

The dialogical character of the extension is especially conspicuous in the law of returning lost property, since it itself is formulated dynamically. It begins with an answer to a predictable question: Is it only an ox or a stray lamb that has to be returned to its owner? No, an ass must also be returned. Another question then arises: Does the obligation apply only to animate goods? No, it applies also to garments. Just to garments? No, it applies to all inanimate goods. Indeed, the commandment to collect lost property and guard it until the identity of the owner is discovered (v. 2) also seems to be

---

of D) is based on grammatical grounds. Deuteronomy 15:17b, for instance, reinterprets the "involuntary bondwoman-marriage" institution (Exod 21:7–11) as a voluntary transaction on the woman's part; Deut 20:15 is an attempt to harmonize the preceding legal regulations with the following law of extermination (vv. 16–18); and 22:3 is part of the Deuteronomist's expansion of the earlier law (Exod 23:4–5) due to his different conceptions (see, e.g., Driver, *Deuteronomy*, 249–50; Fishbane, *Biblical Interpretation*, 177–87, 199–200, 211 n. 99; Jackson, *Wisdom-Laws*, 18, 87). I do not reject that standard scholarly opinion, but propose an approach that examines the extensions as part of a communicative interaction that occurs internally within the laws, an approach that examines the relationship between the primary legal arrangement and its extension within the narrow frame of each law, rather than the broad frame of the entire body of the laws of the Pentateuch.

an answer to a natural question: What if I cannot return it because I don't know who owns it?[124]

I could expand on the latter aspect of the lawgiver's mode of engagement, but my rather selective examination will suffice to demonstrate how he renders his presence constantly perceptible and the function this presence fulfills within the laws.

The Priestly Legislation

To obtain a fuller picture of the perceptibility of the three lawgivers, highlighting the salient characteristics of each, my investigation of the modes of intervention of the Priestly lawgiver focuses on what are deemed to be his distinguishing features. Some of these features are not unique to him; they appear now and again in the laws of Deuteronomy (just as some of the typical modes of engagement of the Deuteronomic laws appear in the Priestly legislation). But their intensive deployment reveals them to be typical representatives of his "intervention mechanism." Such a mechanism may be identified.

Many of the laws reveal the engagement of a guiding hand that organizes, defines, categorizes, or summarizes contents; sometimes it only emphasizes them, doubling and even tripling the volume of text devoted to communicating facts and ideas. All this is achieved through the use of regular linguistic patterns that are repeated like a refrain. The regular rhythm and the symmetrical structures manifested in the recurring linguistic phrases are ample indication of the lawgiver's methodical and pedantic treatment of materials. This point should be clarified. The textual and linguistic features that I treat as signs of the lawgiver's engagement are part of a broader whole that can be called the "linguistic style of the Priestly author." They are not unique to the Priestly lawgiver;[125] however, he harnesses this style to his own ends and uses it to fulfill his role as he understands it.

The Priestly lawgiver, like his Deuteronomic counterpart, is didactic. Or it might be better said that he is a pedagogical lawgiver, because his characteristic interventions do not explicate or illuminate, nor do they have the dialogical character of the Deuteronomic lawgiver's interventions. He does not lead his addressees by the hand, to ensure the reception and internalization of the legal norms. Rather, his interventions (which of course create textual excess

---

124. See Richard D. Nelson, *Deuteronomy: A Commentary* (OTL; Louisville: Westminster John Knox, 2002), 267.

125. On Priestly style as reflected in law and in narrative, see, e.g., Sean E. McEvenue, *The Narrative Style of the Priestly Writer* (Analecta Biblica 50; Rome: Biblical Institute Press, 1971); Meir Paran, *Forms of the Priestly Style in the Pentateuch* (in Hebrew; Jerusalem: Magnes, 1989).

and informational redundancy) are conducted as a "professional-academic" discourse, providing keys for a better comprehension of the legal materials.

Title, introduction, and summary are the three elements that characterize academic texts. They serve to present the topic, the arguments, and central conclusions and to guide comprehension of the issues. The lawgiver too seems to be aware of the advantage of deploying all three devices, since he often begins his recitation of the laws by introducing the topic and only later specifying the relevant norms. More frequently he summarizes the laws by indicating the topics that were previously elaborated. The *"headings"* and the *"summary comments"* are couched in similar formulas. For example:

> *This is the law of* the burnt offering. The burnt offering shall be on the hearth upon the altar . . . [Lev 6:9]; *This is the law of* the burnt offering, of the cereal offering, of the sin offering, of the guilt offering, of the consecration, and of the peace offerings [7:37].
>
> *This shall be the law of* the leper for the day of his cleansing. He shall be brought to the priest [14:2]. . . . *This is the law for* him in whom is a leprous disease, who cannot afford the offerings for his cleansing [14:32].
>
> And *this is the law for* the Nazirite, when the time of his separation has been completed . . . [Num 6:13]. . . . *This is the law for* the Nazirite who takes a vow [6:21].[126]

The headings and the summary comments have no practical legal value, for they contribute nothing to the information imparted in the detailed instructions, yet they do have an interpretive value.[127] The former, which define the subject matter addressed by a certain set of instructions, focus on that which is most important; the latter, which recapitulate the main issues, explain what the specific instructions are addressing.[128] The resulting demarcations—of single

---

126. See in addition, e.g., Lev 6:14, 25; 7:1, 11 ("headings") and Lev 11:46–47; 12:7b; 13:59; 14:54–57; 15:32–33; Num 5:29–30 ("summary comments"). Apart from the uses of the general terms "the law" (. . . ה תורת זאת, התורה זאת), in some cases specific terms appear, such as: "This is the offering" (Lev 6:20); "This is the portion" (7:35); "These are the appointed feasts of the LORD" (23:4). In the Deuteronomic laws, headings (but not summary comments) appear three times: "And this is the manner of the release . . ." (15:2a); "And this shall be the priests' due from the people" (18:3a); "This is the provision for the manslayer (19:4a).

127. They might also have a practical value as didactic aids in memorizing and enacting the texts (see Michael Fishbane, "Biblical Colophons, Textual Criticism and Legal Analogies," *CBQ* 42 [1980]: 445).

128. According to Fishbane, the "summary comments" in the law of the *Sotah*, which refer to two different laws ("This is the law in cases of jealousy, when a wife . . . goes astray and defiles herself, *or* when the spirit of jealousy comes upon a man" [Num 5:29–30]), confirm the conclusion arising (in his opinion) from the opening verses, that the law deals with two separate cases. The first is described in vv. 12–13, to which v. 29 refers, and the second

laws, series of laws, or large units of subject matter—also have an interpretive value, because they mark and classify the instructions according to their specific contents.[129]

Whereas the headings and the summary comments reflect the lawgiver's overarching meta-perspective—the external standpoint from which he regards the legal instructions and provides them with a framework of structure and content—the interventions discussed below reflect his penetrating view of details. They pertain to substantial issues and are therefore integrated into the laws themselves. Some interventions contribute information (we will examine whether and to what extent this information is necessary for the implementation of the law); others repeat the existing information (we will discover what purpose the repetition serves); still others expose the attitude of the lawgiver (we will consider in what manner). All reveal a guiding hand that teaches us how to process the material.

The law of leprosy in Leviticus 13–14, as the "summary comment" indicates (see 14:57), is constructed along a more or less uniform pattern. First, an infectious disease is described (infection of the body, of garments, or of the house), with or without its formal definition; next an instruction is given regarding the requirement to bring the infected object to the priest (the priest comes to the house himself); the priest diagnoses the infection based on the signs that he recognizes and decides the manner of treatment (declaring immediately that the infected object is unclean; quarantining it until its status is decided; observing its conditions until the quarantine period is over; and purifying it when the infection has either been cured or its condition altered). Within each of these units (after describing how the object is brought to the

---

in v. 14, to which v. 30 refers. Both constitute what is called תורת הקנאת (Fishbane, "Accusations of Adultery: A Study of Law and Scribal Practice in Numbers 5:11–31," *HUCA* 45 [1974]: 25–45). Jaeyoung Jeon has offered a different analysis. The law was edited from two laws: the water ordeal law (original stratum) and the ritual oath law (editorial stratum). The former stipulates that when a woman is accused of adultery by the public, she must undergo a water ordeal, whereas the latter is for a case in which a husband only doubts his wife, and she may released with only an oath. The two laws strikingly parallel LH 131 and LH 132. See Jaeyoung Jeon, "Two Laws in the Sotah Passage (Num. V 11–31)," *VT* 57 (2007): 181–207.

129. These lawgiver's interventions, which reveal the significance he accords to defining, classifying, attributing, and demarcating topics, seem to reflect a common convention of ancient Near Eastern scribes. In those scribal traditions, texts of different types—archival, ritual, series of prayers and incantations, catalogues, and inventories—begin with a phrase that serves as a title and ends with a phrase enumerating the chief topics covered (see Fishbane, *Biblical Interpretation*, 32–34). In this context, the sentence that follows the title of the "Shiloah Inscription" may be recalled, "and this is the story of the tunnel," וזה היה דבר הנקבה, as well as the introductory phrase, serving as a general heading, in 4Q251: "concerning immoral unions," על העריות (see Brin, *Studies in Biblical Law*, 124).

priest, and either before, in the course of, or after the description of the treatment) a comment appears that *classifies* the symptoms and *defines* the infection; in some cases an additional comment *declares* the status of the infected object. For example: "it is a plague of leprosy" (e.g., 13:3, 20, 25, 27); "it is a scab" (13:6); "it is the scar of the boil" (13:23); "it is an itch, a leprosy of the head or the beard" (13:30); "it is a malignant leprosy in the house" (14:44); "he is unclean" (13:36, 44, 46); "for he is unclean" (13:11); "it is unclean" (13:51, 55); "he is clean" (13:17, 37, 39, 41); "he is bald but he is clean" (13:40). These comments, which are appended to the rich and colorful descriptions of the infections and the explicit instructions for treatment in each case, again indicate the importance the lawgiver attributes to the classification and definition of the phenomena in question. He is not content merely to describe the symptoms and their treatment, although this would form a self-contained legal unit (the symptoms are the factual data and the priest's treatment is the legal norm), but he adds the diagnoses, pertaining both to the infections and the infected persons/objects, so that the legal norms can be founded on them and deduced from them.[130]

It should be noted that the "*diagnostic comments*," like the other instructions in the law of leprosy, are delivered from the lawgiver's perspective (and therefore reflect his engagement). Yet, since the diagnosis of infection is performed by the priest and it is he who also declares the status of the infected object, these can be regarded as reflections of the priest's actual diagnoses, as statements that are delivered from his perspective.[131]

The illicit sexual practices in Lev 18:6–23 and the sexual offenses in 20:9–21 are replete with the lawgiver's interventions in the "diagnosis form." Some of them condemn the illicit act: "it is depravity" (18:17; 20:14); "it is an abomination" (18:22); "it is a perversion" (18:23); "it is a disgrace" (20:17); "it is impurity" (20:21). Although these labels have no legal significance, since the illicit action bears sanctions even without the condemnation, the lawgiver's negative judgment, through his use of stigmatizing expressions that arouse contempt and shame, adds a deterrent effect to the act.[132]

---

130. On the "diagnosis form" and its medical origin, see David Daube, *Ancient Jewish Law* (Leiden: Brill, 1981), 100–6. Daube claimed that according to ancient medical notions, in order to conquer a sickness it is necessary to discover its name or that of the demon that causes it (p. 104). Bernard Jackson is of the opinion that this means that the naming of the disease was not merely a matter of scientific speculation, but a speech act that formed a necessary part of the treatment (see Jackson, *Semiotics*, 50).

131. This issue is treated at length in the final chapter of this study, which deals with point of view and focalization.

132. These condemnations may also be considered motive clauses explaining the severity of the punishment. HL 187–195, which also deal with sexual behaviors, contain diagnostic comments that indicate the legal status of each behavior. After describing the

Before turning to the Priestly lawgiver's treatment of sexual behavior I wish to fill in a significant lacuna in the preceding discussion of the Deuteronomic lawgiver's interventions. The Deuteronomic lawgiver—perhaps even more than the Priestly lawgiver—often expresses his negative evaluation of and aversion to illicit acts. In some cases he characterizes the acts with condemnatory labels, and at other times he characterizes them only in reference to God's evaluation of them. The lawgiver might describe an action or a thing (idolatry, forbidden forms of worship, forbidden food, sexual illicitness, fraud) as an abomination תועבה (e.g., 13:14; 14:3; 17:4; 18:9) or as an abomination to the LORD תועבת יהוה (e.g., 17:1; 22:5; 23:18; 25:16);[133] an action can be considered an evil thing (e.g., 17:5) and/or evil in the sight of the LORD (e.g., 17:2). In the first case the negative characterization reflects the point of view of the lawgiver, and in the second case the lawgiver adopts YHWH's point of view so that these two points of view are brought into union.[134] The Deuteronomic lawgiver expresses his negative opinion of illicit acts by means of additional characterizations: "[speaking] treason," סרה (13:5);[135] "base [thought]," דבר בליעל (15:9); "outrage," נבלה (22:21); "[performing] injustice," עול (25:16).

---

illicit act (such as having sexual relations with a cow), the law states *kata waštai ḫurkil* ("it is an abomination"), reflecting the lawgiver's aversion to the action; and after describing a permitted action (such as father and son sleeping with the same female slave) the law states *kata waštai ÚL ḫaratar* ("it is not an offense"), providing the legal classification of the act. In Hittite legal and diplomatic documents linguistic formulas are employed stating whether an act is worthy (*āra*) or unworthy (*natta āra*) in the eyes of God and humankind. They represent a moral evaluation of the acts and are therefore close in spirit to the condemnatory comments of the Priestly lawgiver (see Yoram Cohen, *Taboos and Prohibitions in Hittite Society: A Study of the Hittite Expression natta āra ['not permitted']* [Texte der Hethiter 24; Heidelberg: Universitätsverlag C. Winter, 2002]).

133. The term "abomination," which means something improper, loathsome, despicable, seems to have entered biblical literature (wisdom literature, prophecy, and law) under the influence of Mesopotamian and Egyptian wisdom literature. The genres characteristic of this kind of literature (proverbs, wise counsel, poetic fragments, and fables) employ parallel terms—Sumerian *níg-gig*, Akkadian *ikkibu*, and Egyptian *bwt*—which refer to unusual and improper behaviors in the realm of ritual and morality (see William W. Hallo, "Biblical Abomination and Sumerian Taboos," *JQR* 76 [1985]: 21–40; Jacob Klein and Yitschak Sefati, "The Concept of 'Abomination' in Mesopotamian Literature and the Bible" (in Hebrew), *Beer-Sheva* 3 [1988]: 131–48). Frequently one encounters the formulas *ikkib DN, níg-gig-DN-kam*, which mean that conduct X is an abomination to God Y, similar to the expression תועבת יהוה. The sacrifice of impure animals, for example, is *ikkib ilāni kalāma*, that is, the abomination of all the gods (see Klein and Sefati, 135–36, 140–41, 144, 147).

134. See David M. Gunn and Danna N. Fewell, *Narrative in the Hebrew Bible* (Oxford Bible Series; Oxford: Oxford University Press, 1993), 60.

135. In Akkadian, *sarratu* is "deceit, treachery." For the word's etymology, see Paul E. Dion, "Deuteronomy 13: The Suppression of Alien Religious Propaganda in Israel during

Let me now return to the Priestly lawgiver's treatment of illicit sexual acts and other usages of the diagnosis form. Regarding illicit relationships with one's kinswomen, see Lev 18:7–8, 10–17:

> she is your mother . . . it is your father's nakedness . . . for their nakedness is your own nakedness . . . she is your sister . . . she is your father's near kinswoman . . . for she is your mother's near kinswoman . . . she is your aunt . . . she is your son's wife . . . she is your brother's nakedness . . . they are your near kinswomen.

The declarations contribute nothing substantial to the prohibition against uncovering the nakedness of one's kinswomen—neither factual information nor moral evaluation. They only emphasize the familial relationship as a reason for the prohibitions (although there is no need for this in light of the general commandment: "None of you shall approach any one near of kin to him to uncover nakedness" [18:6], in which this rationale is already embedded).[136] However, the declarations that are directed personally to the addressee are useful to illustrate the illicit relationship for him. They reverberate in his mind and act as deterrents—this is not just "any" sister, mother, or aunt, it is *your* sister, *your* mother, *your* aunt.[137]

What remains now is to clarify the status of the diagnostic comment that recurs four times in the law of homicide.

> [16]But if he struck him down with an instrument of iron, so that he died, he is a murderer; the murderer shall be put to death. [17]And if he struck him down with a stone in the hand, by which a man may die, and he died, he is a murderer; the murderer shall be put to death. [18]Or if he struck him down with a weapon of wood in the hand, by which a man may die, and he died, he is a murderer; the murderer shall be put to death. [20]And if he stabbed him from hatred, or hurled at him, lying in wait, so that he died, [21]or in enmity struck him down with his hand, so that he died, then he who struck the blow shall be put to death; he is a murderer. (Num 35:16–18, 20–21)

---

the Late Monarchical Era," in *Law and Ideology in Monarchic Israel* (ed. Baruch Halpern and Deborah W. Hobson; JSOTSup 124; Sheffield: JSOT Press, 1991), 153. For the political background of the expression and its occurrence in the loyalty oaths of the Assyrian royal vassal contracts, see Nelson, *Deuteronomy*, 171.

136. Motive declarations that repeat information already given in the law, emphasizing the familial relation and the illicit nature of the act, appear in the sexual offenses of Leviticus 20: "he has uncovered his father's/sister's/uncle's/brother's nakedness" (vv. 11, 17, 19–21). On motive clauses that convey neither additional information nor the lawgiver's stance, see n. 83.

137. See Milgrom, *Leviticus 17–22*, 1525.

The declaration "he is a murderer," which appears between the factual description in each of the six homicide cases and the establishment of the ensuing punishment (only in the last case does it appear after the punishment), defines the legal status of the perpetrator, although it is explicitly defined in the context of the punishment ("the *murderer* shall be put to death"). It therefore contains no additional information, and the law would be complete even without it (and without the definition in the apodosis, since the sentence, "if he struck him down with an instrument of iron, so that he died, he shall be put to death," matches the standard casuistic form). But on account of his interest in definitions, distinctions, and classifications, the lawgiver is not content to recite the actual punishable deeds, but rather formulates an abstract category that distinguishes between the innocent and the guilty, a category that would seem to belong to the realm of "legal theory."[138]

The murderer (הרצח) in the diagnostic comment is not identical to the one whose action caused the death of a person, nor is he הרצח mentioned in Num 35:25-28 (correctly translated as "the manslayer"), but rather a person whose action engenders guilt. The result is that his punishment is not deduced directly from the facts of the case, but rather from his *classification* as a murderer; he is put to death because "he is a murderer" and not because he struck someone with an iron instrument or hatefully pushed another person. This is one facet of the diagnostic comment.[139] However, it can simultaneously be associated with the level of "judicial practice," since it may reflect the declaration concerning a person's guilt that is voiced in the course of a judicial proceeding, the judgment that is given after the facts are clarified and before the sentencing. Again, as in the law of leprosy, the lawgiver combines theory and practice in his intervention, because the legal category is the very same categorical declaration that reverberates in the judicial tribunal.

To conclude: None of the biblical lawgivers views his role as restricted to the description of the relevant facts and the establishment of legal norms. The laws, so they believe, should not and cannot speak for themselves. This is not by any means because the norms themselves are "weak," nor is it because

---

138. On the transition from concrete legal thinking to more abstract thought, see Jackson, *Semiotics*, 95, 112–13.

139. Other ancient Near Eastern law collections also include comments that define and classify the legal status of perpetrators, or of people whose affairs are subject to legal arrangements—acts, sanctions, or judicial authority. See, e.g., LH 7, *awīlum šû šarrāq* ("that man is a thief"); LH 9, *nādinānum šarrāq* ("it is the seller who is the thief"); LH 13, *awīlum šû sār* ("it is that man who is a liar"); MAL A 23 *sinnilta uššuru zakuat* ("she is clear"); MAL A 33, *almattu šīt* ("she is indeed a widow"); LE 24, 26, *dīn napištim* ("it is a capital offense"); LE 58, *napištum ṣimdat šarrim* ("it is a capital case decided by the a royal edict").

the lawgivers' formulations are inadequate. Rather, it is because from their perspective the laws must be *communicative texts*. The instrument through which this communication is accomplished is intervention. Each type of intervention, as well as the function it fulfills in the laws, constitutes proof that in formulating the laws the lawgivers had the addressees fully in mind. In addition, the interventions, which naturally draw attention to the existence of an intervening personality, permit the addressees to experience the presence and engagement of the lawgivers (each lawgiver with his particular degree of perceptibility, each presence with its distinguishing characteristics); and therefore they are not alone.

Having focused our attention on this vehicle of communication with the purpose of characterizing the personality of the narrator-lawgiver, we have learned to recognize the particular style of each of the lawgivers and his particular approach to the act of legislating.

One final comment: It will be recalled that the participation of the lawgivers (and the addressees) in the contents of the laws is a distinguishing feature of biblical law in contrast to all other ancient Near Eastern law codes. This is not true of their perceptibility. As we have seen from time to time in the course of our discussion, the other law codes also contain marks of the lawgivers' engagement with the substance of the law: comments for clarification or emphasis, various motive clauses, classificatory and definitional remarks. At the same time, it is difficult to compare these with the various "engagement mechanisms" of the Deuteronomic and Priestly lawgivers, and it is equally difficult to discover within them the depth and breadth of exposure that are reflected in the Book of the Covenant's motive clauses.

In this chapter we have acquainted ourselves with the personality of the three lawgivers through the examination of two criteria. We turn now to the other characters featured in the laws, as reflected in their speech and utterances. As we come to know them, we will also deepen our acquaintance with the lawgivers, those who have provided these characters with their voices.

3

Representation of Speech

The Mimetic Illusion

The ability to create an illusion of reality by means of imitation (i.e., *mimesis*) is one of the signal characteristics of narrative. A vivid and dramatic description of the events in which the characters participate affords readers the illusion that they are seeing things with their own eyes, and direct transmission of the characters' conversation produces the (false) sense that they are hearing their voices. Reducing the narrator's role, as it were, to showing or voicing, gives the written text the ability to mimic the verbal and nonverbal events that make up reality.[1]

The casuistic laws are reality-mimicking texts. They describe—and in not a few cases even dramatize, scenes—and although the description is spare in detail, the reader can conjure up the events as they occur: a brawl breaking out between the two men; the blow one delivers to the other with his fist or with a stone clasped in his hand; the wounded lying on his sickbed, his recovery and rehabilitation (Exod 21:18-19); or the stranger who seizes the virgin maiden, the sexual act he forces upon her, their being caught "in the act" (Deut 22:28-29).

What about the conveyance of verbal acts? Does the lawgiver merely show the events and the characters involved, or does he also give voice to them?

Sometimes the lawgiver reports a speech event that occurs in the course of a scene but does not render its verbal content. For example, we do not know what the city elders said to the brother-in-law of a widow to persuade him to retract his refusal to fulfill the duty of levirate marriage (Deut 25:8); nor do we

---

1. The common distinction in narrative between "showing" and "telling" (or "summary" and "scene") is based on Socrates' distinction in the third book of Plato's *Republic*, between two modes of conveying speech: *diegesis* and *mimesis*. The quality that characterizes *diegesis* is that the "poet himself is the speaker," while in *mimesis*, the poet attempts to create the illusion that it is not he who is speaking. See Rimmon-Kenan, *Narrative Fiction*, 103–5.

know the wording of the surrender call that went out to the inhabitants of the captured city (Deut 20:10).

At the same time, in not a few cases, direct rendering of speech takes the place of a bare report that a speech act has occurred. The lawgiver cites the words spoken by the characters, allowing us to form an impression with our own ears. In the law of levirate marriage itself, we hear the widow's utterances (Deut 25:7, 9) as well as the laconic utterance of the husband's brother (v. 8); and in the law introducing the collection of laws of warfare (Deut 20:1–9), we hear the echo of the words of encouragement that the priest addresses to the crowd of warriors (vv. 3–4) and the wording of the exemptions from battle (vv. 5–8).

Moreover, the lawgiver sometimes presents the inner life of the characters—their thoughts, decisions, desires—fashioning these as direct, internal speech. In this manner the people's desire to incorporate Canaanite ritual practices into the worship of YHWH is revealed (Deut 12:30), as is the apprehension regarding the consequences of the fallow year (Lev 25:20).

This chapter discusses a variety of cases in which verbal events are directly communicated. Its purpose is to illustrate how the illusion of reality is produced in the legal texts and to recognize the various ways in which this mode of communication affects us, the readers. We will hear the declarations of the Hebrew slave (Exod 21:2–6; Deut 15:12–18); the clear and incisive statement of the owner of property (Exod 22:8); the priest and the officers before going out to war (Deut 20:1–9); the parents of the rebellious son (Deut 21:18–21); the actors in the family dramas arising in the law of false accusation (Deut 22:13–21) and the law of levirate marriage (Deut 25:5–10); and the two sides taking part in the jealousy ordeal (Num 5:12–31). Later in the chapter, as we become privy to the interior speech of the law's addressees, we will encounter unsuppressible passions (Deut 12:20–28), a desire to "blend in" (Deut 12:29–31), and the hostility shown toward the poor person (Deut 15:7–11). In the final section we will scrutinize five laws—the law of lending to the poor (Exod 22:25–26); the law prohibiting Canaanite worship (Deut 12:29–31); and three laws concerning enticement to idol worship (Deuteronomy 13)—in which we will discover another method employed by the lawgivers in rendering verbal events: combined discourse (an intermediate form combining indirect and direct speech, which brief definition will suffice for now).[2] Let us then observe the speech events closely, listen, and succumb to the illusion of reality.

---

2. For the variety of modes for presenting speech, see Rimmon-Kenan, *Narrative Fiction*, 109–10.

Direct Speech

The utterances of characters conveyed as direct speech are of three kinds: (1) *verba solemnia*, a formal declaration accompanied by a ceremonial action with legal implications; (2) a statement made during a legal confrontation or procedure; or (3) an oath.[3]

Before examining the Pentateuchal laws in order to listen to Israelite voices, I wish to point out a unique appearance of direct speech in one of the Middle Assyrian Laws. It is a singular appearance because the utterance to be cited does not belong to any of the three types described above. It is not an oath, not a declaration accompanied by a ritual action, and not a statement with legal implications.[4] On the other hand, it allows us to become acquainted with the speech style of an Assyrian rapist.

MAL A 12 deals with the sexual assault of a woman. It describes a case in which a man's wife who was walking on the main street was attacked and raped. The rapist is sentenced to death, and the woman upon whom sexual intercourse was forced despite her attempts to defend herself is exempt from punishment. Before the description of the rape the lawgiver presents the man's address to the woman (accompanied by a violent act), in which he expresses his desire to have sex with her: *iṣṣabassu lanīkkime iqtibi* ("a man seizes her and says to her, 'I want to have sex with you'!").

The rendering of the rapist's utterance in direct speech creates a powerful illusion of reality, because the verb *nâku*, serving to voice his desire to have sex, is a vulgar expression for illicit sex,[5] a fitting choice for introducing an act of rape. The use of crude language (planted on his lips by the lawgiver) allows us to hear the words spoken by the rapist, which concretize his blatant behavior, thus painting the events in realistic colors.

What might be the purpose of presenting the man's words in spite of the fact that the utterance does not constitute an essential element of the felony

---

3. In the law of the king (Deut 17:14–20) and in the law of the prophet (18:15–22) another sort of utterance appears in direct speech. The lawgiver cites statements made in the past, by God to the people and by the people to Moses, respectively, providing the law with historical justification or grounding a specific norm. The appearance of both utterances raises questions regarding the relationship between the citation and the "original utterance," which is outside the purview of the study. On this issue, see Meir Sternberg, "Between the Truth and the Whole Truth in Biblical Narrative: The Rendering of Inner Life by Telescoped Inside View and Interior Monologue" (in Hebrew), *Hasifrut* 29 (1979): 111–13; and George Savran, *Telling and Retelling: Quotation in Biblical Narrative* (Indiana Studies in Biblical Literature; Bloomington: Indiana University Press, 1988), 24–25, 114–15.

4. For utterances with legal significance that are presented in direct speech, see, e.g., LE 22, 37; LH 9, 126, 142, 170, 206–7; MAL A 5, 18–19, 22, 47; HL 75.

5. See Roth, *Law Collections*, 192 n. 11.

offense? The lawgiver's motives are undoubtedly not legalistic (and for this reason it is a surprising and unusual example of the use of direct speech in the law). The man is susceptible to severe punishment because of the gravity of the act of rape itself, not because of the blatant utterance accompanying it; had he been silent he would still have been punished. Thus, the presentation of his words carries no legal implications. The voicing of the utterance, which indicates the rapist's crude and aggressive character, aims and also succeeds at enhancing our revulsion at the deed.[6]

Speech is the most specifically human form of action. It allows a person to express his or her individual thoughts and feelings and hence is most conducive to displaying the unique facets of a character. The Assyrian lawgiver knew this as well, and therefore chose to present the rapist's authentic utterance. He did not seek only to present the legal norm and the punitive sanction, but also to exercise an influence over the consciousness of the law's addressee, and to shape his attitude toward the transgressor and his conduct.

Verba Solemnia

"But if the slave plainly says, 'I love my master...'"

The laws of the Hebrew slave in the Book of the Covenant (Exod 21:2–6) and in Deuteronomy (Deut 15:12–18) describe a ritual designed to transform the slave's status from indentured to perpetual slave. The ritual is composed of two elements: an utterance (the slave's declaration) and an act (the piercing of the slave's ear by the master). In both laws the declaration is rendered in direct speech:

> But if the slave plainly says, "I love my master, my wife, and my children; I will not go out free." (Exod 21:5)
>
> But if he says to you, "I will not go out from you." (Deut 15:16a)

Conveying the slave's declaration serves a clear purpose. Such a significant change in a person's status must be performed openly, publicly, leaving no room for doubt that he made the choice consciously, of his own free will (in Exodus it is a universal address; in Deuteronomy the words are addressed uniquely to the master). But the lawgiver is not content only to report the public declaration of the slave. He presents his words "accurately," allowing a reader to hear with one's own ears, as if one had been present at the rite, so that

---

6. The Assyrian rapist's address to the victim is reminiscent of Amnon's address to Tamar before he rapes her, also accompanied by a violent act: "he took hold of her, and said to her, 'Come, lie with me, my sister.'" (2 Sam 13:11).

one might be convinced along with the declaration's original audience about the seriousness of the slave's intentions.[7]

"*I love my master*," the slave begins his declaration, revealing his inner mood to his audience. Does anyone suppose that the slave loves his master more than his wife and sons? Certainly not. But in his desire to emphasize the awareness of his choice, his preference for a life of bondage over freedom, he presents the love of the master first. The love of his wife and children is presented as a second, cumulative justification, but not one of the first order, so as to remove any concern over whether the slave chose eternal bondage only because of his reluctance to lose them (in light of the rule that "the wife and her children shall be her master's and he shall go out alone" [Exod 21:4]). Although the "love scale" rehearsed by the slave is primarily a rhetorical scale, which aims to place his free choice at the center of his declaration, the scale also reflects his life's configuration: first he entered a relationship with his master, and only later did his master give him a wife, who in time bore his children (v. 4). By reflecting back the image of his life in the wording of his declaration, the slave's words testify that he has indeed internalized the life of slavery.

To convince the reader that the slave has consciously and freely chosen slavery, the lawgiver meticulously stylizes his declaration so that it reflects the slave's quintessentially positive attitude toward the crucial decision—this despite the law's negative attitude toward the slave's decision, as can be deduced from the mark of humiliation with which he is branded.[8]

---

7. A document from Nuzi contains a public declaration by a slave, emphasizing that he has become a perpetual slave of his own free will: *u rāmanīma rāmanī ina šeršerreti iddanni* ("So of my free will I have cast myself in chains"). The citation is taken from Paul, *Book of the Covenant*, 49.

8. Maiming of the ear was used in the ancient Near East as a form of punishment and humiliation (see, e.g., LH 282; MAL A 40, 44). However, it is not inconceivable that the piercing of the slave's ear was a mere formal sign attesting to his new social status. The purpose of piercing the ear at the doorpost of the master's house is to symbolize the slave's permanent obedience to the master and his attachment to the household forever (see Edward L. Greenstein, "Introduction and Annotations to the Book of Exodus [Shemot]," in *The HarperCollins Study Bible: A New Annotated Edition by the Society of Biblical Literature* [ed. W. A. Meeks et al.; New York: HarperCollins, 1993], 117; Jackson, *Wisdom-Laws*, 114; see also Victor Avigdor Hurowitz, "'His master shall pierce his ear with an awl' [Exodus 21.6]: Marking Slaves in the Bible in Light of Akkadian Sources," *Proceedings—American Academy for Jewish Research* 58 [1992]: 47–77). Whatever the reasons for maiming the slave's ear (for humiliation, identification, or symbolic purposes), I suggest an additional reason why the lawgiver chose it in particular. According to LH 282 a slave who defies his master's authority is punished by having his ear amputated: *šumma wardum ana bēlīšu ul bēlī atta iqtabi . . . bēlšu uzunšu inakkis* ("If a slave should declare to his master, 'you are not my master,' . . . his master shall cut off his ear"). Adoption of this familiar punishment by the Israelite lawgiver (although in an attenuated form, not as a punishment but at most as a

The verb "love," which is used by the slave, is undoubtedly a sophisticated linguistic choice on the part of the lawgiver, who exploits the dual register of the verb in order to reflect the mixing of domains in the slave's life. The verb originates in the domain of interpersonal relationships—relationships of family or amity. It was transferred from this sphere into a different sphere, that of contract law, where it is used not to express the fierce internal feelings of love, but rather to describe one of the obligations that arise from a contractual relationship—the duty of loyalty.[9] The love of the slave for his master reflects the attitude of loyalty which he must show toward him because of his special status, but the moment he attaches himself permanently to the master's household, thus becoming a member of his family, a new dimension is added, that of familial love, which is not different from his love for his wife or children.[10] The verb "love," therefore, encapsulates both types of relationship, and the fusion of the two meanings illustrates the qualitative and total transformation of his legal-familial status.

The slave's declaration in Deuteronomy is different. It is short, reflecting only the final phrase of the parallel declaration in Exodus ("I will not go out from you"), and it lacks a motive. The laconic citation of the slave's words does not allow the reader to discern his inner mood. However, the two elements that are the focus of the declaration in Exodus—conscious choice and free will—are reflected in the lawgiver's motive clause "because he loves you and your household, since he fares well with you" (Deut 15:16b).[11] Thus, through

---

humiliation—amputation is hence replaced by mutilation) allows him to present his unique set of values, which, instead of condemning someone who defies slavery, as the Babylonian law does, repudiates a person who internalizes the attitude of servitude.

9. See, for example, the loyalty oaths that appear in the legal documents and contracts formulated by the Hittite and Assyrian Kings, which employ the verb "love" (in Akkadian *râmu* and in Hittite *aššiia*). The Deuteronomic commandment to love God also reflects the duty of loyalty to him and to his laws. See William L. Moran, "Ancient Near Eastern Background of the Love of God in Deuteronomy," *CBQ* 25 (1963): 77–87; Moshe Weinfeld, "The Loyalty Oath in the Ancient Near East," *Ugarit-Forschungen* 8 (1976): 382–83; Weinfeld, *Deuteronomy and the Deuteronomic School*, 82–83, 368.

10. It is interesting to compare the slave's declaration to an adjuration of Hittite military personnel (the Hittite text appears in Weinfeld, "Loyalty Oath," 383): "Just as you love your wives, your children, and your houses, so you shall love the king's business (= the king's customs/laws)."

11. The most noticeable difference between the two versions, that is, the mention of the woman and children as opposed to no mention of them at all, results from the fact that according to Deuteronomic law the slave's family status is no longer under the master's control. See Weinfeld, *Deuteronomy and the Deuteronomic School*, 282–83; Patrick, *Old Testament Law*, 113.

the lawgiver's penetration of the slave's mind, the reader is once again convinced that he formed his decision consciously and freely.

Military Speech Acts

Paradoxically, the law concerning going out to war, which opens the collection of laws of warfare (Deut 20:1–9), does not include instructions regarding the conscription and organization of forces before setting out to battle.[12] It describes only a two-phased ritual, composed of two speech events presented in direct discourse: the priest's address, designed to instill confidence and courage in the heart of the warriors (vv. 3–4), followed by the words of the officers, who announce the exemptions from battle (vv. 5–8).[13]

First, the priest's address:

> ³Hear, O Israel, you draw near this day to battle against your enemies: let not your heart faint; do not fear, or tremble, or be in dread of them; ⁴ for the LORD your God is he that goes with you, to fight for you against your enemies, to give you the victory. (Deut 20:3–4)

It is clear that within this address are embedded the introductory phrases of the lawgiver:

> When you go forth to war against your enemies, and see horses and chariots and an army larger than your own, you shall not be afraid of them; for the LORD your God is with you, who brought you up out of the land of Egypt. (Deut 20:1)

As a hortatory speech addressed to the warriors (*oratio directa*), however, it is adapted to the occasion in which it is made and to the function it is meant to fulfill.[14] The lawgiver's address in the second person singular, in accordance with the normal pattern of address in the Deuteronomic Code (the "if-you" pattern), is replaced by an address to the warriors in the second person plural, a form of address suited to a public audience. It is known that alternation

---

12. The law mentions only one real action in preparing for battle: "then commanders shall be appointed at the head of the people" (Deut 20:9b). For the difference between this law and Deuteronomy's other laws of warfare, see Alexander Rofé, "The Laws of Warfare in the Book of Deuteronomy: Their Origins, Intent, and Positivity," *JSOT* 32 (1985): 23–44.

13. The paradoxical nature of this passage is reflected also in its language, for it is somewhat surprising that in a law that deals with going out to war, of all other possible action verbs, it is instead verbs denoting speech—"say" and "speak"—that function as *Leitworte* (appearing seven times in vv. 2–3, 5, 8, 9).

14. For the military oratory in Deuteronomy and the bellicose vocabulary and language reflected in extrabiblical documents, see Weinfeld, *Deuteronomy and the Deuteronomic School*, 45–51.

between singular and plural forms is not unusual in biblical literature, and often no special meaning need be attached to it. But in the current example, it appears to have been designed to emphasize the difference between formulaic language and authentic speech. The substitution reflects the difference between the lawgiver's exposition and the priest's "real" speech. Similarly, the lawgiver's statement "And when you draw near to the battle" (v. 2) undergoes a transformation, when spoken by the priest, to a more concrete and dramatized utterance: "*Hear, O Israel,* you draw near *this day* to battle. . . ."

At the center of the priest's address, as in the lawgiver's opening phrase, are two significant elements: the appeal to the warriors not to fear the enemy, and the promise of YHWH's aid in achieving victory. But since the orator-priest must adapt his words to the place, the time, the audience, and the special circumstances, he embellishes them all. The lawgiver's appeal "you shall not be afraid of them" is expanded in the speech "let not your heart faint; do not fear, or tremble, or be in dread of them," and the words of encouragement promising the help of God, "for the LORD your God is with you," are given much more nuanced color in the priest's words: "for the LORD your God is he that goes with you, to fight for you against your enemies, to give you the victory."

The expansions of these elements—the appeal to fear not, and the promise of God's help—play a vital, if not essential role in the preliminaries to war. First, there is the repetition in four variants, which allows every kind of shade or tone of fear to be entirely preempted. Second, the detailed account (this time in three variants) reiterates God's active role on the path toward victory. The expansion is, therefore, not a literary ornament; it has a clear rhetorical motive, arising from the circumstances and adapted to them. Moreover, it is not unlikely that the absence of the phrase "and see horses and chariots and an army larger than your own," which appears in the words of the lawgiver, also indicates a "true" rhetorical reason, for one can imagine that the priest might omit such information intentionally, realizing that with a battle impending he should avoid describing sights that might only intensify the warriors' fear.[15]

---

15. Of course the absence of the phrase need not necessarily be viewed as a "conscious omission." Even though the priest's speech echoes the lawgiver's words, an exact correspondence between the two is not necessary. Thus, for example, missing from his oration is the phrase appearing in the lawgiver's words "who brought you up out of the land of Egypt." As it is difficult to find a rhetorical reason for this omission (since mention of a past redemption actually strengthens confidence in future salvation), it seems to derive from the author's elliptical style.

To summarize my argument thus far: The rhetorical elements in the priest's address reflect the occasion and circumstance of the speech. But I wish to point out another important matter. One of the hallmarks of the law of the going out to war is its textual excesses, since both speakers, the lawgiver and the priest, say the same things (except for slight variations). This double presentation, which ostensibly has no real use, allows the lawgiver to present a sort of dialogue between his own words and the "real" address of the priest, thus allowing us to experience the rhetorical clout of the address—the actuality of the authentic utterance. The desire to affect our awareness (through repetition and linguistic excess) certainly is not part of the normative-legal plane of the law.

Unlike the priest's address, which deals with mood and *esprit*, the officers' declarations, presented later on, have immediate pragmatic implications for action. As such, I propose to view them not as mere statements, but as what linguists term "performative speech acts," utterances that are in and of themselves the performance of an action by the speaker.[16] What gives the officers' declarations their performative force is the voicing of the words, the speech act that grants the exemptions from going out to war. The officers make four declarations, each of which is composed of four parts (vv. 5–8):

1. An identical introductory question: "What man is there . . ." (מי האיש)?
2. A characterization of the warrior who is eligible for an exemption: "that has built a new house and has not dedicated it"; "that has planted a vineyard and has not enjoyed its fruit"; "that has betrothed a wife and has not taken her"; "that is fearful and fainthearted."[17]
3. A repeated instruction that states the exemption "Let him go back to his house."
4. A motive clause, beginning with the uniform formula "lest he die in the battle," and continuing with a specific justification "and another man dedicate it"; "and another man enjoy its fruit"; "and another man take her"; "lest the heart of his fellows melt as his heart."[18]

---

16. See John L. Austin, *How to Do Things with Words* (William James Lectures 1955; London: Oxford University Press, 1975); on speech acts in biblical discourse, see Hugh White, (ed.), *Speech Act Theory and Biblical Criticism* (Semeia 41; Decatur, Ga.: Scholars Press, 1988); and on speech acts in biblical law see Jackson, *Semiotics*, 47–55.

17. The first three declarations are constructed along one uniform model, according to which the warrior began a certain action but did not have time to complete it. The fourth declaration is different because it refers not to an action performed by the warrior but to his mental state.

18. In the first three declarations the justificatory clauses express the notion that someone who has begun an action is entitled to enjoy its outcomes. The lawgiver has in mind the welfare of the warriors. In the fourth declaration, in contrast, the lawgiver has in sight the general good.

Do we really hear the officers' words? Are we capable of believing that these words were spoken before going out to battle? Or does the repetition of the identical formulas accentuate, rather, the literary stylization of the declarations, thus damaging the mimetic illusion? On the one hand, it stands to reason that whoever was in charge of the warrior corps would announce the exemptions with one blanket utterance, and not with four separate statements.[19] At the same time, the separate, personal addresses (which are the cause of the repetitions) are indeed suited to an occasion of a public verbal declaration, and thus have a real function. At a large convocation, the repetition of the utterance may facilitate the audience's processing of the information, while the "condensation" of the same information into one general utterance could encumber their comprehension. Therefore, the repetition, which appears to be a literary-artistic choice, may in fact reflect a realistic element.

However, questions still need to be asked. Is it likely that, on the eve of battle, the officers would formulate their words through interrogative sentences and support them with justificatory clauses? Is it not to be expected, rather, that because of the circumstances, the exemptions would be announced categorically, with the aid of the formula "a man who" (איש אשר)? Indeed, it appears that even the repetition of the question "What man is there?" reflects a level of realism, for it may mirror the actual, concrete process of identifying the warriors eligible for exemption—the officers using it, in fact, to obtain information not available to them.[20]

The repeated question may have another realistic aspect, for it is unlikely that the syntactical "exploitation" of the interrogative clause is intended only for receiving information. Rather, its purpose is also to affect the audience to whom the question is addressed. The question presented is addressed not only to the exempted soldiers but also (and especially) to the public at large. It creates a type of dialogue between the askers and those questioned and requires the participation of the audience with the intention of receiving its consent. The rhetorical use of a sequence of question and answer, with the addition of a motive clause, shifts the emphasis from the need to locate the warriors to the need to justify the granting of exemptions. Including the audience in the process of decision making allows a public attainment of collective agreement for an action that might normally cause agitation among the body of warriors. The officers' declarations, then, have rhetorical features, deriving first and foremost from the functions they are designed to fulfill. Therefore, despite their literary stylization, they are capable of creating an illusion of reality for us.

---

19. Similar to the one inclusive utterance, addressed to the warriors, as described in 1 Macc 3:55–56.

20. See, e.g., Judg 21:8 (cf. v. 5; 7:3; 10:18).

Legal Confrontation

To hear the following utterance we must abandon the battlefield and relocate to the market square. Here, of course, it is not the lives of warriors that are at stake but the property of citizens.

Two People Holding "It"

In the Book of the Covenant, between two casuistic laws—the law of deposit of goods (Exod 22:6–7) and the law of deposit of animals (22:9–10)—appears a legal stipulation that presents something of a stylistic anomaly:

> For every breach of trust, whether it is for ox, for ass, for sheep, for clothing, or for any kind of lost thing, of which one says, "This is it," the case of both parties shall come before God; he whom God shall condemn shall pay double to his neighbor. (Exod 22:8)[21]

According to the law's provision, any dispute over ownership of movable property or animals, resulting from theft or loss of the property, will be decided through an adjudicated procedure, and the party whose ownership of the property is not recognized will pay the other party double restitution. The law deals with a dispute between someone who has possession of property and another who claims ownership over it, though it is not in his possession.[22] While the first part of the verse is formulated in generic language, removed and abstracted from the concrete case in question ("for every breach of trust"; "any kind of lost thing"), the second half depicts a scene in which an utterance is delivered in direct speech—in a style that draws the reader closer to the incident at hand: "of which one says, 'This is it' [כי הוא זה]." What is the nature of this scene? What is the meaning of the statement "This is it"?[23] Who utters it?

---

21. According to Dale Patrick, v. 8 formulates in general language and in terms of principle the cases spelled out in vv. 7 and 10 (*Old Testament Law*, 81). Brevard Childs suggests that it expands the principle stated in v. 7 (*Book of Exodus*, 475–76). It is possible to see in v. 8 the glimmerings of a transition from concrete thinking to abstract thinking, as reflected in the transformation of the verbal sentence (in vv. 7 and 10): "whether or not he has put his hand to his neighbor's goods" to nominal phrases: "For every breach of trust," "or for any kind of lost thing" (see Jackson, *Semiotics*, 93–95). Principally for these reasons v. 8 is regarded as a late addition (see Boecker, *Law and the Administration of Justice*, 170; Horst Seebass, "Noch Einmal zum Depositenrecht Ex 22, 6–14," in *Gottes Recht als Lebensraum: Festschrift für Hans Jochen Boecker* [ed. Peter Mommer et al.; Neukirchen-Vluyn: Neukirchener Verlag, 1993], 24; Jackson, *Wisdom-Laws*, 342–43, 470).

22. See Sprinkle, *Book of the Covenant*, 149–50.

23. According to some commentators the phrase should be rendered "This is *he*," referring to the person accused of theft, rather than the property. See Bernard Jackson,

The law, as mentioned above, deals with a dispute over ownership. It addresses the question whether someone legally possesses property, or whether that property belongs to another person, who deposited it for safekeeping, or the property was stolen from him, or lost. The legal dispute has two phases: in the first phase the parties recognize the existence of the dispute regarding specific property (this is the ex-tribunal phase); and in the second phase the dispute is clarified and decided before a judicial forum (the tribunal phase). The scene in question belongs to the first phase, the phase of recognition of the dispute, before a formal legal mediation is sought.

Before discussing the content and wording of the statement, I wish to clarify its status as direct speech, lest any doubt be entertained regarding the meaning of the connector *kî*, which does indeed sometimes introduce indirect speech.[24] However, there are cases in which *kî* forms part of the utterance itself, in various functions such as introducing an explanation, a temporal phrase, or as an asseverative particle. When it appears following the verb "to say," as in the case under discussion, it should always be viewed as part of the direct speech; as the first word of the quoted utterance.[25]

What is the relationship between the content and wording of the utterance and the scene in which it is uttered? In other words, is the utterance consonant with the nature of the situation? Since we are speaking of a dispute over the right of ownership of specific property (movables or livestock), the utterance must refer to the identity of the property and the type of right claimed for it. Does the sentence "This is it" really denote these elements?[26] It is a nomi-

---

Theft in Early Jewish Law (Oxford: Clarendon, 1972), 239–40; Raymond Westbrook, "The Deposit Laws of Exodus 22, 6–12," *ZAW* 106 (1994): 396. Westbrook is of the opinion that "he" refers to the depositee of v. 7. To remove any doubt, I consider the phrase under discussion as referring to property rather than to a person.

24. The common wisdom that views כי as the standard way to introduce indirect speech in biblical Hebrew is, according to Cynthia Miller, unfounded. She claims, rather, that כי has this function only in thirty instances, and its more common use is following verbs of cognition and perception (remember, know, see, hear) and verbs denoting a mental state (relent). See Cynthia L. Miller, *The Representation of Speech in Biblical Hebrew Narrative: A Linguistic Analysis* (Harvard Semitic Monographs 55; Atlanta: Scholars Press, 1996), 81.

25. For this linguistic feature, defined as "style direct lié," see Gideon Goldenberg, *Studies in Semitic Linguistics: Selected Writings* (Jerusalem: Magnes, 1998), 203. For particular cases of direct speech in which *kî* can belong to the citation framework (termed *kî* recitativum) or to the citation itself (as the initial word in the quote), see Miller, 103–16. On *kî* recitativum, see also Samuel A. Meier, *Speaking of Speaking: Marking Direct Discourse in the Hebrew Bible* (SVT 46; Leiden: Brill, 1992), 19–21.

26. In LH 9, the equivalent of the law under discussion, the utterance of the adversarial parties is cited, reflecting these elements: *nādinānummi iddinma maḫar šībīmi ašām*

nal clause, composed of personal and demonstrative pronouns, indicating something proximate to the speaker. Both pronouns are used by the speaker to identify the property,[27] and the connector *kî*, which is conjoined to them, fulfills an asseverative or affirmative function, as if to say, "This is certainly it."[28] Although the identification of the property is focused, it lacks specification. Moreover, the utterance does not denote the right claimed, namely, the relationship or the type of relationship the speaker claims with the property. Whereas the absence of the first element—specification—is understandable (since the utterance is pronounced in the presence of the object being identified), leaving out the second element is unexpected. Is it not surprising that the speaker makes no assertion regarding his ownership of the property? Does such lack of explicit reference not risk creating a misunderstanding between the parties?

Elliptical utterances, which omit linguistic and substantive elements, are characteristic of human speech. The speakers, who share common insights, know what the subject of their conversation is and therefore do not take care to include all elements of the sentence. The omitted elements are completed by thought processes.[29] In addition, in face-to-face conversation, an allusion is often sufficient to clarify the speaker's intention (this is why demonstrative pronouns abound in oral communication).[30] In the represented scenario, when the speaker points to a specific piece of property with the use of incisive and focused language, the nature of the dispute is apparent to both parties, and the speaker need not clarify that he is making a claim of ownership in respect to the goods. The utterance reflects the speaker's spontaneous response at the sight of his property. Only later, when facing the tribunal, will he produce the supportive evidence for his claim. Such an utterance is realistic, befitting a situation where a man identifies specific property and makes a claim of

---

("A seller sold it to me, I purchased it in the presence of witnesses"); *šībī mūdē ḫulqīyāmi lublam* ("I can bring witnesses who can identify my lost property").

27. See "And the LORD said, 'Arise, anoint him; for this is he'" (1 Sam 16:12b) and other verses, such as Judg 7:4b; Ps 24:10; Esth 7:5.

28. Asseverative כי appears, for example, in Josh 2:24 and 1 Kgs 20:6. For uses of כי, see Carl M. Follingstad, *Deictic Viewpoint in Biblical Hebrew Text: A Syntagmatic and Paradigmatic Analysis of the Particle Kî* (Dallas: SIL International, 2001), 51–52, 98–99. In the second utterance quoted in LH 9, a grammatical form appears that also stresses the speaker's intention—the form *lublam* ("I will indeed bring.")

29. For the elision of linguistic elements in biblical speech, see Frank Polak, "The Style of the Dialogue in Biblical Prose Narrative," *JANES* 28 (2002): 61–62, 79–80. On the elliptical structure of answers to questions, see Edward L. Greenstein, "The Syntax of Saying 'Yes' in Biblical Hebrew," *JANES* 19 (1989): 51–59.

30. See Frank Polak, "The Style of the Dialogue in Biblical Narrative" (in Hebrew), *Teʿuda* 16–17 (2001): 49–51.

ownership vis-à-vis his interlocutor. We can imagine the speaker pointing his finger at the property, which is held in the hands of another person.

In addition to the realistic justification, can this utterance also be explained on literary-artistic grounds? (For one should never lose sight of the fact that the "world" in a literary text is first and foremost an intentionally fashioned artifact.[31]) I believe it can. In a legal ordinance that is not formulated according to the casuistic model but rather determines a general principle regarding property disputes, an utterance lacking specification is consonant with the stylistic framework in which it appears. The generic character of the utterance meshes stylistically with the generality of the legal instruction. Thus, the wording of the utterance, initially dictated by the strictures of reality, also sits well with the language and style of the law. The principle of generality is also preserved because the lawgiver does not attribute the statement to either one of the parties. Indeed, it seems logical that the speaker would be the one not in possession of the property, who by claiming ownership of it declares the existence of a dispute. But, by the same token, it could be spoken by the one in possession of the property, who also claims ownership. The lack of specification allows the utterance to be attributed to both sides simultaneously, thus granting both of them the right to argue within the framework of the law.[32]

Judicial Procedure

From the confrontation between these two parties, who may be acquainted or may be strangers, we turn to highly charged and strident confrontations between intimates.

Mutiny in the Family

> [18]If a man has a stubborn and rebellious son, who will not obey the voice of his father or the voice of his mother, and, though they chastise him, will not give heed to them, [19]then his father and his mother shall take hold of him and bring him out to the elders of his city at the gate of the place where he lives, [20]and they shall say to the elders of his city "This our son is stubborn and rebellious, he will not obey our voice; he is a glutton and a drunkard." [21]Then all the men of the city

---

31. See Hanna Hertzig, *The Fictional World: Mimesis vs. Artifice* (in Hebrew; Tel Aviv: The Open University Press, 1989), 15–26.

32. Unlike in this law, in LH 9 the claims of the two parties are differentiated. In the mishnaic law that treats the case of two people who simultaneously have possession of a single garment (*m. B. Meṣiʿa* 1:1) each party voices his claim separately but the claims are identical: "One of them says, 'I found it,' and the other says, 'I found it'; One of them says, 'It is all mine,' and the other says, 'It is all mine.'" This stylistic choice reinforces my opinion that the claim "This is it" can be attributed to both sides simultaneously.

shall stone him to death with stones; so you shall purge the evil from your midst; and all Israel shall hear, and fear. (Deut 21:18–21)

The law of the rebellious son limits the authority and freedom of action of the parents by determining that the son's sentence will be decided through a public adjudicative procedure.³³ At the same time, the parents have a clearly defined role in this procedure, for they initiate it by making a statement describing their son's behavior—"This our son is stubborn and rebellious, he will not obey our voice; he is a glutton and a drunkard"—a statement that will be used as an indictment against him.³⁴

The son's behavior, which provokes the parents to initiate the judicial proceedings, includes, according to their statement, three features: rebelliousness, disobedience, and unrestrained eating habits.³⁵ While the first two characteristics appear in the lawgiver's preamble ("If a man has a stubborn and rebellious son, who will not obey the voice of his father or the voice of his mother"), the third appears only in their words.³⁶ The relationship between the first characteristic and the two others is a relationship of whole to part. Just as disobedience may characterize the behavior of someone who does not accept authority, ³⁷ unrestrained eating habits can be seen as another example of a

---

33. On the issue of limiting parental authority, see Tigay, *Deuteronomy*, 196. Also according to LH 168–169, the father's authority to act against his son is subject to judicial decision (in contrast to *patria potestas* operative in ancient Roman law, which reflects the father's absolute authority).

34. The rationale behind giving the injured party a role and turning him into an official arm of the judiciary system is the desire to restrain familial/tribal law and subordinate it to public law. A similar "treatment" is accorded to the "blood avenger" (see Deut 19:12; Num 35:19–24).

35. The participial forms in the Hebrew text, סורר ומורה, שמע, זולל וסבא, emphasize the recurrence of his behavior to the extent that it has become a permanent state.

36. LH 168 is formulated according to a similar pattern. At first the lawgiver's words appear, and later the father's statement is delivered in direct speech, initiating the judicial process against the son. Among other differences between the Babylonian law and the law under discussion (which will not be fully enumerated here) there are two differences that relate to the content of the statement, and the relation between that content and the lawgiver's preceding words. In the law of the rebellious son, the statement relates to the conduct of the son, and in the Babylonian law to the sanction that the father wants to apply to him—disinheritance: *mārī anassaḫ iqtabi* ("I will disinherit my son"). Unlike in the law of the rebellious son, in the Babylonian law the content of the father's statement is identical to the lawgiver's words *šumma awīlum ana mārīšu nasāḫim* ("If a man should decide to disinherit his son").

37. In an adoption contract from the Late Babylonian period (*Ana Ittishu* III:10–16) we find a different course of rebellion—escape from the home of the adoptive parents (see

rebellious behavior.³⁸ For what reason, if so, did the parents see fit to present another example of their son's rebelliousness? Is not the first example, also given in the authoritative words of the lawgiver, sufficient? And why was this feature in particular chosen, among many others that might have illustrated his rebelliousness?

We must listen to the parents and attempt to understand their frame of mind, for therein lies the key to understanding the addition of the third attribute. We must, therefore, pay attention to the phrase with which they begin their statement—"This our son" (בננו זה). It is not impossible, of course, that the demonstrative pronoun is used as a neutral demonstrative, whose sole purpose is to point to the son who is present at the proceedings. But since the words "our son" renders the word "this" superfluous (for he is their only son present at the proceedings), and based on our familiarity with other biblical verses in which "this" (זה or הזה) reflects a negative attitude of distancing or scorn toward the person referenced,³⁹ it is clear that its use here expresses the parents' estrangement from and revulsion toward their son. In contrast to the lawgiver's official preamble, their declaration is a statement by those who suffer daily from the son's conduct and have to contend with its destructive effect on the family unit; it is they who know the son at first hand, and for whom "rebellious and stubborn" is not merely a legal definition but a vivid experience. The characteristic "glutton and drunkard" reflects, then, the subjective position of those who are at the eye of the storm, who experience their son as a reckless bully and an unproductive squanderer.⁴⁰ But the reason for adding the third characteristic is not simply to illustrate how intolerable life with

---

David Marcus, "Juvenile Delinquency in the Bible and the Ancient Near East," *JANES* 13 [1981]: 37).

38. See Driver, *Deuteronomy*, 247–48; A. D. H. Mayes suggests that the phrase "a glutton and a drunkard" (influenced by the hendiadys "winebibbers," and "gluttonous eaters of meat" in Prov 23:20–21) is a late accretion, intended to give greater specification to the general accusation (Mayes, *Deuteronomy*, 304). According to Elizabeth Bellefontaine's (original) idea, the source of the expression is in a broader law dealing with antisocial behavior, and it was imported into the law of the rebellious son as part of a conventional repertoire of terms (Elizabeth Bellefontaine, "Deuteronomy 21:18–21; Reviewing the Case of the Rebellious Son," *JSOT* 13 [1979]: 20–22).

39. See, e.g., Exod 32:1; 1 Sam 10:27; 21:16; Jer 7:16; 26:11; and also Gen 24:65 הלזה. Alongside these texts are other verses where the use of the demonstrative pronoun does not have a negative connotation (Gen 24:58; Judg 19:23–24; Jer 26:16). Below, in my discussion of the law of false accusation I will refer again to the significance of adding the demonstrative pronoun.

40. The combination of rebelliousness, disobedience, and unrestrained eating and drinking matches one modern characterization of the psychopathic and antisocial personality (see Marcus, "Juvenile Delinquency," 49).

this son is, and how destructive his influence is to the family's integrity. The parents append it as a rhetorical flourish intended to make clear that this is the last resort, and that he represents a threat to society as a whole. The daunting image they project aims, and succeeds, at alienating the tribunal from the rebellious son, persuading them to remove him from the community. It removes all doubt from the heart of the judges (and of the readers) regarding the necessity of the death penalty.

Finally, I must address the interpretation that views the third attribution of the son as bearing a normative legal meaning (rather than a "mere" rhetorical flourish), by determining the limits of the legal norm. In other words, the third attribution appears in the parents' statement in order to determine that only someone who is *both* "a glutton and a drunkard" *and* is disobedient toward his parents is to be considered a rebellious son according to the law.[41] This position seems untenable to me, since the limits of the legal norm are stated in the lawgiver's opening words, according to which a rebellious son is one who does not obey his parents (the requirement of obedience is taken for granted by a patriarchal society, and someone who disobeys the head of the family is seen as someone who rebels against society's foundations.) Therefore, it is sufficient to characterize the son as a rebel who is disobedient toward his parents, in order to sentence him to death (as emerges also from the parallel laws in the Book of the Covenant and in the Priestly Code, which deal with violations of parental authority [Exod 21:17; Lev 20:9]).

The third attribute, although it adds nothing to the legal norm, adds much to its comprehensibility and assimilability, as it addresses itself to the sensibility of the law's addressee—to the sense of fear and intimidation in the face of anyone who threatens the social order.

"This Woman," "This Man"

Our discussion of the rebellious son naturally leads to discussion of the rebellious daughter, who is accused by her husband of harlotry, and indeed the two laws appear to have several elements in common.

> [13]If any man takes a wife, and goes in to her, and then spurns her, [14]and charges her with shameful conduct and brings an evil name upon her, saying, "I took this woman, and when I came near her, I did not find in her the tokens of virginity," [15]then the father of the young woman and her mother shall take and bring out the tokens of her virginity to the elders of the city in the gate; [16]and the father of the

---

41. See Joseph Fleishman, *Parents and Children in Biblical and Ancient Near Eastern Law* (in Hebrew; Jerusalem: Magnes, 1999), 256–65. This position is in line with the early rabbinic interpretive outlook, which did all it could to limit the applicability of the law.

young woman shall say to the elders, "I gave my daughter to this man to wife, and he spurns her; [17]and lo, he has made shameful charges against her, saying, 'I did not find in your daughter the tokens of virginity.' And yet these are the tokens of my daughter's virginity." And they shall spread the garment before the elders of the city. [18]Then the elders of that city shall take the man and whip him; [19]and they shall fine him a hundred shekels of silver, and give them to the father of the young woman, because he has brought an evil name upon a virgin of Israel; and she shall be his wife; he may not put her away all his days. (Deut 22:13–19)

In the main clause of the law dealing with a man's accusation against his wife of having engaged in sexual intercourse before marriage, the lawgiver presents two utterances in direct speech. The first comes from the husband: "I took this woman, and when I came near her, I did not find in her the tokens of virginity"; and the second from the father-in-law: "I gave my daughter[42] to this man to wife, and he spurns her; and lo, he has made shameful charges against her, saying, 'I did not find in your daughter the tokens of virginity.' And yet these are the tokens of my daughter's virginity."

The husband initiates with his statement a judicial procedure to annul his marriage, while the father's utterance, pronounced in the course of the proceedings, is designed to present a defense in the woman's favor. At the end of his statement, he presents evidence proving her innocence. In addition to the legal-functional element embodied in each of the utterances, they allow us to "attend" a colloquium in which husband, father, and lawgiver are panelists, and whose title is "Reality and Its Tendentious Presentation." By means of the statements made by each of the (male) protagonists, the lawgiver reveals different points of view to the reader, all of which bear implications for the presentation of reality—the same reality presented by him in the opening lines of the law.

Let us begin with the lawgiver's utterance. His words, "If any man takes a wife, and goes in to her, and then spurns her, and charges her with shameful conduct and brings an evil name upon her," describe a sequence of events that led to the initiation of legal proceedings. This sequence contains two causal-chronological links and one observation—the three elements that constitute reality. We know that the husband began to hate his wife *after* having sexual relations with her; that his hatred is what *caused* him to accuse her; and that

---

42. The Septuagint version reflects the textual variant "*this* my daughter," most probably under the influence of the phrases: "this woman," "this man." The Masoretic Text is to be preferred (as I will explain below), although it could be argued that the repeated appearance of the demonstrative pronoun reflects a conventional legal formula for pointing at the defendant or at any party to a legal dispute.

the accusation is *false*.⁴³ The disclosure that the accusation is false prepares us for the way in which the husband will present (the same) reality.

The husband's utterance is a distorted mirror image of the picture painted by the lawgiver. His opening words, "I took this woman, and when I came near her," ostensibly follow the lawgiver's phrase "If any man takes a wife, and goes in to her"; however, the seemingly neutral opening reflects his true attitude toward his wife—the hatred that he attempts to camouflage with the grave accusation "I did not find in her the tokens of virginity." His choice of the expression "this woman" (as opposed to "my wife") attests to the alienation he feels toward her; and the more remote expression "I came near her" (as opposed, for example, to "I came to her") accentuates his revulsion toward her, as though he is incapable of reenacting the intimate act.⁴⁴ We must bear in mind that admitting his hatred toward his wife would have enabled him to divorce her, but at the same time it would require him to return the brideprice. Therefore, by taking advantage of the concealed nature of the private domain, he chooses to present a different, false and tendentious reality.

Interestingly, the father's statement is a "mosaic" in which the voices of the other participants in the colloquium can be heard. In the opening words, "I gave my daughter to this man to wife," he reverses the husband's words, "I took this woman [to wife]"—a reversal reflecting his attitude to the situation and toward the protagonists. The alienated expression used by the husband, "this woman," is replaced by "my daughter," an expression of intimacy;⁴⁵ and

---

43. The English translation, "charges her with shameful conduct," does not reflect the falseness of the husband's allegation. The Hebrew expression עלילת דברים (lit., "wantonness of words," i.e., "baseless charges" [see *BDB*, s.v. עלילה, 760a]) can also be interpreted as "words of torment" or "excuses" (based on the Aramaic ʿillaʾ [Arabic ʿillah], as reflected in the Septuagint, the Vulgate, the Peshitta, and the Aramaic Targum]). See S. R. Driver's discussion of v. 14a (*Deuteronomy*, 254–55) and William W. Hallo's reading of this law in the light of ancient Near Eastern documents ("The Slandered Bride," in *Studies Presented to A. Leo Oppenheim, June 7, 1964* [ed. R. D. Briggs and J. A. Brinkman; Chicago: Oriental Institute of the University of Chicago, 1964], 95–98).

44. According to Jacob Milgrom, the verb "to come near/approach" (קרב) is euphemistic language for sexual intercourse (e.g., "Now Abimelech had not approached [קרב] her" [Gen 20:4]; "And I went [אקרב] to the prophetess" [Isa 8:3]). He adduces support for this view from the alternation between the verbs "come near" and "lie" (קרב and שכב) (Lev 18:6, 14, 19; 20:11, 16, 18, 20), and also in the Akkadian verbs *qerēbum*, *ṭeḫûm*, which also appear in sexual contexts (*Leviticus 17–22*, 1534). Apart from Isa 8:3, in the rest of the verses listed the verb קרב does not denote the actual sexual act, but rather approaching with sexual intent (see *BDB*, s.v. קרב, 897a, 1a). If so, it seems to me that one can attribute to the husband a deliberate use of the more remote verbal root, semantically speaking.

45. The Septuagint's harmonizing version ("*This* my daughter," following the husband's expression, "*This* woman") obscures the difference between the husband's alienating

through the use of the phrase "this man," the father pays the husband back for first using the expression of contempt toward his daughter. Moreover, the shift of agency from the husband to himself, from "I took" to "I gave," indicates the sense of responsibility that weighs upon him, and his understandable involvement in the situation.

The second part of the father's utterance, "and he spurns her; and lo, he has made shameful charges against her," echoes the words of the lawgiver. He understands what is understood by the lawgiver (and reader), that the husband actually hates his wife and that his hatred causes him to distort reality. Therefore, he emphasizes the causal connection between the hatred and the false accusation with the words "and lo" (והנה).[46] His understanding, which coincides with the knowledge of the lawgiver, turns him, unlike the husband, into a reliable character. Even so, it appears that this understanding is not complete (or maybe he prefers to present it only partially), because the statement does not reflect the causal link that explains the nature of the reversal in the husband's attitude, the appreciation that he rejected her only after he had satisfied his sexual passion, as has been made explicit by the lawgiver in the opening verse.[47]

As part of the father's statement, another utterance is delivered in direct speech, a quotation of the husband's words, "saying, 'I did not find in your daughter the tokens of virginity.'" A comparison between the latter and the original utterance shows that the quotation pretends to be accurate, but it is in fact not. The quotation, rather, indicates the subordination of the original utterance to the framework of citation and to the citer's motives.[48] First, it is a paraphrase of the husband's words, which reflects not his perspective but rather the father's perspective—the perspective of the quoter. The husband did not implicate the father in his own utterance. The father, however, having a sense of responsibility for his daughter's actions and for her fate, changed the word "her" ("I did not find in her the tokens of virginity") to the words "to

---

and demeaning language and the father's more familial and endearing wording. Therefore the Masoretic Text, "my daughter," is to be preferred.

46. On the use of wĕhinnēh to express causality, see Dennis J. McCarthy, "The Uses of wᵉhinnēh in Biblical Hebrew," *Biblica* 61 (1980): 333–34.

47. A similar shift occurs in Amnon's attitude toward Tamar, from great infatuation before the sexual act, to great hatred after the rape (2 Sam 13:14–15).

48. A quotation is a joining of two independent situations: the one in which the words were spoken by the first speaker and the second one in which they are presented by another speaker. The act of citation involves the combination of two perspectives: that of the original speaker and that of the quoter, while the perspective of the first is always subordinated to the second. See Sternberg, "Between the Truth and the Whole Truth," 111–13.

your daughter," a reflection of his own feelings.[49] Second, and most important, the father transforms the husband's original utterance in a way that betrays his attitude toward him and his evaluation of the husband's claim. Two elements that appeared in the original utterance are missing from the father's quotation: the opening phrase "I took this woman" and the words "I came near her." While the omission of the opening phrase need not be given too much weight and can be explained away as the father's reluctance to repeat information that he already conveyed at the beginning of his speech (although had he preserved that phrase, he would certainly have refrained from using the alienating locution "this woman," and would have chosen a different pronoun), the omission of the words "I came near her" is not coincidental. It reveals, rather, the father's attitude toward the husband's claim and his point of view. The latter, as to be expected, linked the sexual act to the failure to find her tokens of virginity—the intimate act is presented by him as the moment of discovery. The omission of any mention of the sexual act in the quotation means that the claim about the missing maidenhead remains without any factual substantiation and highlights its arbitrary nature. The husband's accusation appears in the quotation as detached and decontextualized, and so the father underscores the distortion of his presentation.

The phrase concluding the father's utterance, "And yet these are the tokens of my daughter's virginity," constitutes the climax of the utterance, because the father's main purpose is to present the exonerating evidence and to deflect the accusation. The question, therefore, arises why the lawgiver is not satisfied with this and chooses to put in the father's mouth a long and complex utterance that contains no additional information. There is no legal justification for the lawgiver's conveyance of the father's long utterance, with all of its rhetorical elements (just as the formulation and stylization of the husband's arraignment bear no legal meaning). It would have been sufficient to present only the final functional section. It is clear that the presentation of these utterances has a different value. Their purpose is to evoke the presence of the reader within the events—to allow the reader to take part in the perspectival colloquium, to hear the different voices, and to become exposed to the different points of view. The father's long utterance is first and foremost a stylized artistic template, intended to realize the nonlegalistic values of the law, but at the same time it is a realistic, verisimilar reaction. His utterance is detailed, because an authentic father, whose daughter had fallen prey to a grave false accusation, would not

---

49. The characters in the law under discussion are given different appellations: "man," "this man," "wife," "this woman," "young woman," "my daughter," "your daughter," "a virgin of Israel," "the father of the young woman," "her father." The alternation of appellations will be considered in the final chapter, which discusses point of view and focalization.

respond with a brief, functional, matter-of-fact utterance, for his response is an emotional one. He is not satisfied with proving his daughter's innocence; he wishes rather to underscore that an evil deed has been perpetrated against her. This emphasis, which in fact amounts to a counteraccusation against the husband, requires him to pronounce his long and complex utterance.

The Dead Man, His Wife, and His Brother

From a failed relationship we turn to a different sort of disappointment and grief.

> ⁵If brothers dwell together, and one of them dies and has no son, the wife of the dead shall not be married outside the family to a stranger; her husband's brother shall go in to her, and take her as his wife, and perform the duty of a husband's brother to her. ⁶And the first son whom she bears shall succeed to the name of his brother who is dead, that his name may not be blotted out of Israel. ⁷And if the man does not wish to take his brother's wife, then his brother's wife shall go up to the gate to the elders, and say, "My husband's brother refuses to perpetuate his brother's name in Israel; he will not perform the duty of a husband's brother to me." ⁸Then the elders of his city shall call him, and speak to him: and if he persists, saying, "I do not wish to take her," ⁹then his brother's wife shall go up to him in the presence of the elders, and pull his sandal off his foot, and spit in his face; and she shall answer and say, "So shall it be done to the man who does not build up his brother's house." ¹⁰And the name of his house shall be called in Israel, The house of him that had his sandal pulled off. (Deut 25:5–10)

The secondary law in the law of levirate marriage (vv. 7–10) describes a judicial procedure enacted against the brother-in-law who has shirked his duty in levirate marriage, as stipulated by the principal law (vv. 5–6). As part of the procedure, three utterances are delivered in direct speech:

1. An accusatory utterance by the widow, which instigates the judicial procedure: "and say, 'My husband's brother refuses to perpetuate his brother's name in Israel, he will not perform the duty of a husband's brother to me.'"⁵⁰

---

50. In the Hebrew text one finds a similarity both in content and in alliteration between the opening and closing phrases (the two verbs denoting refusal and the root יבם), which create the tight structure of the utterance. The tight structure of the law as a whole is enhanced by the many repetitions of the verb יבם (seven times), and the intensive alliteration of the two consonants [b] and [m] of which it is formed (ב appears in twelve words, and מ in twenty-one), as well as the way in which the words שם ("name") and אח ("brother") recur as *Leitworte* (each appears four times). On "cohesion" and "cohesive chain," see Frank Polak, *Biblical Narrative: Aspects of Art and Design* (in Hebrew; Jerusalem: Bialik Institute, 1994), 90–106.

2. The brother-in-law's response to the accusation: "and if he persists, saying, 'I do not wish to take her.'"
3. A further statement by the widow, which together with the accompanying symbolic acts (removal of the shoe and spitting) creates a new legal status and exempts the parties from the duty placed on them: "and she shall answer and say, 'So shall it be done to the man who does not build up his brother's house.'"[51]

Had the lawgiver wished to present the reader only with the problem and its solution, or in other words, had he desired only to fulfill his role as lawgiver, by setting down the legal norm in the matter of a noncompliant levir, he would have formulated the law as follows:

> And if the man does not wish to take his brother's wife, then his brother's wife shall go up to the gate to the elders, and the elders of his city shall call him, and then his brother's wife shall go up to him in the presence of the elders, and pull his sandal off his foot, and spit in his face, and the name of his house shall be called in Israel, The house of him that had his sandal pulled off.

It can be seen that in the above formulation a problem is presented—the brother-in-law's defaulting on his obligation to take his brother's widow in levirate marriage. Next a legal procedure is described that is the means to remedy the problem, and a legal solution is given—the new social status of the brother-in-law. The only thing that is missing is the attitude of the parties to their new position, regarding the difficult situation that has transpired following the death of the husband or brother, and regarding one another. This attitude can be found only within their speech.

What function do these three utterances fulfill? Indeed, on the level of legal practice, each one of them is vital for the legal procedure. The widow's statement is an indictment; the brother-in-law's statement is a writ of defense, and the widow's second utterance is part of the legal sanction. Thus, through these utterances, the lawgiver outlines the three phases of the judicial procedure. But at the heart of the utterances, what reverberates is actually a question regarding human distress and the parties' incompatible interests (a secondary question, considered from the purely legal standpoint): Why does the brother-in-law not fulfill his duty? The lawgiver "utilizes" the parties' answers to show us that he balances different interests, that he takes into account personal and human distress.

---

51. According to Rashi, the verse concluding the law, "and the name of his house shall be called . . . ," describes a speech event; in his terms, "It is required of all present there to say: 'him that had his sandal pulled off' [חלוץ הנעל]."

In what way does the widow respond to this question? She replies on two levels: on the level of the relationship between the brother-in-law and his deceased brother, and on the level of his relationship with her. First, she characterizes his behavior as an act of defiance—"My husband's brother *refuses*";[52] and she anchors his refusal in the first level—"*to perpetuate his brother's name in Israel*." Her words, which echo the lawgiver's statement in v. 6, have rhetorical power in their juxtaposition with the brother-in-law's refusal to fulfill his duty and the social rationale that underpins this duty. He is depicted as someone who is not prepared to produce an offspring for the sake of his brother's inheritance,[53] as someone who does not respect his family's needs. In her second utterance, which accompanies the symbolic act, the widow once again focuses on the implications of the brother-in-law's refusal for her dead husband's household ("So shall it be done to the man who does not build up his brother's house"). On the other hand, her claim that "he will not perform the duty of a husband's brother *for me*" belongs to a different plane.[54] She anchors his refusal in the relationship between him and her (the second level), as though she had said: "he refuses to marry *me*." With her variant claim she presents an alternative that softens the reader's attitude toward the recalcitrant brother-in-law and diminishes the severity she had attributed to his behavior when she first spoke. Thus, seemingly against her will, she paves the way toward accepting his position.

What is the brother-in-law's response to the said question? With his laconic statement "I do not wish to take her," he clarifies that his failure to

---

52. For the use of the verb *m'n* (מאן) to describe rebellion and stubborn resistance, see Exod 7:14; 1 Sam 8:19; 1 Kgs 21:15; Isa 1:20; Ps 78:10; Esth 1:12. Also in the law concerning seduction of a virgin (Exod 22:16–17) the verb appears as part of the secondary law and describes the resistance to upholding the primary law. However, unlike the law of levirate marriage, it is the lawgiver who characterizes the behavior as refusal, not one of the characters.

53. According to Raymond Westbrook, the word שם should not be translated by the standard meaning of "name," but rather by its legal meaning of "inheritance." See Raymond Westbrook, *Property and the Family in Biblical Law* (JSOTSup 113; Sheffield: JSOT Press, 1991), 71–77. Evidence that a person derived his name from his land can be found in the claim of Zelophehad's daughters: "Why should the name of our father be taken away from his family, because he had no son. Give to us a possession among our father's brethren" (Num 27:4). In Ezekiel 48 the word שם appears in the context and perhaps as a synonym of landed inheritance.

54. Unlike the English translations, in the Hebrew original לא אבה יבמי the word "duty" (the duty of a husband's brother) does not appear. Rather, the Hebrew reflects the husband's reluctance to fulfill the act of levirate marriage, while the act itself receives no special characterization. Therefore, I propose a different translation: "he is not willing to take me in levirate marriage."

fulfill the obligation is not tantamount to a refusal to reproduce for the sake of his brother's inheritance but derives, rather, from his unwillingness to marry a woman under such difficult circumstances. He locates his reason for refusal in the emotional life of the individual (and not in the failure to honor the custom of patriarchal society). In using the verb "wish" in the negative, he underscores the intensity of his unwillingness.[55]

Interestingly, the brief words of the brother-in-law correspond to the lawgiver's words: "and if the man *does not wish* to take his brother's wife." It seems that the lawgiver adopts the brother-in-law's standpoint in regard to the reasons for his failure of duty, rather than the widow's view, for he does not state "and if the man *refuses*." The congruence between the brother-in-law's claim and the lawgiver's formulation accords legitimacy to his behavior, while it is understood that against the interest of the dead brother's household stand his own needs and the needs of his own family.[56]

Before conveying the brother-in-law's utterance, the lawgiver reports another speech event, but this time without revealing its content: "Then the elders of his city shall call him, and speak to him" (naturally, the reader fills in the gap and treats the elders' words as persuasion, an attempt to talk the brother-in-law out of his refusal).[57] The difference in the manner of conveying speech events in this law—direct speech, on the one hand, and summary report, on the other—highlights the role each of these types of discourse plays within the law. While the widow's statements and the brother-in-law's declaration have operative implications in regard to the sociolegal status of the speaking character, the elders' speech has no such practical effect, for the brother-in-law does not change his mind after hearing it. Perhaps for this reason the lawgiver refrains from rendering the content of the elders' speech. Since it effects no change and the reader's cognizance of it bears no consequence, its content and wording become secondary, and the lawgiver can be satisfied with the reader's general insight in regard to its import. But the very presentation of the elders' address (despite its nonspecification) has importance within the framework of the law, for it allows the law to reflect its ambivalence toward the brother-in-

---

55. The Hebrew employs the verb חפץ ("have delight in"). Use of this verb in relation to a woman appears in Gen 34:19; Deut 21:14; Esth 2:14 (and together with חשק ["desire"] in 1 Kgs 9:1).

56. For the socioeconomic causes behind the failure to perform the duty of levirate marriage, see Tigay, *Deuteronomy*, 232–33.

57. The difference in the presentation of the speech acts is reflected also in the different verbs employed to report them: for the widow and brother-in-law the verb "say" (אמר) is used, whereas for the elders the verb "speak" (דבר) is used. This choice of verb aligns with the rule according to which direct speech appears in the Bible only after the verb "to say," and not following other verbs that report speech. On the rules, the exceptions, and the verbs introducing direct or indirect speech, see Goldenberg, *Studies in Semitic Linguistics*, 203–5.

law's behavior. On the one hand, the elders attempt to persuade him to fulfill his obligation (to this we must add the expression with which the lawgiver prefaces the brother-in-law's utterance, "and if he *persists*, saying," which attributes to his behavior an aspect of willfulness and rebellion).[58] Yet, on the other hand, his brief and laconic utterance illustrates that he is not required to justify his unwillingness—mere unwillingness is sufficient to exempt him from his obligation.

I think that the utterances presented in the law of levirate marriage allow us to anticipate the reform that occurred in relation to the obligation of levirate marriage—from an absolute requirement that sanctifies a social principle and takes a single family consideration into account (as reflected in Genesis 38) to a more limited obligation, which, in light of an appreciation of the difficulties in implementing the principle, includes the right of refusal.[59] The symbolic act that concludes the judicial procedure also reflects the balanced and moderate stance of the law toward failure to fulfill the obligation. On the one hand, this is a sanction that is intended to tarnish the honor of the brother-in-law and to express disapproval of his behavior,[60] but, on the other hand, it is an act that releases him from the obligation and is therefore desired by him.

Oath

I have chosen to present only one oath, or more precisely, one long and complex adjuration. So as not to dull its strong impact, I have forgone discussion of two other oaths.[61]

---

58. The Hebrew text uses the verb "to stand" (עמד). For the prefacing of a speech verb with עמד as an expression of defiance and rebellion, see 1 Sam 17:8; 2 Kgs 10:9; 18:28; 2 Chr 26:18.

59. Over the years levirate marriage became a custom so obsolete that eventually it was completely prohibited (Lev 18:18 and 20:16), and the removal of the shoe came to replace it as obligatory custom. See Daube, *Studies in Biblical Law*, 39–62.

60. On the intensity of the humiliation and degradation implied by each element of the symbolic act: removal of the shoe, spitting, name-calling, and their far-reaching impact on the status of the dissenting brother-in-law, see Jonathan P. Burnside, *The Signs of Sin: Seriousness of Offence in Biblical Law* (JSOTSup 364; Sheffield: JSOT Press, 2003), 113–19. For another view concerning the significance of the removal of the shoe, see Paul A. Kruger, "The Removal of the Sandal in Deuteronomy XXV 9: "A Rite of Passage?" *VT* 46 (1996): 534–39.

61. Two oath-taking procedures are presented in the deposit laws of the Book of the Covenant. The first reads as follows: "the owner of the house shall come near to God, to show whether or not he has put his hand to his neighbor's goods" (Exod 22:7); and the second ordains that, "an oath by the LORD shall be between them both to see whether he has not put his hand to his neighbor's property" (v. 10). The lawgiver does not convey the formula of the oath of innocence, but rather paraphrases its content, rendering the oath in

"And the woman shall say 'Amen, Amen'"

The law of the jealousy ordeal (Num 5:11–31) is not a substantive law that either prohibits or permits an action, but a procedural rule dealing with evidentiary law. The law establishes a mechanism for ascertaining the guilt of a woman suspected of adultery by her husband, in cases where there is no evidence for proving guilt.[62] The mechanism of divine examination, the ritual ordeal described by the law (similar to other known ritual ordeals)[63] is composed of two elements: an act (or series of actions) and an utterance (an oath). The oath ensures the realization of the ordeal's outcome—it enacts divine power and allows magic to take over the action.[64]

At the basis of the law are two alternative accounts: according to one, the woman committed adultery; according to the other, she did not. Both accounts are presented four times; three times on the part of the lawgiver:

> ¹²If any man's wife goes astray and acts unfaithfully against him, ¹³if a man lies with her carnally, and it is hidden from the eyes of her husband, and she is undetected though she has defiled herself, and there is no witness against her, since she was not taken in the act; ¹⁴and if the spirit of jealousy comes upon him, and he is jealous of his wife who has defiled herself; or if the spirit of jealousy comes

---

indirect speech. At the same time, his use of the word אם as a marker of indirect speech (instead of the more prevalent כי) creates the illusion of having preserved some aspect of the original oath. Since oaths in the Bible begin with the word אם followed by a verb, or with the words אם לא followed by a verb (similar to the Akkadian *šumma, šumma la* [see *CAD*, Š III, 276b]), אם has here a poetic function of preserving, even to a small degree, the illusion of *mimesis*, of imitating the original utterance within the lawgiver's paraphrase. On the polyvocality of indirect speech that reproduces the style of the reported utterance, see Mikhail Bakhtin, "Discourse in the Novel," in *The Dialogic Imagination: Four Essays by M. M. Bakhtin* (ed. M. Holquist; trans. C. Emerson and M. Holquist; Austin: University of Texas Press, 1981), 340–42.

62. The lawgiver presents the lack of evidence in four variations (v. 13), thus emphasizing that the husband's jealousy is the motive for undertaking the ordeal (v. 14). The Mishnah limited the applicability of the rite, stating that the husband cannot subject his wife to the "water" ordeal simply because he was gripped with suspicion that aroused his jealousy (*m. Sotah* 1:1).

63. On the judicial ordeal, see Jacob Licht, *A Commentary on the Book of Numbers, 1–10* (in Hebrew; Jerusalem: Magnes, 1985), 67–69; Jacob Milgrom, *Numbers-Be-midbar: The Traditional Hebrew Text with the New JPS Translation* (JPS Torah Commentary; Philadelphia: Jewish Publication Society, 1990), 346–48.

64. The description "Then the priest shall write these curses in a book, and wash them off into the water of bitterness" (v. 23) reflects the symbiosis between deed and utterance. In LH 131–132 one finds two separate evidential instruments. In the absence of evidence substantiating the husband's suspicions, the wife must take an oath of innocence, and the ordeal is enacted only when the source of guilt is a third party.

upon him, and he is jealous of his wife, though she has not defiled herself. . . . (Num 5:12b–14)

²⁷And when he has made her drink the water, then, if she has defiled herself and has acted unfaithfully against her husband, the water that brings the curse shall enter into her and cause bitter pain, and her body shall swell, and her thigh shall fall away, and the woman shall become an execration among her people. ²⁸But if the woman has not defiled herself and is clean, then she shall be free and shall conceive children. (vv. 27–28)

²⁹This is the law in cases of jealousy, when a wife, though under her husband's authority, goes astray and defiles herself, ³⁰or when the spirit of jealousy comes upon a man and he is jealous of his wife. (vv. 29–30a)

and once more, from the lips of the priest, as he administers the oath:

¹⁹Then the priest shall make her take an oath, saying, "If no man has lain with you, and if you have not turned aside to uncleanness, while you were under your husband's authority, be free from this water of bitterness that brings the curse. ²⁰But if you have gone astray, though you are under your husband's authority, and if you have defiled yourself, and some man other than your husband has lain with you. . . . (vv. 19–20a)

The woman, on the other hand, does not present her story. As against these repeated accounts hers is a laconic utterance: "Amen, Amen" (5:22b). This situation, where her brief utterance stands over against four statements that are linguistically aligned, reflects "collaboration" between the lawgiver and the priest (a functional extension of the husband), which allows the weaving of a male web that entraps the helpless woman.[65] Lest I create the impression that I am ignoring the original context of the passage, and that I am guilty of an anachronistic interpretation (feminist or otherwise), I base my argument on the wording of the two utterances that are conveyed in direct speech, pointing out how they are exceptional and so present an unbalanced position (like the passage itself).

The act of making the woman take the oath is composed of two opposite conditional clauses. In each of them her behavior is described in detail in the conditional clause, while the results of her behavior are stated in the conse-

---

65. Ostensibly my position is incongruent with the view that the priest's involvement is designed to prevent the jealous husband from subjecting his wife to the law of the mob, and therefore the two do not share a common interest (see Milgrom, *Numbers*, 350). However, the two views are not necessarily at odds. Even if the rationale underpinning the law is to prevent the husband from taking the law into his own hands, the priest may still see the husband's interest as foremost, and may thus serve as his agent, in activating the procedure required by law.

quential injunction. The priest begins with a negative conditional clause pointing to her innocence (*the alternative of innocence*):

> If *no man* has lain with you, and if you *have not* turned aside to uncleanness, while you were under your husband's authority, be free from this water of bitterness that brings the curse.

and ends with an affirmative conditional clause pointing to her guilt (*the alternative of guilt*):

> But if you *have gone astray*, though you are under your husband's authority, and if you *have defiled yourself*, then ... the LORD make you an execration and an oath among your people ... may this water that brings the curse pass into your bowels and make your body swell and your thigh fall away.

Thus he deviates from the order given in the lawgiver's presentation, which in each of the three references to the woman's behavior places her guilt first and concludes with her innocence.[66] The reversal of the order, which presents the option of her innocence first and might ostensibly indicate a positive evaluation of the woman, actually allows the other option to dominate.[67] The first alternative begins with the word "if" (אם), a seemingly neutral linguistic choice, but the second option begins with emphatic "but [as for you] if" (ואת כי) and later "and if" (וכי), which echoes for our ears the alteration in the priest's intonation. Giving precedence to the option of innocence allows, therefore, the option of guilt to be accentuated.[68] The woman (and the reader) is left

---

66. This "deviation" produces a chiastic structure formed of the priest's and lawgiver's utterances, which parallels other chiastic structures in the passage. On the general chiastic structure of the entire segment, see Milgrom, *Numbers*, 351. Through the use of the nested, latticelike chiastic structures the male web is woven more and more densely.

67. In addition to its divergence from the lawgiver's presentations, the priest's utterance contains a unique element compared to other similar statements. As a whole, in statements composed of two opposing conditional clauses, the speaker opens with an affirmative conditional, "if," and ends with a negative conditional, "if not" (see, e.g., Gen 24:49; 42:15–16; 43:4–5; Jer 38:17–18; Ps 137:5–6 [the last two verses present oaths]). Not so with the priest's oath formula.

68. Baruch Levine calls the repeated כי form "assertive *kî*" (although probably asseverative *kî* is what is meant), similar to the emphatic כי appearing in Gen 3:14; 13:17; 21:17–18. See Baruch Levine, *Numbers 1–20: A New Translation with Introduction and Commentary* (AB 4; New York: Doubleday, 1993), 197. Such a כי is so foreign to conditional clauses (the three aforementioned verses are not conditional clauses) that it obscures the hypothetical element underlying the utterance and points up the element of certainty. Therefore, the balance between the two alternatives is disturbed, since the option of innocence is presented as more hypothetical and her guilt as certain. The balance would have been maintained

with the terrifying impression of the concluding alternative—the alternative of guilt.

Moreover, the oath formula chosen by the priest is exceptional not only vis-à-vis the lawgiver's formulations, that is to say, in the narrow contexts of this passage, but also (and perhaps especially) in the broader context of oath formulas and imprecations. The oaths that appear in the Bible and in other ancient Near Eastern literatures are usually divided into two main classes, according to the function they fulfill: assertory (or declaratory) oaths and promissory oaths. The first type confirms declarations or statements in respect to an event or conduct that occurred in the past, affirming the content of the information, while the second type grants validity to future commitments, testifying to the seriousness of the oath taker's intentions.[69] Oaths that confirm contents include exculpatory oaths (or oaths of innocence)—oaths that are taken in the course of judicial proceedings in cases where it is impossible to decide based on the standard evidentiary laws. The oath, which is usually cast upon the suspect or the accused, completely exempts from liability and in this sense serves as a decisive piece of evidence that brings the process to a close. Unlike modern legal process, where the burden of proof rests on the prosecution, in the ancient world it is not uncommon for a person against whom either insufficient evidence, or even no evidence at all exists, to carry the burden of proof and to take an exculpatory oath, according to which he did not commit the transgression/s of which he is suspect or with which he is charged.[70]

Now let us return to our passage. Substantially speaking, and in terms of the function it fulfills, the woman's oath is an exculpatory oath.[71] Nevertheless,

---

had the second alternative been phrased in like manner "And if [ואם] you have gone astray. . . ." On asseverative *kî* in oath formulas, see Follingstad, *Particle Kî*, 49–51; on uses of the asseverative *kî* in the Bible, see Edward L. Greenstein, "The Poem on Wisdom in Job 28 in Its Conceptual and Literary Contexts," in *Job 28: Cognition in Context* (ed. Ellen van Wolde; Biblical Interpretation Series 64; Leiden: Brill, 2003), 265.

69. See John A. Wilson, "The Oath in Ancient Egypt," *JNES* 7 (1948): 129–30; Westbrook, "Deposit Laws," 392.

70. Such, for example, are the exculpatory oaths described in the Book of the Covenant (Exod 22:7, 10) and in other ancient Near Eastern laws (LE 37; LH 20, 206; MAL A 22). Alongside the legal exculpatory oaths are other declarations of innocence that are not uttered in the context of formal judicial proceedings (see, e.g., Num 16:15; 1 Sam 12:3; 22:15; Job 31). For other examples of judicial and nonjudicial oaths of innocence, see Wilson, "Oath," 131–40. On the pattern of declarations of innocence and their ancient Near Eastern parallels, see Michael B. Dick, "Job 31: The Oath of Innocence and the Sage," *ZAW* 95 (1983): 31–53; Edward L. Greenstein, "A Forensic Understanding of the Speech from the Whirlwind," in *Texts, Temples, and Traditions: A Tribute to Menahem Haran* (ed. Michael V. Fox et al; Winona Lake, Ind.: Eisenbrauns, 1996), 246–47.

71. See Dick, "Job 31," 39; Jackson, *Theft*, 248.

it is not formulated as one. Unlike the standard pattern, in which the oath taker makes only one claim—a claim of innocence—the woman's oath presents two alternatives, a claim of innocence and a claim of guilt. Such a simultaneous presentation, while emphasizing the option of guilt turns the utterance into an "*oath of guilt*." But this is not enough, for her guilt is underscored also through the very repetition of the depiction of the act of adultery in three linguistic variations.[72] What value could the priest find in repeating the description of the act of adultery twice, even when reciting the innocent option, if not to augment the "guilty language," as Alice Bach has noted?[73]

The imbalance between the two alternatives (i.e., the guilty option being more heavily weighted) is even more salient in the apodosis of each alternative, beginning already with the option of innocence, "be free from this water of bitterness that brings the curse." Commentators have interpreted the word "be free" (הנקי) in two ways, which are not mutually exclusive: you will not be punished by the water, you will be immune from its harmful properties; or you will be cleansed of guilt, you will be exonerated by its examination.[74] Without ruling out these interpretations, I offer a third, indicated by the context, that is, by the drinking of the water, as well as by the grammatical imperative form.[75] The original meaning of the verb נקה is "to eliminate," "to rinse."[76] It therefore would seem that the meaning of the word is not metaphorical (exoneration from guilt or inoculation against punishment) but rather literal, rinsing and elimination from impurities. The phrase "then she shall be free and shall conceive children" (v. 28) illustrates this idea more clearly, for only after rinsing off the impurities does her womb become available for legitimate sperm.

---

72. "But if you have gone astray, though you are under your husband's authority"; "and if you have defiled yourself"; "and some man other than your husband has lain with you." To these three variants a fourth may be added that appears only in the statements of the lawgiver "and acts unfaithfully against him."

73. The author notes that such a vivid description of illicit sexual congress (such as the repeated verse "under your husband's [authority]," which serves as a pictorial allusion to the act of coitus) makes it difficult for the reader to remember that the woman may be innocent. The repeated descriptions serve as "verbal punishment" (Alice Bach, "Good to the Last Drop: Viewing the Sotah [Numbers 5. 11–31] as the Glass Half Empty and Wondering How to View It Half Full," in *The New Literary Criticism and the Hebrew Bible* [ed. David J. A. Clines and J. Cheryl Exum; JSOTSup 143; Sheffield: JSOT Press, 1993], 37–41).

74. See Licht, *Numbers 1–10*, 78; Milgrom, *Numbers*, 40; Levine, *Numbers 1–20*, 197. In light of the ambiguity of the term עון ("iniquity," both sin and punishment) the verse concluding the law, "The man shall be free from iniquity, but the woman shall bear her iniquity," reflects both interpretations.

75. In all of the many occurrences of the verb נקה in the *nipʿal* conjugation, it appears in the imperative form only here.

76. See *BDB*, s.v. [נָקָה], 667a.

The imperative form makes more sense this way, because the woman is commanded to rinse herself of impurity; it is less logical to demand that she be exonerated from guilt or avoid punishment.

One might well wonder why the suspected wife must be rinsed of impurity, though she is not impure (or be cleansed of guilt despite her innocence). The reason lies in the fact that the cloud of guilt hovers over the option of innocence as well. The water affects her internal organs—adversely in the case of guilt but also positively—in the case of innocence, in order to eliminate any doubt in the matter (and even though it is technically unnecessary). Moreover, the characterization of the water as "this water of bitterness that brings the curse" also imposes an element of guilt on the option of innocence, because it is clear from the circumstances that the examining water becomes bitter only in the case of guilt and not in the case of innocence (as clearly noted in v. 27, although not necessarily in v. 24). Therefore, the water's examination seems to be weighted toward guilt from the outset. Is there any chance that the woman will emerge pure when she is drinking "this water of bitterness that brings the curse" and not, for instance, "holy water of testing"?[77]

The imbalance between the apodosis spelling out the option of innocence and its much longer and more detailed equivalent in the option of guilt (v. 21) is extremely prominent, therefore, in view of the invocation of God and the explicit threat to amplify the curse to the woman's social status as well. The brief option of innocence (and, as explained above, in itself problematic) must face a flood of curses that leaves the woman no chance. It is important to note, to remove any doubt, that the imprecations are not in themselves an unusual element of oaths. The contrary is true, although there are cases when they are not explicitly mentioned, since the natural fear of the consequences of the oath (i.e., divine punishment) is sufficient. The role of the imprecations is to deter one from taking a false oath (and in the case of promissory oaths from violating one's commitment). But this is not the role they play here. The imprecations fall upon the woman because of the act of adultery, not in order to validate the oath. This is what makes them an exception.

To sum up: Such a wording of the oath, which reflects an imbalanced presentation of the matter at hand,[78] is intended to deter the humiliated and

---

77. The lawgiver uses tendentious wording also in his characterization of the water (vv. 18, 23, 24a). Neutral language can be found in vv. 17, 26b, 27a. For an interpretation of the term "the water of bitterness that brings the curse," see Eryl W. Davies, *Numbers* (NCBC; London: M. Pickering, 1995), 53–54.

78. The lawgiver is also an "accomplice" in the unbalanced presentation. The presentation of the case in the initial part of the law (vv. 12b–13a), which makes clear that the woman committed adultery, is incongruent with the question mark hovering over v. 14, whether perhaps an obsessively jealous husband has unjustly suspected his wife. The description of

already terrified woman from actually completing the ritual act. Its purpose is to persuade her to confess the sin, without having recourse to the divine ordeal.[79]

As mentioned earlier, the woman's version of events is not heard. Had she formulated the oath, certainly, a different utterance would have been produced, but she does not couch the oath of innocence in her own words, but rather accepts the priest's formula.[80] Therefore, all she is left with is to affirm the dictated terms and answer "Amen Amen." Commentators have treated the affirmative nature of the utterance as natural and have not noted how foreign it is to the character of the passage as a whole.[81] They have not wondered how, in a passage so elaborately detailed and filled with repetitions, the woman is furnished with such a brief formula. Evidently she is not the protagonist of this affair but merely the object of the husband and the priest's actions, and it is difficult not to hear her rehearsal of "Amen Amen" as a terrified stammer.

Interior Speech

Up till now we have listened to the characters' explicit statements—words that they directed toward others with whom they interacted. Now we encounter

---

the act of adultery in three linguistic variations leaves the reader with a clear impression that the case is one of adultery and not merely a suspicion of adultery. The illogic implicit in the opening verses of the law is usually explained through textual criticism and the suggestion of conflations or late accretions (see Licht, *Numbers 1–10*, 71–72, 75; Jeon, "Two Laws in the Sotah Passage"), but it seems that it can (also) be attributed to the tendency toward lopsidedness that marks the entire passage.

79. If so, the trend exhibited in the Mishnah, to reduce the applicability of the rite to as few cases as possible is already perceptible in the biblical law. More pertinently, the woman's confession cannot substantiate her guilt (the law of adultery is not applicable to her) but it plays into the hands of the husband, who has the right to divorce her even without releasing her bill of divorce. Modern law also does not allow a conviction to be based on a confession extracted under duress or intimidation.

80. It is interesting to note that only in this passage does the adjuration by a third party refer to an assertory/declaratory oath. In all other cases where adjurations are described they refer to promissory oaths (see, e.g., Gen 24:3; Exod 13:19; Josh 2:17; Neh 5:12).

81. Licht, *Numbers 1–10*, 80; Milgrom, *Numbers*, 41; Levine, *Numbers 1–20*, 198; Davies, *Numbers*, 54. Answering "Amen" is indeed typical for confirmations of oaths, contracts, and covenants with YHWH (see, e.g., Deuteronomy 27; Jer 28:6; Neh 5:13), but a double affirmation is rarer. "Amen and Amen" appears in three psalms of praise to God (Pss 41:14; 72:19; 89:53), and "Amen, Amen" only in Neh 8:6 (in this verse the reduplication appears as part of a blessing to God, and it presents an irony vis-à-vis our passage; perhaps the double affirmation suits the general context of Nehemiah 8, a rite for acknowledgment of guilt). Reduplication of a verb can also connote self-debasement (e.g., the cry of the leper "Unclean, unclean" [Lev 13:45]).

the words people say to themselves. We accompany the all-knowing and all-hearing lawgiver, peer through the window he opens into the interior world, and listen to the characters' interior speech. Thus, through direct speech we will learn the thoughts and beliefs of the protagonists, their decisions and their wishes.

Three examples (all from the Deuteronomic Code) were chosen to illustrate the phenomenon of internal speech.[82] In each of them (and also in additional cases where internal speech is quoted in the laws), the lawgiver penetrates the consciousness of the character (who is always the addressee of the law). The report of what is happening there allows him to respond to the thoughts and feelings that lead to an action, even before this action is performed by the character. Let us become acquainted with these thoughts, feelings, and the responses they evoke, before they turn into actions.

Craving for Flesh

[20]When the LORD your God enlarges your territory, as he has promised you, and you say, "I will eat flesh," because you crave flesh, you may eat as much flesh as you desire. [21]If the place which the LORD your God will choose to put his name there is too far from you, then you may kill any of your herd or your flock, which the LORD has given you, as I have commanded you; and you may eat within your towns as much as you desire. (Deut 12:20–21)

The law of profane slaughter (Deut 12:20–28) provides an answer to a problem caused as a result of the law of the centralization of the cult (with which the Deuteronomic Code opens).[83] According to this law, it is compulsory to slaughter sacrificial animals in "the place which the LORD your God will

---

82. It is important to emphasize that the rules for conveying internal speech in the framework of the laws are identical to those that apply in the context of narrative prose. In the law, as in narrative, the determination that what is reported is internal speech depends first and foremost on the context of the speech and its inherent logic, since most occurrences of internal speech appear following the verb "say" (אמר) alone, in the exact same manner in which external speech is quoted (see, e.g., Gen 21:16; 1 Sam 18:21; 25:21–22). Having said that, there are occurrences where it is entirely clear that the discourse is internal speech, since it is explicitly noted that the discourse occurs within the heart of the speaker (see e.g., Gen 17:17; 27:41; Deut 7:17; 1 Sam 27:1; 2 Kgs 5:11; Eccl 1:16). The only example for such an occurrence within the laws appears in the law of the prophet (which I shall not treat here): "And if you say in your heart" (Deut 18:21). It is worthy of note that verbs of cognition such as "think," "remember," "imagine" (חשב, זכר, הגה) are not generally used for presenting thoughts (see Miller, *Representation of Speech*, 291).

83. The law is a repetition and expansion of the permission to perform profane slaughter that is legislated earlier in the context of the law of cult centralization (Deut 12:15–16).

choose," such that only those living in proximity to the "place" may consume meat from the sacrifice. The law of profane slaughter equates the status of animals offered as sacrifices (sheep, goats, bulls) to the status of those that are not fit for sacrifice (hunted animals) and allows the former to be slaughtered and eaten outside of a ritual context.

Already in the opening verse of the law "your" utterance—an utterance of the law's addressee—is rendered in direct speech: "and you say, 'I will eat flesh.'" The discourse is internal speech because apparently it has no external addressee, and it expresses something that belongs to the realm of desires—the speaker's wish to eat meat.[84] His strong wish is reflected in the use of the modal form אכלה ("I would eat, Let me eat"),[85] while the choice of the imperfect tense provides his words with a dramatic flourish, as though the wish and the decision to act upon it occurred simultaneously, at the very moment it was uttered.

The utterance is undoubtedly dramatic. But is it in and of itself sufficiently clear? Does it make explicit why the speaker wishes to eat meat? The answer to both questions is no. Although the words constituting the wish are certainly clear, the context is not, and were it addressed to an external interlocutor, in a face-to-face conversation, a misunderstanding could arise between the parties to the conversation. The external addressee might not know why and under what circumstances the speaker desired meat.

As opposed to the hypothetical external addressee, the reader's situation is different. In cognizance of the utterance's textual environment—that is, the law of centralization of the cult—and with appreciation of its context, which is the absence of secular slaughter, the reader can make do with such an elliptical utterance. The lawgiver completes the gaps for us, of which more will be said later.

Two characteristics of internal speech should now be pointed out: the first pertains to the plane of reality. It illustrates how internal speech is a verisimilar construction, a realistic utterance reflecting the speaker's psychology; the second relates to the artistic plane and instructs us about the manner in which the lawgiver conveys internal speech to the reader, about the features of the citation of such a discourse.

In internal speech the speaker tends to elide segments of sentences. The utterance may suffer from syntactical errors or from an ellipsis in content, because one who addresses oneself employs "shortcuts" and is not in need of a

---

84. The utterance can be viewed as a personal wish of the speaker-addressee of the law, but also a merging of the personal desires of those who make up the "collective you."

85. For the use of the modal form for expressing a wish, see Bruce K. Waltke and M. O'Connor, *An Introduction to Biblical Hebrew Syntax* (Winona Lake, Ind.: Eisenbrauns, 1990), 347 (20.2f), 455 (29.1). Also in the law of the king, the law's addressee makes use of the modal form for expressing a wish אשימה עלי מלך (Deut 17:14).

well-grounded statement that clarifies the context. Exactly for that reason, our speaker, who knows in which context he has said to himself "I will eat meat," does not need to include any explanation of the motivating circumstances in his speech. The brevity of the utterance reflects, therefore, one of the realistic elements of internal speech. The utterance is "true" because, in such a formulation, a person might express a wish on which he had resolved to act. But the brevity of the utterance is not only a result of its verisimilar construction. The internal utterance is short and lacks context because the lawgiver penetrates the speaker's consciousness, not at the phase of internal debate that preceded it and led to it, but at the culmination of the process; not in the course of deliberation, but at the moment of decision, when he resolves to fulfill the desire to eat meat.[86] The utterance is future-oriented, looking forward to action, but not revealing the speakers motives, reasons, or deliberations. Only by using the information that is revealed through the lawgiver's entry into the speaker's mind ("because you crave flesh") and under the cover of one of the two conditions making the legal arrangement applicable ("If the place which the LORD your God will choose to put his name there *is too far from you*") is the reader made cognizant of the speaker's fierce desire to eat meat and of the difficulty he encounters when seeking to fulfill this desire. By means of these phrases authored by the lawgiver we are exposed to the speaker's internal debate, which is not expressed in the interior speech.[87]

Not only does the lawgiver open a window for the reader into the inner life of the speaker, but it seems as though he himself is affected by the latter's feelings. The recurring phrases "because you *crave flesh*," "you may eat as much *flesh* as you *desire*," "you may eat within your towns as much as you *desire*,"[88] which exhibit again and again the strong craving that cannot be stifled, testify to the fact that the lawgiver is not merely granting legitimacy to the addressee's feelings; he does not merely create a sublimation under the cover of a legal arrangement. His repeated mention of the desire to eat flesh displays his identification with the addressee of the law, as if he had said to him and to us: "you and I are alike in our appetites."

---

86. Meir Sternberg labeled this type of penetration into the character's consciousness "terminal penetration" ("Between the Truth and the Whole Truth," 142).

87. The second condition for the applicability of the legal arrangement, "When the LORD your God enlarges your territory," is not part of the interior world of the speaker, since it is unlikely that someone who fiercely desires something but encounters an obstacle in the attempt to realize this desire would examine the problem through the historical lens of border expansion. This condition (with which the law begins) reflects, therefore, only the perspective of the lawgiver.

88. To this may be added the phrase "you may slaughter and eat flesh within any of your towns, as much as you desire" (v. 15).

The Imagination of Man's Heart Is Evil from His Youth

The additional disclosure of the inner world of the law's addressee leads to an utterly different response on the part of the lawgiver. Be cautioned!

> ⁷If there is among you a poor man, one of your brethren, in any of your towns within your land which the LORD your God gives you, you shall not harden your heart or shut your hand against your poor brother, ⁸but you shall open your hand to him, and lend him sufficient for his need, whatever it may be. ⁹Take heed lest there be a base thought in your heart, and you say, "The seventh year, the year of release is near," and your eye be hostile to your poor brother, and you give him nothing, and he cry to the LORD against you, and it be sin in you. ¹⁰You shall give to him freely, and your heart shall not be grudging when you give to him; because for this the LORD your God will bless you in all your work and in all that you undertake. ¹¹For the poor will never cease out of the land; therefore I command you, You shall open wide your hand to your brother, to the needy and to the poor, in the land. (Deut 15:7–11)

As part of the law's instruction whose purpose is to defend the rights of the poor, the lawgiver directs several warnings to the law's addressee, reflecting his inner world: "you shall not *harden your heart*"; "Take heed lest there be a *base thought in your heart*";[89] "and *your eye be hostile*"; "and *your heart shall not be grudging*."[90] Among these warnings the addressee's own internal utterance is integrated "*and you say, 'The seventh year, the year of release is near.'*"

Like the internal speech in the law of profane slaughter, this utterance too can be characterized as elliptical (mentioned earlier as one of the realistic features of internal speech). The speaker mentions a time—the arrival of the year of release—and no more. He does not explain why he mentions this time or why it is relevant for him. But here, too, the brevity and the insularity of the utterance are no cause for wonder, for the speaker is aware of his own train of thought and has no need to explain the context (to himself); a glimmer of a thought is sufficient for him to encapsulate his idea. He does not need to say, as though rehearsing a well-thought-out philosophy: "the year of release is near, if I make a loan now I will lose my money, therefore I will not." Knowing the context, a minimal utterance is all he needs.

---

89. This segment of the verse appears to be corrupted; the variant, reflecting a different word order דבר בליעל עם לבבך seems to be preferable (see Pss 41:9; 101:3).

90. In the chapter dealing with other cases where the lawgiver penetrates the mind of the characters I will discuss the semantic fields of body parts—heart, hand, eye—which metaphorically reflect the two elements that constitute any deed: the physical and the intentional.

And again, like the role he assumed in the law of profane slaughter, in this law, too, the lawgiver completes for us (as external addressees) what the speaker has omitted in his utterance. First he makes the static utterance, the temporal adverb, into a future-oriented verbal statement. By stating "and you give him nothing," revealing the action planned by the speaker (or, more precisely, the lack of action), the lawgiver indicates what implication the thought holds for the world of action. Second, he shows the utterance in its true light: it is not an "innocent" time reference but rather a "code," intimating for the speaker the lack of profitability in giving close to the year of release. The lawgiver penetrates the speaker's thought process and clarifies (to us) the rationale and the position that are the basis for his words.

In addition (and herein lies the difference between the lawgiver's relationship to the internal utterance in the law of secular slaughter and his relationship to the present utterance), he belies his negative position toward the speaker's thought by characterizing it as a "base thought" and adding "and your eye be hostile to your poor brother." The speaker does not perceive his own thought as a "base thought" (nor does he probably consider the poor man as his brother), but the lawgiver lends it a negative charge by declaring it a malicious thought, and not a legitimate appraisal of the profitability of the deal.

In contrast to the law of secular slaughter, here the lawgiver shows no identification with the difficulty that the speaker must confront; he is not affected by his feelings, but rather wishes to affect them. By clarifying his opinion of the thought or feeling, he hopes to prevent the unworthy action it precipitates and to direct the addressee toward the worthy action, "You shall surely give him."[91] And since the lawgiver began his "journey" into the inner world of the addressee with the goal of influencing the external world of action, he comes full circle and reenters his mind, encouraging the proper mind-set, "and your heart shall not be grudging when you give to him."

The intriguing question remains of why, within the internal utterance, characterized as an "elliptical" utterance, the speaker actually protracts his speech and twice repeats the temporal marker by saying "the seventh year, the year of release." This repetition can of course be justified on artistic grounds; that is, it can be attributed to the author's style and his tendency to duplicate phrases for the sake of emphasis (e.g., "you shall not harden your heart or shut your hand").[92] But I wish to offer another justification, this time on the plane of realism (although ostensibly people do not tend to stylize their

---

91. The RSV renders "You shall give to him freely," which is distant from the Hebrew text נתן תתן לו.

92. For the relationship between direct discourse and poetic parallelism, and the

thoughts through parallelism). It appears to me that the repetition of the temporal marker reflects two different phases in the speaker's thought process. At first he calculates and realizes that the seventh year is drawing near; this is reflected by the "naïve" temporal marker, "the seventh year." Only later, when he understands and internalizes the practical implications of its arrival, does the seventh year become the year of "release," a much more meaningful temporal phrase.

In Remembrance of Rites Past

And so the dialogue continues, because the lawgiver speaks about everything, even the worst of all.

> ²⁹When the LORD your God cuts off before you the nations whom you go in to dispossess, and you dispossess them and dwell in their land, ³⁰take heed that you be not ensnared to follow them, after they have been destroyed before you, and that you do not inquire about their gods, saying, "How did these nations serve their gods? that I also may do likewise." ³¹You shall not do so to the LORD your God; for every abominable thing which the LORD hates they have done for their gods; for they even burn their sons and their daughters in the fire to their gods." (Deut 12:29–31)

The dialogue that the lawgiver conducts with his addressee by conveying his internal utterances is forcefully represented in the law prohibiting the imitation of Canaanite cultic practices. The addressee's utterance: "saying, 'How did these nations serve their gods? that I also may do likewise,'" reflects his desire to integrate the cult of the gods of the land with the worship of YHWH. However, as the cult is no longer familiar (after the destruction of the land's inhabitants no one practices it any longer), the speaker must inquire and uncover its essence in order to realize his wish. In search of the lost rites, the speaker encounters the challenge of ignorance, which he expresses with the following question: "How did these nations serve their gods?"[93] Obviously he does not ask this question for the sake of acquiring information (the normal function of an interrogative sentence), for if he knew the answer, presumably he would not have asked the question at all. The question fulfills another purpose; it functions as a sort of declarative introduction to the "journey" of search and

---

tendency to fashion the speech of characters out of parallel phrases, see Greenstein, "Direct Discourse and Parallelism," 33–40.

93. The imperfect form יעבדו (translated by the RSV as past tense) does not indicate a future action, but means rather "used to serve" (see Deut 11:10).

discovery on which he is about to embark, as though announcing to himself, "I wish to discover how they worshiped their gods."

The choice of placing an interrogative sentence on the lips or in the mind of the speaker enables the lawgiver to simulate a real dialogue between him and his addressee, the speaker. In the absence of an external addressee, the speaker does not expect an answer, but the lawgiver surprises him and answers his question (as if he were a counterpart in a conversation), revealing to him the nature of the Canaanite cult: "for every abominable thing which the LORD hates they have done for their gods."[94]

The dialogue between the lawgiver and his addressee is not exhausted in referring to the first part of the internal speech, which reflects the speaker's difficulty. The lawgiver responds to the second part of the utterance, that is, to its action part, as well. The speaker declares to himself: "that I also may do likewise,"[95] and the lawgiver "adopts" his style and responds to him: "You shall not do so to the LORD your God." In view of the explicit prohibition, the transgression itself, that is, imitation of Canaanite rites, is articulated only at the level of intention—it is not carried out. The prohibition, then, plays a preventive role in relation to action. But the lawgiver is not content with merely preventing the transgression; he also wishes to influence the realm of thought. By exposing the negative values of the Canaanite cult, which make it inappro-

---

94. Another example of a question asked within the frame of internal speech and its answer is Deut 7:17–19 ("If you say in your heart, 'These nations are greater than I; how can I dispossess them?' you shall not be afraid of them, but you shall remember what the LORD your God did"). In this case, too, the purpose of the question is not to receive information. The question has a rhetorical and expressive function; it expresses an anxiety, and the answer is meant to assuage this anxiety. The same technique is used in two other laws: the law of the prophet (Deut 18:15–22) and the law of year of release (Lev 25:19–22). The lawgivers report the addressee's internal speech, couched as an interrogative sentence ("And if you say in your heart, 'How may we know the word which the LORD has not spoken'" [Deut 18:21]; "And if you say, 'What shall we eat in the seventh year, if we may not sow or gather in our crop?'" [Lev 25:20]), and answer the question by providing a solution to the distress described in the utterance: "when a prophet speaks in the name of the LORD, if the word does not come to pass or come true, that is a word which the LORD has not spoken" (Deut 18:22); "I will command my blessing upon you in the sixth year, so that it will bring forth fruit for three years" (Lev 25:21). A similar technique appears in prophetic literature. The prophet presents the common wisdom by delivering it as a statement in direct speech and responds to it polemically with his own statement, which negates it (see, e.g., Isa 40:27–28; Jer 5:19; 8:8–9).

95. According to S. R. Driver, the pronoun אני, deviating from the prevalent usage of אנכי in Deuteronomy, is used here for emphasis (see *Deuteronomy*, 150). This view fails to appreciate the personal nature of the statement, which reflects the speaker's personal style and not that of the lawgiver (or the "implied author").

priate for the worship of YHWH, he seeks not only to prevent an action but also to undermine the desire to perform such acts.

At the margins of the discussion of internal speech, I wish to demonstrate how the appearance or absence of direct speech in the law (internal or external speech) may assist our understanding of the nature of the law.

The law prohibiting the Canaanite cult is similar in theme to four other laws: the laws of enticement to idolatry (Deut 13:2–6, 7–12, 13–19), and the law of the idolater (Deut 17:2–7), all of which share common language and themes.[96] Like the law in question, the laws of enticement also communicate utterances in direct speech—the words of the enticers, conveyed as external speech (13:3b, 7b-8, 14). On the other hand, the law of the idolater does not represent direct speech and includes only a summary verse, reporting the statement after which the fact of the transgression is publicized: "and it is told you and you hear of it" (17:4).[97] Appearance of direct speech in the laws of enticement is understandable. After all, enticement is a "speech transgression," and therefore it is no wonder that the utterances that are the focus of the transgression are presented in direct speech. Not so in the case of the violations presented in the law of the idolater and in the law under discussion; these laws are not predicated on speech acts. The reason for direct speech in the law against the Canaanite cult, and for its absence in the law of the idolater, is that the latter treats the completed transgression—idolatry itself—while the former addresses a transgression that is "under way," as yet inchoate. And as this process may be likened to "self-enticement," the lawgiver chooses to express it through internal speech. Only in this manner are both thought and intention properly given expression.

Combined Discourse

Combined discourse is one of the modes for presenting speech—external or internal. It is a mixed form, intermediary between indirect and direct speech (it is therefore also called "free indirect discourse"), which appears without the marker that subordinates indirect speech and without the quotation marks proper to direct speech. An utterance will be considered combined speech if, in a statement that grammatically speaking pertains to one speaker, two statements are actually involved, two perspectives (although there is no formal separator between them, and they belong to one syntactical framework).[98]

---

96. See Dion, "Deuteronomy 13," 158–60, 192.

97. The verb "to tell" (הגיד) is used in biblical prose to report a speech act and for presenting indirect speech, but it does not introduce direct speech. For the presentation of direct speech the infinitive form לאמר (= "saying") follows the speech verb.

98. Bakhtin, "Discourse in the Novel," 304–8.

Combined discourse serves in literary texts as a bivocal or polyvocal form, presenting a multiplicity of speakers and of attitudes—usually a fusion of the narrator with one of the characters.[99] The capacity of combined discourse to reflect within the narrator's utterance the personal style of the character (style of speech, thought, or opinion) renders it a central tool for entering into the characters' psyches. Thus, as Meir Sternberg argues, it originates in biblical narrative.[100] Is it possible to point to its use in the genre of law as well? Scrutiny of five laws—one from the Book of the Covenant and four from Deuteronomy—demonstrates that it is.

In What Else Shall He Sleep?

I find the following example touching, perhaps because one can sense how it touched the heart of the lawgiver.

> [26]If ever you take your neighbor's garment in pledge, you shall restore it to him before the sun goes down; [27]for that is his only covering, it is his mantle for his body; in what else shall he sleep? And if he cries to me, I will hear, for I am compassionate. (Exod 22:26–27)

The law of lending to a poor person allows the lender to seize movable property as a pledge, but it also hedges this right, by forbidding the lender to withhold property that the debtor needs for basic bodily needs. In the concrete case provided by the law, a lender who received a garment in pledge must return it to its owner by evening, and this obligation is explained in a motive clause: "it is his mantle for his body; in what else shall he sleep?"

From a grammatical point of view the motive clause is pronounced by the lawgiver. But the intimate language, which describes the distress of the poor person in such a vivid and graphic manner so that the evening chill on his exposed body can be sensed, suggests that it does not reflect the lawgiver's own style but rather assimilates the intentions of another speaker. The lawgiver's utterance reflects a different, additional point of view. This other speaker is the poor person, approaching the home of the lender when evening falls, requesting his garment back. Only his identity can account for the personal attitude,

---

99. On the various functions of combined discourse in a literary text, see Rimmon-Kenan, *Narrative Fiction*, 113–14; Martin Wallace, *Recent Theories of Narrative* (Ithaca, N.Y.: Cornell University Press, 1986), 136–42.

100. Sternberg, "Between the Truth and the Whole Truth," 111. See, e.g., "And God saw everything that he had made, *and behold it was very good*" (Gen 1:31); "And a man *found him wandering in the fields* [והנה תעה בשדה]" (Gen 37:15); "And when the captains of the chariots saw that *it was not the king of Israel*" (1 Kgs 22:33).

the entreating voice incorporated into the lawgiver's. The rhetorical question "in what else shall he sleep?" seems to belong to a scene of dialogue between two parties. The question, which in grammatical terms is addressed by the lawgiver to the lender, his addressee (as is the rest of the motive clause), in fact reflects the rhetorical question presented to the lender by the poor man, who stands at his doorstep and depicts his life's reality. The question aims at persuading him that returning the garment is a matter of survival. As combined discourse allows the narrator's speech to reflect a character's own words, the lawgiver can replace the reporting of the speech event with a summary transmission, that is, with a motive clause, which merges his mind with the mind of the poor man.

The lawgiver does not render the poor man's words in direct speech, "If ever you take your neighbor's garment in pledge, and *if he says: 'it is my mantle for my body; in what else shall I sleep?'*"; nor does he report it as indirect speech: "If ever you take your neighbor's garment in pledge, and he says to you *that it is his mantle for his body; in what else shall he sleep?*" Instead of employing one or the other of these options, he employs discourse that combines both (while omitting the verb introducing speech and other markers of indirect speech, and by using third person personal and possessive pronouns). Presenting the poor man's words in direct speech would have brought the reader closer to his point of view, arousing identification and sympathy with him; a motive clause reflecting the lawgiver's moral position would help the reader understand the relationship of patronage the lawgiver has to the poor man. But only combined discourse, which colors the discourse of the lawgiver with the voice of the poor man, allows the achievement of both goals, by presenting both voices, both positions, simultaneously.[101]

Comparison of this motive clause with other motive clauses in the Book of the Covenant reveals the uniqueness of combined discourse in the context of biblical legal literature. While the other clauses reflect only the style, position, and ethical or legal perspective of the lawgiver, the clause in question integrates another voice, the voice of one of the characters, an engaged and personal voice, which illustrates the engagement of the divine lawgiver and his concern for the welfare of the poor person.[102]

---

101. On the human drama sketched in this law, seen from a different point of view, see Jonathan Ben-Dov, "The Poor's Curse: Exodus XXII 20–26 and Curse Literature in the Ancient World," *VT* 56 (2006): 431–51.

102. An example of the incorporation of a character's "voice" as part of the lawgiver's motive clause can be found in the Deuteronomic law of the Hebrew slave (Deut 15:12–18), and also in LH 136, which deals with an entirely different matter (a husband who abandoned his town and therefore cannot reclaim his wife, who went with another man). See

The "Mingling" Lawgiver

In four Deuteronomic laws the lawgiver employs the technique of combined discourse to achieve other goals. Unlike the combined discourse of the type discussed above, where the voice of the character is incorporated into the lawgiver's discourse, in these four laws the lawgiver insinuates his voice into the utterances of the characters, which are conveyed in direct speech. The hypothesis of combined discourses allows us to identify an additional voice, a voice that is mingled with the direct speech, since the utterance includes language that is incongruent with the speakers' identities, or that deviates from the positions they present.

As was said above, in the law prohibiting Canaanite cults, the inner voice of the law's addressee is delivered in direct speech "saying, 'How did these nations serve their gods? that I also may do likewise'" (Deut 12:30). The phrase "these nations" is a common phrase in Deuteronomic literature, appearing always in a negative context in connection with the sins of the other nations and the requirement to destroy them.[103] One might wonder, therefore, why the speaker, in expressing his desire to emulate the cult of the neighboring nations, would characterize them precisely with a phrase carrying a negative connotation. The speaker could have used a neutral expression "the nations that are round about me" (used, for example, by the speaker-addressee in the law of the king [Deut 17:14]).[104] This question forces us to examine the status of the phrase, and identify its author. Is it the addressee, as the grammar would suggest? Is it the lawgiver? Or does it belong to both speakers, reflecting two perspectives simultaneously?

To attribute the phrase to the voice of the addressee, although grammatically correct, ignores its negative connotation. The reader who is familiar with the locution is sensitized to the negative attitude it conveys toward the neighboring nations, and when this attitude is incommensurate with the position presented by the speaker, the reader will find it difficult to see the phrase as an integral part of his speech. It will be easy for him, rather, to attribute it unhesitatingly to the voice of the lawgiver, since it matches his entire outlook.

Why does the lawgiver adopt the technique of combined discourse? Why does he choose to mingle his voice with the addressee's words rather than voicing his disapproving stance independently? It seems that the reason for the employment of combined discourse in this case is to be sought in the dan-

---

my discussion of these laws in Assnat Bartor, "The Representation of Speech in the Casuistic Laws of the Pentateuch: The Phenomenon of Combined Discourse," *JBL* 126 (2007): 238–42.

103. See, e.g., Deut 7:17, 22; 9:4–5; 11:23; 18:14; 20:15; 31:3.
104. See also Lev 25:44 (but also 2 Kgs 17:15, and other verses).

ger embodied in the speaker's stance, as perceived by the lawgiver. Therefore the lawgiver senses the need to neutralize this position from the outset, from within the speaker's utterance, and he is not content with his own independent utterance, as resolute as it may be, which appears later on (v. 31). By using the familiar pejorative phrase, which produces dissonance within the utterance, the lawgiver injects into the reader's mind a negative judgment toward the speaker's position—an attitude that will be "officially" presented later.

At the same time, by characterizing the speaker's utterance as combined discourse, one could also argue that the phrase "these nations" simultaneously reflects two voices: "the voice" of the lawgiver, as explained above, and the voice of the speaker, who employs the phrase neutrally, as an ethnic/geographic label. This latter option also increases the polyvocality of the text.[105]

The three laws dealing with enticement to idolatry (Deut 13:1–6, 7–12, 13–19) have similar features. The utterances conveyed through direct speech include phrases that lead one to wonder whether they reflect the quoted voice of the speakers, or whether they belong to the speech of the lawgiver.[106] The three laws share a similar verbal construction.[107] In the center of the protasis, after the identity of each of the enticers is given, the utterances which constitute the act of enticement are presented. These utterances are phrased more or less identically and mirror each other both linguistically and thematically. The first utterance is made by a "prophet or dreamer of dreams": "and if he says, *'Let us go after other gods,' which you have not known, 'and let us serve them* (v. 2b). The second utterance is made by "your brother, the son of your mother, or your son, or your daughter, or the wife of your bosom, or your friend who is as your own soul": "saying, *'Let us go and serve other gods,' which neither you nor your fathers have known* (v. 6). And the third utterance is made by "certain base fellows," conveyed as part of another utterance, a rumor: "If you hear in one of your cities . . . saying, *'Let us go and serve other gods,' which you have not known*" (vv. 12–13).

The first phrase that prompts us to examine the status and identity of the speaker is "other gods," which appears in all three utterances. On the one hand, this phrase (like "these nations") is a common phrase in Deuteronomic literature,[108] and this fact may point to the infiltration of the speaker's utterances by the "official voice" of the lawgiver. But, on the other hand, when the

---

105. Bakhtin, "Discourse in the Novel," 304.
106. For a discussion of this issue, see Tigay, *Deuteronomy*, 130.
107. See Nelson, *Deuteronomy*, 166–67. See in addition the synoptic presentation of the laws in the appendix to Paul Dion's article (Dion, "Deuteronomy 13," 207–10).
108. See, e.g., Deut 5:7; 6:14; 7:4; 8:19; 11:16, 28; 17:3; 18:20; 28:14, 36, 64; 30:17; 31:18, 20. For the notion of "other gods" in Deuteronomic law, see Yair Hoffman, "The Conception of 'Other Gods' in Deuteronomistic Literature," *Israel Oriental Studies* 14 (1994): 103–18.

speakers entice their audience to worship a different god, other than YHWH, it is difficult to think of an alternative way of saying "other gods." It does not therefore have to be attributed to a voice other than that of the speakers. Nevertheless, it seems to me that to attribute the phrase to the enticers impairs the logic of their discourse. Is it logical that the inciters would use a generic, idiomatic phrase and not point their audience toward a specific god? It would seem not. Therefore, this phrase "deviates" somehow from the text one would expect to hear. On the other hand, attributing it to the voice of the lawgiver seems natural and logical.

Unlike the ambiguous status of the phrase "other gods," the status of the other phrases the speakers use to characterize the "other gods" ("which you have not known," "which neither you nor your fathers have known") is indisputable. To attribute them to the speakers entails a grammatical and stylistic incongruence and reveals a discrepancy with the position they present, whereas attributing them to the lawgiver's voice is congruent both grammatically and stylistically and is consonant with his outlook. First, each of the three speakers' utterances is couched in the first person plural ("Let *us* go after" and "Let *us* go and serve"). Therefore their use of the second person (singular or plural) of the verb "to know" reveals an inconsistency. Substantively, the use of the second person is inappropriate in the context of the enticers' speech, for the lack of knowledge of other gods is not unique to the audience of potential idolaters but is shared by the enticers themselves. On the other hand, the use of this verbal form is consistent with the style of the lawgiver's address in these laws, and in the Deuteronomic Code in general (i.e., the "if-you" pattern characteristic of the Deuteronomic laws). Second, to the stylistic incongruence one must add the incompatibility of the ideas expressed. One would hardly suppose that speech aimed at persuading someone to follow another god would include statements questioning the desirability of abandoning YHWH, or arguments presenting the ineffectuality of other gods. Such statements, of course, are congruent with the lawgiver's theological outlook.

In these three laws, characterized by a total and uncompromising approach, it is little wonder that the lawgiver feels obliged to "infiltrate" the utterances of the enticers. He must express his utter disapproval from the outset, before directly presenting his views (in the apodosis). In the end, the insertion of the "foreign" phrases, which implicate the utterances' meanings, create an ironic distance between the speakers and their words. The common approach in biblical criticism, which sees these phrases as belonging to a later redactor, does indeed recognize the multilayered character of the enticers' speech,[109] but this solution is less interesting from a literary point of view, because it denies the

---

109. Dion, "Deuteronomy 13," 189–90.

possibility of recognizing the polyvocal character of the text, achieved through the use of combined discourse.[110]

In sum: "show and tell" is the mandate of the lawgiver who formulated the casuistic laws. "Listen attentively" he commands the reader in a long line of laws in which he presents the external and internal speech of the characters. The presentation through scenes of the characters' utterances and the possibility of hearing their words confer a vivid and dramatic quality upon the events described in the laws. The careful stylization of the character's speech, and even more so, the revelation of their inner thoughts, creates the illusion of reality.

We hear the slave and are persuaded of the profound seriousness of his intentions; along with the owner of the property we identify the object held by another; we listen to the priest's "order of the day," and the declarations of the officers reverberate in our ears; we sense revulsion and fear of the son who turned his parents' life into hell and agree that he must be expunged from the community; we encounter truth and falsity, reality and its tendentious presentation; we are exposed to passions and needs, to stimulation, curiosity, and miserliness; we succeed in hearing another, concealed voice that coaxes us into adopting the right attitude.

The events described in the laws are borrowed from the reader's daily reality, and the utterances voiced in them are mimetic utterances reflecting the psychology of the characters. Therefore, when reading the laws, we do not have to cajole ourselves to "identify strongly"; our identification may be spontaneous, as we take part in the dialogue unfolding among the characters, and between them and the lawgiver.

---

110. The fact that combined discourse is a recognized literary phenomenon weakens the theoretical basis for a source-oriented analysis of the passage. The presence of two different voices can be characteristic of a textual integrity and not necessarily a sign of compositeness.

4

Representation of Inner Life

The Lawgiver as Psychologist

Every action of ours occurs on two planes: the overt level of external activity, and a covert level that involves the emotions, thoughts, and intentions that accompany action. Since laws are concerned with actions, it is only to be expected that they will reflect both external and internal levels of activity. Modern law does not ignore the private wishes of a father who is composing his last will and testament, the intentions of a woman who negotiates a contract, or the rage of a betrayed husband who assaults his wife's lover. But is modern law truly interested in our mental and emotional reality? It would appear so, and this is evidenced in the wealth of modern legal terms that describe mental states. I shall mention only a few: "in good faith," "of one's free will," "knowingly," "with malevolent intent," "frivolously," "premeditated," "fraudulently." These concepts as well as others reflect modern law's deliberate treatment of the two mental dimensions that inform human behavior: the cognitive dimension, that is, awareness and understanding of the meaning and nature of behavior, and the emotional dimension, that is, the emotional attitudes that induce and accompany it.

At the same time, modern law seems not to evince an interest in the world of the psyche as such, in a person's emotional turmoil or mental processes. Its attitude toward an individual's interiority arises chiefly from the functional need to define and typify action as proper or improper, as guiltless or guilt bearing, in different manners and to different degrees. The interior world of the soul or the mind does not figure in modern law as an autonomous domain but rather as the "servant" of the external world. Its role is to illuminate, clarify, and attach attributions to external actions and events. Therefore modern laws seldom raise questions about the complexity of mental life, and they do not deal with the way in which external circumstances influence thoughts and feeling; this is the domain of psychology and of literature, and of narrative fiction in particular.

My introductory remarks pertain especially to modern law. Are they also applicable to the laws of the Pentateuch? Do these laws also presume a similar hierarchical relationship between the internal and external world? What is the status of the inner mental world in the laws of the Pentateuch, and how is it portrayed there?

Before answering the questions that form the focus of this chapter, I would like to respond preemptively to some of the questions that might occur to some of my more skeptical or meticulous readers. The first type of reader may puzzle over the relevance of the life of the psyche to a literary reading. Is the life of the mind considered a narrative phenomenon? The second type of reader, who surely remembers our joint foray into the internal life of the characters, may wonder whether we have not already covered the topic of thought and feeling. Why then go back and devote a whole new chapter to this subject? My answer to the skeptics is brief. Psychic life in all its depth and complexity is one of the central tools of literary characterization and, as such, plays an important role in the poetics of narrative. For the meticulous reader I add a clarification. Although we have dealt with the inner life of our characters on more than one occasion, we have revealed only a fraction of a much broader repertoire of the ways by which psychological life is represented in the laws; the current chapter will bring many more elements to light. By following the ways in which the lawgiver probes the inner world of the characters we will encounter different levels of human consciousness and different types of attitudes and moods that accompany behavior, thereby gaining more intimate knowledge of our characters. We will also come to appreciate the degree to which the lawgiver evinces an interest in the psyche, and we will interrogate the nature of this interest and its goals, thus deepening our appreciation of the lawgiver.[1]

However, before acquainting ourselves with the various ways in which the lawgiver reveals the characters' inner life, I will present a few cases in which he treats the inner world "functionally," in the same manner that his modern colleague does, namely, by drawing on the inner life to typify external action. I begin the chapter on the psyche with these cases, even though the discussion is not narrative by nature but rather legalistic, out of my admiration for the original psychological insights of the biblical lawgiver. In any event, it would be fitting to entitle this brief discussion "An Introduction to Criminal Law."

When examining the biblical laws of homicide, one cannot fail to be amazed at the comprehensive and methodical treatment they give to one of the basic concepts of criminal law—*mens rea* (criminal thought/intent). The Priestly law of homicide accomplishes this in the most fully developed form,

---

1. In the present chapter I have chosen to examine the laws as a monolithic unit, rather than as separate collections; therefore, unless otherwise specified, the singular "lawgiver" refers to the lawgivers in each of the law collections.

but in the Deuteronomic law, and even in the brief law in the Book of the Covenant, one encounters expressions of principles and rules that belong to the domain of the practice and theory of criminal law, principles and rules that are still valid today. Criminal intent is the element used to determine whether a forbidden act (*actus reus*) bears guilt; its cognitive and emotional qualities determine the severity of the deed, as well as the type and degree of guilt. The laws of homicide are the only laws in the Pentateuch that present different levels of cognizance and different levels of intention side by side;[2] this presentation is accomplished in one of two ways: (1) through the use of *verbs* that express the slayer's feelings and his attitude toward the victim before, close to, or at the time of the perpetration of the deed: act willfully; attack; hate; lie in wait for; seek harm;[3] (2) through *terms* that typify the *actus reus* by describing the state of mind or emotional state that led up to the act or accompanied it: treacherously; unintentionally;[4] without intent;[5] suddenly; without seeing;[6]

---

2. Most of the laws of the Pentateuch do not directly address the issue of *mens rea*, but in some of them the mental dimension can be indirectly inferred from the circumstances of the case, or from the punishment entailed. The description "When men fight, and one of them pushes a pregnant woman" (Exod 21:22) leads to the conclusion (in my opinion at least) that the law deals with an inadvertent injury that was caused in the heat of the brawl. The language "When a fire is started and spreads to thorns . . ." (22:5) reveals that the law deals with a negligent, unintentional act; and the harsh sanction "he shall make restitution from the best in his own field and in his own vineyard" (22:4) might mean that the law attributes a certain degree of intentionality to a person whose livestock caused damage (without attributing a true desire to cause damage).

3. Some of the verbs contain an independent semantic element that endows them with a specific meaning. Such is the element of evil intent embedded in the verbs ארב, יזיד, צדה. Following Esther Borochovsky, I call them "adverbial predicates." See Esther Borochovsky, "The Specific Meaning of Verbs: Incorporation of Arguments and Fusion of Downgraded Predicates" (in Hebrew) (diss., Tel Aviv University, 1988).

4. "Unknowingly" is a more appropriate translation of the Hebrew idiom בבלי דעת. A similar idiom appears in LH 206-207, 227: *ina idû la amḫaṣu*; ("I did not strike him intentionally [= knowingly]"); *ina idû la ugallibu* ("I did not knowingly shave it off"). MAL A 23-24 present the cognitive elements of knowing or unawareness with a verb: *a'īlu kî aššat a'īlenni īde* ("the man knows that she is the wife of a man"); *bēl bēte kî aššat a'île ina bētīšu usbutûni la īde* ("the householder is not aware that it is the wife of a man").

5. The priestly concept of שגגה (see Lev 4:2, 13, 22, 27; 5:15, 18; 22:14; Num 15:22-29) expresses two types of lack of awareness: lack of awareness of the nature of the act and of its consequences (the case of the inadvertent manslayer); or lack of awareness that the act is a sin (ignorance of the law). See Baruch Levine, *Leviticus-Va-yikra: The Traditional Hebrew Text with the New JPS Translation* (JPS Torah Commentary; Philadelphia: Jewish Publication Society, 1989), 18-19; Jacob Milgrom, *Leviticus 1-16: A New Translation with Introduction and Commentary* (AB 3; New York: Doubleday, 1991), 228-29, 264-69, 319-20, 334.

6. On the relationship between seeing and knowing, see Robert Sekuler and Randolph Blake, *Perception* (2nd ed.; New York: McGraw-Hill, 1990), 12; Meir Malul, *Knowledge,*

out of hatred; [without] lying in wait; in [without] enmity.[7] In addition, alongside the patent figures of speech concerning *mens rea* (Exod 21:13a, 14; Deut 19:4, 11; Num 35:11, 15, 20–23) in all three laws it also appears implicitly. When the lawgiver in the Book of the Covenant describes the machinations of a higher power—"God let him fall into his hand" (Exod 21:13b)—he does not explicitly describe the state of mind of the killer, but one can infer that it is a state of lack of awareness and loss of control.[8] The way the Deuteronomic lawgiver sets the stage, as just another working day in the forest that ended with a lethal accident—"and his hand swings the axe to cut down a tree, and the head slips from the handle and strikes his neighbor so that he dies" (Deut 19:5)—means that he does not need to characterize the manslayer's state of mind, because the lack of intent is implied in the description of the circumstances. Finally, in the Priestly law *mens rea* is implied in the last three verses that describe the murder that was caused by blows from tools (Num 35:16–18) or, more precisely, the legal presumption reflected therein, according to which whoever makes violent use of a lethal tool (of iron, stone, or wood) must have intended to cause the fatal outcome that ensued.

In summary: the manner in which the lawgiver penetrates the intrapsychic world in the context of the laws of homicide allows us to distinguish between different types of homicidal acts and, in accordance with this typology, to determine the appropriate response—whether a punishment or an alternative legal arrangement.[9] The lawgiver condenses into a verb or an adverb an entire state of mind—both cognitive and emotional—reflecting the killer's attitude toward the victim at the moment he takes a life, or prior to that moment. Actu-

---

Control, and Sex, Studies in Biblical Thought, Culture, and Worldview (Tel Aviv/Jaffa: Archaeological Center Publication, 2002), 144–45.

7. In the laws of Exodus and Deuteronomy, the *mens rea* is presented almost exclusively with verbs, and in the Priestly Law mostly with abstract nouns. Both forms of presentation appear in other law collections from the ancient Near East. See n. 4 above and LE 6, 33; LH 227, 265, which describe fraudulent acts: the first law says the act was performed in *ina nulāni* ("fraudulent circumstances"), and the three others describe the mental aspect with two verbs: *surrurum* ("to defraud") and *dâṣum* ("to misinform"). For the transition from a concrete formulation with the use of a verb to a more nominal and abstract formulation, see Jackson, *Semiotics*, 93–97.

8. HL 3–4, which deal with accidental manslaughter, also contain references to the cognitive element. The description *aki kešaršiš waštai* ("his hand sins") reflects a distinction between the acting hand, which is responsible for causing the death, and the person, who acted unintentionally.

9. As we have seen, other law collections from the ancient Near East also contain several references to *mens rea*. However, a systematic presentation of criminal intent, as one finds in the biblical laws of homicide, is undoubtedly a unique phenomenon.

ally, this kind of mental penetration is no different from the way the biblical narrator enters the mind of the characters. That narrator, too, condenses feelings and psychological processes into a mere verb or an adverb, leading some commentators to the view that the author takes very little interest in psychological reality. This sort of minimalism in biblical narrative usually produces an imbalance between the intensity of feelings or complexity of mental processes and their spare textual representation (since the reader receives only partial and selective information about the character's interiority). In the laws of homicide, in contrast, the penetration into the psyche is merely "functional" and is therefore sufficient and adequate for the law's purposes—presenting the *mens rea* that accompanies the *actus reus*.

HEART AND SOUL

The law of homicide in the book of Deuteronomy (19:2–7) presents one episode that reveals a considerably less "legalistic" dimension of this law (and of others). In a number of cases the lawgiver depicts the inner life of the characters even though this contributes little to the legal understanding of the law. The glimpse into the characters' inner world supplies the background or motive for their behavior, explains their attitudes toward other characters, and reveals what they expect to achieve by their actions. These matters, belonging as they do to the narrative plane of the law, also have relevance and importance for the lawgiver. We therefore ought to become acquainted with them, as they will contribute to our appreciation of the psychological aspects of the law and of the lawgiver's psychological sensibility.

The establishment of three cities of refuge is intended to guarantee access to asylum for any unwitting manslayer who seeks to escape blood vengeance. The territorial distribution of the cities is designed to prevent the manslayer's apprehension by the blood avenger, or at least to increase his chances of arriving at a safe haven unharmed. As the law ordains:

> ²you shall set apart three cities for you in the land which the LORD your God gives you to possess. ³You shall prepare the roads, and divide into three parts the area of the land which the LORD your God gives you as a possession, so that any manslayer can flee to them. (Deut 19:2–3)

The blood avenger's pursuit of the manslayer, for the purpose of taking the life of the person who killed a member of his family, is both a familial duty and a social right. This is the reason for his pursuit and the grounds for creating cities of refuge. But the episode presented subsequently gives a different reason for the chase:

⁶lest the avenger of blood in hot anger [lit., while his heart is hot] pursue the manslayer and overtake him because the way is long, and wound him mortally. ⁷Therefore I command you, You shall set apart three cities. (Deut 19:6–7)

Here the behavior of the blood avenger, as described by the lawgiver, is not anchored in a familial duty or social right, namely, in external reality, but is rather motivated by fiery passions—anger, enmity, and the sheer desire for vengeance. The lawgiver penetrates into the blood avenger's psyche and uses the metaphorical expression "his heart is hot" to describe his mood, his emotional turmoil, and his inability to control it.[10] Unlike the presentation of the manslayer's mental profile, which defines the limits of criminal liability (see vv. 4, 11), the "hot heart" of the blood avenger is not mentioned in order to explicate the *mens rea* of his deed; such a characterization would be irrelevant, since the blood avenger is not criminally liable for killing the manslayer. What, then, is the purpose of revealing his interior state? Is there a legal need for it? Or in other words, is the reflection of his psychological state crucial or useful for comprehending the motivation for establishing the legal norm—the requirement of three cities of refuge?

These two questions may be answered in the affirmative by suggesting that the commandment to establish *no fewer than three* cities derives from the understanding that, while the law's intervention may impose a limit on the custom of blood vengeance, it does not have the power to restrain the formidable passions and impulses of the avenger. The lawgiver's recognition that such stormy passions can and do exist dictates the conditions of the legal arrangement—perhaps not the very principle of asylum but certainly the number of cities of refuge needed (as in v. 7).[11] In other words, psychological realities are taken into account in legislative considerations.[12]

---

10. The feelings of the blood avenger are transferred metaphorically to the heart, as the organ that represents the inner life. In the law of warfare and the law of the king, too, heart metaphors appear: "your heart faint," "fainthearted," "the heart of his fellows melt as his heart" (Deut 20:3, 8), "his heart turn away," "his heart may not be lifted up above his brethren" (17:17, 20). The first three phrases reflect the warriors' state of mind, and the final two describe an attitude toward another, which has a concrete expression in external behavior. The law of the king differs from the law of homicide and the law of warfare in one additional respect. While the latter two describe the influence of psychic life on behavior, the former describes the possible effect external acts may have on the psyche (polygamy can adversely affect worship of YHWH, and learning and obeying YHWH's commandments can positively affect the king's attitude toward the people).

11. This, for example, is Rashi's view. See also Tigay, *Deuteronomy*, 181.

12. The authority given to the blood avenger to execute the intentional murderer (v. 12) is a clear example of how inner life is taken into account as part of legislative con-

The foregoing example demonstrates the significance that the lawgiver accords to intrapsychic life and the decisive influence it can have on legal arrangements. But the picture may be even more complex and interesting. Even were we not granted a glimpse into the emotional turmoil of the blood avenger, we would know that the unwitting manslayer is in mortal danger and that a place of asylum must be made accessible. This is reflected in the fact that the commandment to set apart *three* cities is spelled out at the very beginning, before any reference is made to the tormented heart of the blood avenger. This indicates that the *general* legal arrangement stems from recognition of the power of the institution of blood vengeance and the obligatory force that the custom still holds over people. The law seeks to restrain custom and set limits on it but does not prohibit it. It is therefore likely that even if passions are not ignited, the blood avenger will still attempt to fulfill his duty or realize his right in accordance with the rule of tribal custom. Accordingly, the representation of the blood avenger's vengeful passion is not strictly necessary for establishing or even rationalizing the legal norm. Either way, the raging emotions and uncontrollable impulses prove that an entire realm exists in which the law has no sway, and that despite its power to set limits, law remains a limited instrument of social control. Could it be that the lawgiver makes use of intrapsychic reality not as a rationalization of the legal order, but rather in order to dispute its effectiveness? If so, he practically undermines the legal instrument that he himself has devised.

Let us turn away now from the loss of life and indulge in life's pleasures. The psyche (נפש), like the heart, is perceived as the seat of the feelings. This is reflected in several laws: the Israelite psyche is presented as desiring meat (the law of secular slaughter [Deut 12:15, 20–21]);[13] the (collective) psyche of the pilgrim desires food and drink (the law of tithing [14:26]); the psyche of the Levite repeatedly desires to serve in the sanctuary (the law of the Levite [18:6]); and the psyche of the passerby desires to satisfy itself with fruits of the vine (the law prohibiting theft of agricultural produce [23:24]). The four events, in which the psyche is invoked as an organ of desire, passion, and appetite, describe the emotional intensification that occurs in a situation of material want or powerlessness. The Israelite's inability to fulfill his desire for meat, because of his physical remoteness from the temple, intensifies that experience of want and transforms a natural desire into a true craving. The option of converting the tithes, which addresses the pilgrims' difficulties in transporting

---

sideration. The law turns the blood avenger into the authorized party in order to create a sublimation of his impulses.

13. In the Hebrew source the expressions אות נפשך and נפשך תאוה do appear, but this locution is not apparent in the English translation—either in this law or in the other laws chosen to illustrate the phenomenon.

provisions to the remote temple, leads them to crave for a feast of meat and wine. The unexpected opportunity to eat grapes turns the passerby's simple state of non-eating to a nagging hunger that must be satisfied. The unemployed Levite's powerful desire to serve in the sanctuary, which only intensifies as time goes by, requires little elaboration. When the lawgiver invades these characters' inner life and presents it as an arena of passions, appetites, and desires, he proves how attuned he is to the emotional intensity of his audience, and how responsive he is to their needs. In these cases, intrapsychic reality is not merely one among other considerations that contribute to the legislative process, but actually motivates the legislation.

The process of emotional intensification is painted even more boldly in the law prohibiting delay of wages.

> [14]You shall not oppress a hired servant who is poor and needy, whether he is one of your brethren or one of the sojourners who are in your land within your towns; [15]you shall give him his hire on the day he earns it, before the sun goes down for he is poor, and sets his heart upon it; lest he cry against you to the LORD, and it be sin in you. (Deut 24:14–15)

To justify the injunction to give the poor person his wages on a daily basis the lawgiver probes his psychological state and describes his attachment to his wages: "and sets his heart upon it" (lit., "lifts up his soul to it"). Every laborer deserves to receive his pay on time, but where a poor person is concerned this is a question of survival; if his need is unfulfilled, this may have disastrous effects for him and his family. One can therefore observe a process of emotional intensification of his inner state. The poverty and deprivation that engender a daily dependence on money turn money or exchangeable goods into an object of intense expectation and longing.[14]

What is the purpose of presenting the process of intensification? Why does the lawgiver choose to describe it even though the first part of the motive clause, "for he is poor," sufficiently explains the importance of paying a daily wage on time? It would seem that by adding a verse depicting the poor person's special attachment to his wages, the lawgiver attempts to guide the protagonist toward the correct action and to prevent him from straying from it. Here the lawgiver reveals the character's state of mind, not as an explanation for his own behavior but rather in order to influence the behavior of another character. I will leave unanswered the question whether despite his attempt to elicit empathy toward the poor person, by adding this descriptive content, the lawgiver ultimately does not really trust its efficacy, and therefore appends

---

14. The English translation of the verse in question invokes the heart, as the organ of desire, while the Hebrew invokes the soul/psyche.

another threatening and admonishing verse: "lest he cry against you to the LORD, and it be sin in you."

Male and Female He Created Them

Intimate relationships are a focus of interest of many of the Pentateuch's laws—legitimate conjugal relationships, but even more so prohibited relationships. Those laws dealing with legitimate relationships present a variety of patterns of relationships in which a spectrum of emotions is given play—positive feelings, as well as not a few negative ones. In the law of the Hebrew slave alone (Exod 21:2–6) two relationships are described—the slave's conjugal-familial relationship before becoming a slave, and the relationship that is formed during the period of slavery—with different legal principles applying to each situation (as will be recalled, the slave's feelings are revealed through the citation of his declaration: "I love my master, and my wife and children").

In the following discussion my task will be to reveal the life of the psyche as depicted in laws pertaining to relationships between men and women. I will not only uncover what occurs inside the characters' hearts and minds, but will also attempt to clarify what legal or other function is served by exposing them. To this end we will accompany the lawgiver as he enters into the minds of eight different characters, where we in turn will meet another eight characters. The intrapsychic world is represented in the seven laws of intimate relations, as follows:

1. "If *she does not please her master*,[15] who has designated her for himself"[16] (law of the female slave [Exod 21:8]).
2. "... and *you have desire for her* and would take her for yourself as wife. . . . Then, if *you have no delight in her* . . ." (law of the captive woman [Deut 21:11, 14]).
3. "If a man has two wives, the one *loved* and the other *disliked* . . ." (law concerning the rights of the firstborn [Deut 21:15]).
4. "If any man takes a wife, and goes in to her, and then *spurns her*" (law of false allegation [Deut 22:13]).
5. "When a man takes a wife and marries her, if then *she finds no favor in his eyes* because he has found some indecency in her . . . and if she goes and becomes another man's wife, and the latter husband *dislikes her* . . ." (law on divorce [Deut 24:1, 3]).
6. "And if the man *does not wish* to take his brother's wife . . ." (law of levirate marriage [Deut 25:7]).
7. "and if *the spirit of jealousy comes upon him*, and *he is jealous of his wife* . . ." (law of the *Sotah* [Num 5:14]).

---

15. Lit., "If she is evil/bad in the eyes of her master."
16. The translation is based on the *qere* אשר לו יעדה (cf. the *ketib* אשר לא יעדה, "who does not keep her").

All of the laws exhibit an identical pattern. The lawgiver penetrates the mind of the *man* and reveals his attitude toward the *woman*. The man's state of mind and feelings provide the background for his behavior toward the woman (and in one case toward his children). In addition, the intrapsychic world is presented as a dynamic space, in which changes occur, always for the worse: the master who bought a concubine with whom to cohabit is not interested in her; the warrior who desired and married a captive woman no longer wants her; the husband who satisfied his sexual urges and then immediately, so I surmise, began to despise his wife; the vacillations of the two men who each married (by turn) a woman who pleased them, but with time changed their feelings toward her and sought to terminate the marriage (each for his own reasons); and finally, the dramatic change that occurred in the emotional state of the man who felt a fierce jealousy toward his wife.[17]

The gender identity of the characters whose inner life becomes transparent is the key to understanding the role that the revelation of intrapsychic content plays in these laws. The internal world of the man induces a change in the intimate relationship (in one case he tries to create a change in the children's status), but most importantly, it affects the woman's social status. This is why the lawgiver reveals someone's inner reality; he does so when it has the potential to affect another person's life. When a woman's inner life has no bearing on her personal or social situation, the lawgiver apparently has no reason to reveal it.[18]

It is important to note that when the internal life of the characters is on display, we are exposed not only to different kinds of emotions but also to different intensities of emotion, which can explain (external) actions. Only an intense emotion such as hate can explain the decision of a husband to blame his wife with a false charge, which affects not only their conjugal relationship and her social status, but even her life itself. On the other hand, a feeling of

---

17. Only in the case of two men is the emotional world described as a stable space (even if fraught with difficulties), without vacillations from one state to another: the husband simultaneously feels the polarized emotions of love and hate toward his wives, and the brother-in-law consistently expresses lack of desire to marry his brother's widow.

18. The only woman whose inner world is not closed to us is the widow. Her stance and her interpretation of the brother-in-law's state of mind are presented directly, in her words. The reason for this is that, unlike the other women, she initiates a legal procedure against the man and precipitates a change in his and her status. In this context, I mention LH 142, according to which the woman's attitude toward her husband is an element that can precipitate a change in the marital relationship and in the status of the woman: *šumma sinništum mussa izērma ul taḫḫazanni iqtabi . . . šeriktaša ileqqēma ana bīt abīša ittallak* ("If a woman repudiates her husband, and declares, 'You will not have marital relations with me' . . . she shall take her dowry and she shall depart for her father's house").

minor intensity, such as lack of desire, is justification enough for ending a marriage or refusing to perform a levirate marriage.

In this context it is interesting to observe the emotional nuances that are described in the law that forbids a man to remarry a woman he has divorced, once she has been married to another man (the law designated briefly as the "law on divorce"). The attitude of the first husband, who is said to have found an indecency in her, implying that his change of heart was motivated by some external-objective factor, is described in minor negative terms—she no longer pleases him. The intense negative feelings of the second husband, on the other hand, which are not said to have an external reason, are much stronger—he hates her.[19] Is this distinction between the levels of emotional intensity significant, and does it contribute to our understanding of the law? It would appear so, since it allows one to recognize various legitimate reasons for terminating a marriage. When the husband has found some indecency in his wife, it is sufficient to note his negative feelings in a minor key; on the other hand, in the absence of an external cause on which to pin the second husband's desire to divorce her, it is more fitting to introduce a fierce negative feeling.[20]

Two central conclusions emerge from my discussion of the "laws of intimate relationship": the lawgiver presents the inner world of the men because of the decisive influence they have on women's lives; and there is a significant correspondence between the type of feelings and their intensity and external behavior. The latter conclusion leads us into a deeper exploration of the way in which the lawgiver presents the attitude of the master toward his female slave.

According to the law, a man who bought a young woman to serve him as a concubine but then did not follow through with the declared purpose of the purchase, must allow her to return to her family. Essentially this law deals with a case of contract law, according to which an essential violation of the purchase agreement obligates the violator to make amends by restoring the original state of affairs. One can sense, so it appears to me, that when compared to the last six cases presented above, this latter case is less emotionally charged. It can therefore be assumed and expected that the master's attitude toward his girl-slave will be characterized by the lawgiver as a moderately negative one; for example, he does not want her or she does not please him.[21] In contrast to our expectations (or my expectations at least), the master's state of mind is presented in the harshest and fiercest terms: רעה בעיני אדניה she is "evil in the

---

19. The English translation "dislikes her" is not accurate and does not convey the phrase's intensity; "hates her" is a better option.

20. According to S. R. Driver, the second husband's attitude is also subordinated to the condition "he has found some indecency in her," that is, it is a response to external circumstances (Driver, *Deuteronomy*, 271–72).

21. This is precisely how Rashi, Rashbam, and Ibn Ezra describe the master's attitude.

eyes of her master."[22] Why is it not sufficient to describe the master's behavior from an external point of view as merely, say, "if he does not desire to take her as a wife?"[23] Why does the lawgiver, who is free to make a stylistic mark on the mind-set he is describing, choose to present the master's attitude in this particular way, rather than another?[24]

The presentation of such extreme negativity is exceedingly puzzling. But perhaps this puzzle can be resolved relatively easily, if we follow a few commentators in interpreting the word "bad" as referring to her external appearance. In this case, the position presented certainly makes sense under the circumstances; he does not want her because she is unattractive and sexually unappealing to him.[25] This interpretation can seemingly be supported by verses such as Gen 41:3, 4, 19, 20, 21, 27, where the word "bad" refers to external appearances (the bad-looking cows and stalks of grain that Pharaoh saw in his dream). But whereas in those verses there is no doubt that this is an external characterization, because the word appears in collocations such as מראיהן רע, רעות תואר, רעות מראה (lit. "have a bad appearance"), in the law of the concubine it does not say her appearance was bad in the eyes of her master. In addition, the adjective רע alone is never used to characterize a person's

---

22. I prefer to translate this part of the verse literally, because the standard translation, "If she does not please her master," neutralizes the emotional intensity and obscures the uniqueness of this negative attribution.

23. It should be noted that the law does not present the master's external behavior. (I base this statement on the *qere*, אשר לו יעדה, "who has designated her for himself." According to the *ketib*, אשר לא יעדה, "who does not keep her" or according to the formulation suggested by a few commentators, אשר לא ידעה, "who knew her not" [see the discussion in Jackson, *Wisdom-Laws*, 90–91], the law does indeed refer to behavior.) The fact that he does not take the young woman as a wife/concubine is a conclusion that the reader draws in light of the revelation of the interior state of mind. This of course illustrates the connection between the interior world and external behavior, since understanding the state of mind is sufficient for surmising what followed.

24. It should be noted that, unlike in the six previous examples, the presentation of the master's state of mind does not describe what he *felt* toward the female slave (desire, indifference, love, or hatred), but rather expresses the way in which she is *perceived by him*. Thus, the law deals not with revealing the man's attitude toward the woman but rather with a direct characterization of a female character by a male character. It goes without saying that such a description displays the personal point of view of the person making the characterization, and it is different from an objective and "authorized" characterization by the lawgiver.

25. This is Rashbam's view. See also Propp, *Exodus 19–40*, 197. Support for this position can be found in LL 28, which states that if there is a deterioration of the woman's appearance the man may take another wife. It should be noted that, unlike in the law of the female slave, in the Sumerian law the change is not presented as the husband's personal appreciation, but is rather described by the lawgiver.

external appearance, whether a man or a woman. This fact, too, makes it difficult to attribute the word רעה to the concubine's looks.

The aforementioned locution resonates with two other verses: "So when Esau saw that the Canaanite women *did not please Isaac his father*" [lit., "(were) evil in the eyes of Isaac"] (Gen 28:8); and "to preserve you from *the evil woman, from the smooth tongue of the adventuress*" (Prov 6:24). In both cases the use of the adjective רעות/רעה refers to the detrimental influence of women, whether because of their unsuitability (foreign women), or whether because of inferior moral conduct.[26] In light of this intertextual reading, my puzzlement over the lawgiver's linguistic choices remains, and perhaps is even greater.

The way in which the inner life is exposed in the law of the *Sotah* also deserves a more probing inquiry. Mental life is here presented three times (Num 5:13–14): twice explicitly, when the lawgiver reveals the husband's mental and emotional state ("and it is hidden from the eyes of her husband"; "the spirit of jealousy comes upon him, and he is jealous of his wife"), and another time implicitly, when one of the characteristics of the wife's behavior is described with the use of an adverbial predicate[27] that contains a mental state ("she is undetected," נסתרה).

Let us begin with the (tormented) soul of the husband, in which two polar states coexist: a cognitive vacuum and a surfeit of emotion. First the lawgiver reveals the husband's mind in the cognitive dimension, pointing out his deficit, in that he is not cognizant of any act of adultery.[28] The lawgiver next penetrates the husband's psyche at a later point in time, to reveal the emotion of jealousy. Between these two points a psychological process is under way, which explains what seems inexplicable—how the man makes the transition from a mental vacuum to a state of overwhelming emotion; from a state where the mind is void of information, and therefore also free of any reference, to a tempestuous soul inundated with destructive impulses.[29] The lawgiver does not spell it out, but allows the reader to fill in the gaps and to imagine a slow

---

26. Another verse may be added here: "But Er . . . was *wicked in the sight* [in the eyes] of the Lord" (Gen 38:7). Compare Greenstein's comments regarding the expression טוב בעיני פלוני: "The common biblical expression 'to be good in the eyes of someone' relates to personal appreciation not moral evaluation" (Edward L. Greenstein, "Presenting Genesis 1, Constructively and Deconstructively," *Prooftexts* 21 [2001]: 13–14).

27. See n. 3 above.

28. Penetration of the character's consciousness that reveals lack of knowledge as well as lack of awareness about this lack of knowledge has been designated by Meir Sternberg as a "minus penetration" ("Between the Truth and the Whole Truth," 117).

29. On "spirit" as an uncontrollable impulse, see 1 Sam 16:14–15, 23 ("an evil spirit"); on the jealousy of a betrayed husband, see Prov 6:34.

process beginning with ignorance, followed by a suspicion that steals into his heart and takes over, breeding fierce feelings of jealousy.[30]

The law contains repeated descriptions of the adulterous act, as reported by both the priest and the lawgiver (Num 5:13, 20, 27, 29). The descriptions are lively and lifelike, and they are rephrased each time, because they reflect, as in an X-ray, what is transpiring in the inner world of the husband—the visions that horrify his spirit and the images that incessantly taunt his mind.

In light of this, the law's position is clear. The dreadful scenarios that torment the jealous husband allow him to initiate judicial proceedings against his wife. His jealousy is sufficient reason and, in fact, the only reason for activating the ordeal.[31] The ordeal is not a means of identifying adulteresses but rather an instrument devised for husbands who cannot cope with uncertainty, uncontrollable fears, and destructive feelings.[32] Either way, the husband's emotional life plays an important, even vital, role, in the law of the suspected wife. Whereas in the other six laws the disclosure of the men's inner world is meant to explain the background or the motive for their behavior toward the woman—a function of the narrative dimension of the law—in the law of the *Sotah* the man's emotions are displayed not in order to explain his behavior but rather in order to explain the ruling, so that the reader understands the background for the unusual legal arrangement provided by the law.[33]

---

30. Baruch Levine is not content with such a minimalist supplementation of the gap. According to him, the husband's jealousy must be based on some grain of reality and, according to the dynamic of the ordeal, he concludes that this must be the woman's pregnancy (*Numbers*, 193). See also Tikva Frymer-Kensky, "The Strange Case of the Suspected Sotah (Numbers V 11–31)," *VT* 34 (1989): 11–26.

31. It would appear that this is the reason that the lawgiver designates the law as תורת הקנאת (v. 29) "cases of jealousy" and not תורת הסוטה, "the case of *Sotah*" (as we call it). On the issue of jealousy, see Richard S. Briggs, "Reading the Sotah Text (Numbers 5:11–31): Holiness and a Hermeneutic Fit for Suspicion," *Biblical Interpretation* 17 (2009): 288–319. Because of the mention of two offerings, "the offering of jealousy" and "the offering of remembrance" (vv. 16, 18), and of course in light of the many repetitions, some have argued that the law has combined two cases: the case of remembrance, which dealt with methods of proving the guilt of adulteresses in cases where no witnesses existed to their actions, and the case of jealousy, which determined how to establish the guilt or innocence of a woman whose husband was jealous of her (Licht, *Numbers 1–10*, 74).

32. See Bach, "Viewing the Sotah," 46–47.

33. In three additional laws the lawgiver describes situations of incognizance: the law of the supreme court, "If any case arises . . . which is *too difficult for you*" (Deut 17:8); the law of the expiation for an untraced murder, ". . . and *it is not known* who killed him" (21:1); and the law of returning a lost possession, ". . . or if you *do not know him*" (22:2). Similar to its function in the law of the *Sotah*, here too the lack of knowledge serves as a point of departure for deciding the ruling—this is the problem the law is meant to resolve. But unlike the incognizance presented in the law of the *Sotah*, in each one of these laws, the character is aware

What, then, of the woman's internal world? The ordeal itself, with all of the rituals and speech acts that constitute it, contains vast potential for dealing with psychological materials; the woman is disgraced, humiliated, intimidated, perhaps even remorseful or guilt-ridden. But since the woman's internal reality has no bearing either on the judgment or on the narrative unfolding of events, the lawgiver tells us nothing at all about her feelings. On the other hand, he does attach importance to her mental state during the adulterous act itself and therefore reveals one aspect of it. I refer here to the statement "she is undetected."

To be undetected (or to hide oneself) means to be in a certain place with the intention of not being caught or exposed. This intention is embedded in the verb and gives it its central meaning. Such an element connoting the goal of an action is called an "adverbial predicate of purpose." Adverbial verbs describe external actions while disclosing the actors' state of mind. They are therefore useful as an additional means of revealing the inner life of characters. At the same time, it is important to note that this mode of revelation is implicit, almost hidden, since the mental state is indicated by a simple verbal phrase and receives no unique linguistic form.[34]

Let us return to the adulteress's state of mind. Why does the lawgiver choose to describe an aspect of her behavior that is so self-explanatory and obvious? Do we not understand that hiding is integral to the act of adultery?

---

of his incognizance and is disturbed by it. A penetration of consciousness that reveals this sort of incognizance has been called by Meir Sternberg "negative penetration" ("Between the Truth and the Whole Truth," 117). It is important to understand that a state of consciousness represented through a "minus penetration" (see n. 28) cannot arouse the character to action, while a state of awareness represented by means of a "negative penetration" usually seeks a solution to its problem. Another example of presenting a state of consciousness, this time a dynamic and changing one, appears in the laws of gleaning: "When you reap your harvest in your field, and have *forgotten* a sheaf in the field, you shall not go back to get it; it shall be for the sojourner" (Deut 24:19). In the beginning the character is not aware of his incognizance, that is to say, of having forgotten (for such is the nature of forgetting, when it occurs), but as the commandment not to return to collect the sheaf implies, at some point the character becomes aware of his own forgetfulness. In the two following laws (vv. 20–21), it is not a state of lack of awareness that is described—the abandonment of the grain in the field is a deliberate and fully aware action.

34. It should be noted that adverbial predicates not only serve to expose a character's stance or intention but sometimes also allow the lawgiver to "sneak" an ethical tone into the description of actions without harming the neutral appearance of the description. When the lawgiver uses, for instance, the verbs "to entice" or "to lead astray" (Deut 13:6, 13), he clarifies his negative attitude toward the words of enticement; and when in apodictic prohibitions he employs verbs belonging to the semantic field of abuse, oppression, and exploitation (e.g., "to wrong," "to afflict" [Exod 22:21–22]; "to oppress," "to rob" [Lev 19:13]), he gives expression to his values and ethical stance.

Moreover, the fact that "she is undetected" is not crucial for understanding the situation and seems superfluous, since three other pieces of information apprise us of the fact that no one knew about the act of adultery: "it is *hidden from the eyes* of her husband . . . there is *no witness* against her, since she *was not taken in the act*" (Num 5:13). It appears as though here, too, as when the husband's state of mind was revealed, the implicit revelation of the adulteress's mental state is meant to help warrant the ruling. The presentation of the four facts sequentially, cumulatively, each reiterating that the act was not known and could not have been known, draws a thick, impenetrable curtain of opacity around the event, persuading us of the need for a legal ordeal. This is the only way the reader will understand the meaning and implications of this incognizance, namely, the unavoidable necessity of recourse to the unusual legal procedure. It goes without saying that, despite the woman's efforts to maintain the opacity surrounding the event, it does not provide protection for her at the ultimate test.

Before examining one of the more interesting cases where the lawgiver penetrates the mind of a female character, I shall take a brief detour to discuss an adverbial verb of attitude. The verb קלה, which means to be lightly esteemed, or dishonored,[35] is chiefly a verb of emotion. It connotes not necessarily the external behavior that accompanies the feelings of disregard but rather the mental attitude of lack of respect. Let us examine the verb's appearance in the law of corporal punishment (in the explanatory verse).

> ¹If there is a dispute between men, and they come into court, and the judges decide between them, acquitting the innocent and condemning the guilty, ²then if the guilty man deserves to be beaten, the judge shall cause him to lie down and be beaten in his presence with a number of stripes in proportion to his offense. ³Forty stripes may be given him, but not more; lest, if one should go on to beat him with more stripes than these, *your brother be degraded in your sight.* (Deut 25:1–3)

This text raises the question of whose mind is revealed by the lawgiver's use of the verb קלה here. Is it the mind of the protagonist, in which case the adverbial predicate reflects the disregard and disparagement of one person toward another, or is it perhaps the mind of the punished offender, in which case the verb represents a subjective sense of degradation? The answer lies in our understanding of the idiom לעיניך "in your sight" ("before your eyes"). This expression denotes physical sight, and we can therefore infer that the lawgiver is speaking of the physical presence of the observer, who witnesses the stripes administered to the offender. He sees the humiliation of the beaten

---

35. See *BDB*, s.v. II קָלָה, 885b.

man, but this does not mean that he does not therefore respect him. Had the lawgiver wished to represent the observer's internal vision, that is, his emotional attitude toward the man receiving the punishment, he would have used the idiom בעיניך, "in your eyes." Therefore, in this instance the adverbial predicate reveals what is going on in the psyche of the beaten man—a sense of humiliation caused by the protracted public beating. And if I am asked (with a certain measure of justification), why any of this makes a difference, and why it is important to decide whether the adverbial predicate reflects an external or, alternatively, a subjective sense of humiliation, I would reply that for the stricken body of the punished offender it certainly does not make a difference. But the nuances that I have identified make a significant difference for the reader, as they reveal the lawgiver's special sensitivity toward the offender's feelings, his wishes to prevent even a subjective sense of humiliation.

Impure Touch from Pure Motive

In the law of the woman who grasps a man's genitals, we encounter an interesting example of the lawgiver penetrating the mind of woman.

> ¹¹When men fight with one another, and the wife of the one draws near to rescue her husband from the hand of him who is beating him, and puts out her hand and seizes him by the private parts, ¹²then you shall cut off her hand;³⁶ your eye shall have no pity. (Deut 25:11–12)

This law does not deal with the legal aspects of the marital bond. The relationship between the husband and his wife does indeed form the background of this scenario, but that background belongs to the narrative level of the law and has no bearing on the legal plane. Three questions arise in reference to the way in which the lawgiver penetrates the woman's psyche: What is revealed by this

---

36. The English translation follows the standard view (also adopted in the present discussion) that the Hebrew וקצתה את כפה refers to the amputation of the woman's hand. Having said that, another view (first introduced by Lyle Eslinger) regards כף as a term for a sexual organ; therefore the punishment inflicted on the woman is some degree of genital mutilation (see Lyle Eslinger, "The Case of an Immodest Lady Wrestler in Deuteronomy XXV 11–12," VT 31 [1981]: 269–81). Recently, Jerome Walsh has suggested an original reading for וקצתה את כפה. He argues that the phrase is to be understood to mean "you shall shave [the hair of] her groin." According to Walsh, reducing the severity of the punishment from the permanency of amputation to a temporary humiliation allows the punishment to be seen as both talionic and corresponding to shamefulness of the woman's deed. Since she has humiliated a man publicly by an assault on his genitalia (presumably without serious injury to them), her punishment is public genital humiliation, similarly without permanent injury (see Jerome T. Walsh, "'You Shall Cut Off Her ... Palm'? A Reexamination of Deuteronomy 25:11–12," JSS 49 [2004]: 47–58).

penetration? What characterizes it in this unique case? What is its purpose? Before responding to these questions, however, let us delve more deeply into the relevant text.

The verse segment "to rescue her husband from the hand of him who is beating him" indicates the reason that the woman performed the illegal act. In order to understand what caused her unusual behavior, we must recognize that her motive was not only concern and solidarity, feelings that are typical of a bond between a husband and wife, but that it arose from a different perception of the event. In other words, she perceived the event differently from the way it is presented by the lawgiver. The lawgiver describes the brawl as a balanced and mutual confrontation, in which each side is equally responsible and equally at risk.[37] The woman, however, does not see things this way. She does not see before her eyes a contentious man who is beating his friend, but a beleaguered husband who is in immediate danger at the hands of his rival. Therefore she rushes to save him. As she sees it, her action is motivated by necessity.

In many instances where the psyche is penetrated in this way, the internal world is represented through the processing and organization (including the verbal formulation and stylization) of raw psychological materials, until at times little remains of the intrinsic qualities of the character's own consciousness, and the perspective of the penetrating lawgiver takes over.[38] This is not the case here. Despite the fact that the content of the woman's consciousness is not identical to the lawgiver's, he tries not to overwhelm hers and takes care to preserve (for us) a sense of her subjective experience. The verse that presents her personal motive colors the event with the tones of her thoughts and feelings and does not attempt to impose his official, "true" description of the events. In so doing he endows her motives with the mark of credibility and good faith. The presentation of the motive as a snapshot of the woman's mental perception, which allows us to sympathize with her fear for her husband's

---

37. The expressions יחדו (together) and איש ואחיו (lit., "man with his brother"), which appear in the opening sentence convey a sense of brotherhood and tone down the depiction of a violent confrontation, giving the fight an almost idyllic feel. It is difficult to shake the impression that the choice of these expressions, which produces a dissonant description, was influenced by the opening phrase of the adjacent law of levirate marriage: "When brothers dwell together" (v. 5). Both laws have similar narrative foundations: a social triangle composed of a woman and two men; a woman who approaches a man, touches him (removing the shoe), and performs a violent act against him (spitting). Since it is difficult to imagine that the opening phrase of the law under discussion reflects its original version, I propose that law of levirate marriage was juxtaposed to this law initially because of its similar plot elements and that only later, in order to fasten the associative link, was the formulation of its opening sentence revised in this anomalous fashion.

38. Sternberg, "Between the Truth and the Whole Truth," 113.

safety, leads us to expect that this will have a bearing on the question of guilt, or at least on the punishment to be meted out for the forbidden act. In other words, presenting the motive "from the inside" produces an illusion for the reader, namely, that the lawgiver views this as an "extenuating circumstance"; this is an illusion because ultimately the purity of her motive has no bearing on the question of guilt or of punishment.[39] Why then, does the lawgiver bother to present it when it has no impact on the ruling? It appears that he does this precisely in order to show that the motive has no bearing on the ruling! This is the only way he can emphasize that an action that offends modesty is absolutely forbidden, and that there are no circumstances that could justify it. Presenting the motive, which we might at first expect to be used as a basis for exoneration from guilt, or a mitigated punishment, in fact has the ironic effect of substantiating the absolute and unrestricted responsibility of the offender.

The law, therefore, presents two seemingly opposing values—offering succor and respecting modesty—and determines that in case of conflict the second value supersedes the first. But would it not be correct to say that these values are presented side by side rather than in opposition? A close examination of the lawgiver's description of the woman's behavior suggests that he thought that under the circumstances these values do not in fact collide, and that both could have been upheld, that is, succor could have been offered without offending modesty (in fact, perhaps he even wants to insinuate that this was her original intent but that she deviated from it).

The woman's actions are described by way of indicating four different elements: "draws near"; "to rescue her husband from the hand of . . ."; "puts out her hand"; "seizes him by the private parts." Seizing the genitals is not the only action, and not even the first, but one that concludes a series of actions. In addition, the sequential ordering of these elements places the motive in the middle, between drawing near and extending her hand. It therefore refers back to the act of drawing near, and not to grasping the genitals. In other words, the woman approached the fighting men in order to save her husband (and not to seize the other man's private parts)—this action is legitimate. Her second

---

39. MAL A 8, the parallel law that describes a woman harming a strange man's testicles—*šumma sinniltu ina ṣalte iška ša a'île taḫtepi* ("If a woman should crush a man's testicle during a quarrel")—does not refer to any motive. The essential difference between the two laws lies in the verb describing the action. While the biblical law uses the verb "to seize," denoting forbidden touch, the Assyrian law, which is focused on the bodily harm that the man sustains, uses the verb *ḫepum*, which means to crush or press. Anthony Phillips and Lyle Eslinger are of the opinion that the Deuteronomic law also indicates that the woman has damaged the man's testicles; both of them think that the *hipʿil* of the verb חזק (to seize) denotes an intense, violent act (see Anthony Phillips, *Ancient Israel's Criminal Law: A New Approach to the Decalogue* [Oxford: Blackwell, 1970], 95; Eslinger, "Deuteronomy XXV 11–12," 272).

action, too, reaching out her hand, is blameless and seems to be an appropriate response under the circumstances. The law does not state that "she puts out her hand *to seize* him by the private parts," namely, that she extended her hand in order to seize his genitals.⁴⁰ Therefore one cannot rule out the possibility that she extended her hand in order to separate the two men, and that this physical contact is deemed legitimate. When the expression "put out her hand" appears in conjugated form, the extension of the hand is a prior preparatory act leading to the main action.⁴¹ Here too the woman puts out her hand as a preface to a second action, but rather than choosing a correct and legitimate action in order to rescue her husband (such as striking or deflecting the other man's hand) she chose a forbidden act. Having chosen this maneuver, after blamelessly drawing near and extending her hand, she deviated from the proper course of action and is punished for it.

To summarize: the presentation of the woman's personal motive, alongside the description of her actions as a gradual process in which choice is possible, constitutes a special example of the lawgiver's interest in interior reality. It is special because it is an example of a pure "intellectual" interest (and a moral interest as well), for neither the motive nor the chain of actions serves any special legal purpose.⁴²

---

40. Compare, e.g., 1 Sam 22:17; 2 Sam 1:14; 1 Chr 13:9 (and in this case, as in the law under discussion Uzza is punished for actually seizing YHWH's ark, and his pure motive is of no avail to him).

41. See, e.g., Gen 19:10; 22:10; Exod 4:4; 9:15. For the locutions "put out PN's hand" and "stretch out PN's hand," see Paul Humbert, "'Etendre la Main': Note de Lexicographie Hébraïque," *VT* 12 (1962): 383–95.

42. I have found that an intrinsic interest in the inner world exists in appearances of what is termed the "ethical dative" or "dative of feeling." This refers to an idiom that focuses on the actor; it emphasizes the meaning that the action has for the actor, the interest he takes in it, or his need for it. In not a few laws the injunction or prohibition to perform an action appears with the addition of the words לך or לכם ("for you," "for yourself"), e.g., in the laws of the pilgrimages and the year of jubilee (Exod 34:22; Lev 23:15, 40; 25:8; Deut 16:9, 13), in the laws of idolatry and forbidden worship (Exod 34:17; Lev 19:4; 26:1; Deut 12:30; 16:21–22), and in other laws (e.g., Deut 16:18; 19:2–3, 7, 9). The use of this linguistic element is another example of the lawgiver's attitude toward psychological reality, because in employing it he expresses the relationship of the protagonist to the actions that he is either enjoined to perform or from which he is to refrain. It is important to note that the ethical dative has no effect on the status or the legal validity of the injunction or prohibition to which it is attached; from a legal point of view there is no difference between the commandment "You shall count seven weeks of years ..." and the original injunction "You shall count *for yourself* seven weeks of years ..." (Lev 25:8), or between the prohibition "You shall make no molten gods" and the original prohibition "You shall make *for yourself* no molten gods" (Deut 16:21). This may be the reason the ethical dative is not reflected in the English translation of most of the laws in which it appears. On the ethical dative, see Wilhelm Gesenius and Emil Kautzsch, *Hebrew Grammar* (trans. A. E. Cowley; Oxford: Clarendon, 1910),

The Lawgiver Colonizes the Psyche

When I discussed the phenomenon of "internal speech," namely, when the lawgiver penetrates a character's mind and conveys his thoughts and desires, I observed that the lawgiver sometimes not only describes the mind's contents but also attempts to shape them, in order to direct the protagonist toward correct behavior. In some cases the degree of intervention is even greater; the lawgiver seems to have taken initial control over the character's interior space and determines what the contents of the psyche will be and what will be absent from it. He not only enjoins an action but decides what state of mind will accompany it. He therefore commands the protagonist to feel or not to feel a certain thing—to experience a feeling that somehow completes or contributes an element of seriousness and enthusiasm to the act, or to refrain from a feeling that might raise doubts or prevent him from carrying out the necessary action. Sometimes it appears as though the psyche itself is the object of the commandment, when the protagonist is enjoined to feel or not to feel a certain feeling, even if no action accompanies this feeling at all: "You shall not abhor an Edomite . . . you shall not abhor an Egyptian" (Deut 23:7); "You shall not hate your brother in your heart . . . you shall love your neighbor as yourself" (Lev 19:17–18); ". . . you shall love him [the stranger who sojourns with you] as yourself" (Lev 19:34). At the same time, and despite the importance the lawgiver attributes to it, emotional life is not treated in these cases as separable from the behavior that follows it. In the final analysis, the invasion of psychological terrain is meant to influence the world of deeds (for example, to enable the acceptance of an Edomite or an Egyptian into the Israelite congregation [Deut 23:8] or to prevent the fraud of a sojourner [Lev 19:33]).

The fusion of inner and outer reality, in which one's state of mind and actions coalesce, is expressed most powerfully in the commandment to rejoice, attached to several "religious" laws—the law of centralization of the cult, the law of tithing, and the law of pilgrimage,

> and you shall rejoice before the LORD your God in all that you undertake (Deut 12:7, 12, 18)
>
> and you shall eat there before the LORD your God and rejoice . . . (Deut 14:26)
>
> you shall rejoice in your feast . . . because the LORD your God will bless you in all your produce and in all the work of your hands, so that you will be altogether joyful (Deut 16:11, 14–15; 26:11)
>
> and you shall rejoice before the LORD your God seven days (Lev 23:40)

---

381 §199s; Waltke and O'Connor, *Hebrew Syntax*, 208 (11.2.10d); Paul Joüon, *A Grammar of Biblical Hebrew* (trans. T. Muraoka; Rome: Pontificio Instituto Biblico, 1996), 487–88 (133d).

The joy that the protagonists are commanded to feel as part of their relationship with God involves actions of giving and receiving. It is combined with thanksgiving for the bounty that God grants them, and it accompanies the worship of God and the gifts presented to him. The commandment to rejoice does not mean that one should accompany one's actions with laughter and gaiety, but rather that one should perform them with enthusiasm and a total will.[43] This joy fulfills two functions—it motivates the actions and accompanies them, but also, with a sort of feedback mechanism, it influences the mood of the actors by inducing satisfaction and high spirits.

However, whereas joy motivates action and also serves as a catalyst for fulfilling the requirements of the law, some feelings have an opposite effect—they prevent or delay action. For this reason the lawgiver commands the protagonist to eschew them: "your eye shall have no pity,"[44] "you need not be afraid of him"—do not pity the relative who incited you to idol worship (Deut 13:8), nor the murderer (19:13), the false accuser (19:21), nor the woman who seized a man's private parts (25:12), and do not fear the false prophet (18:22). One must administer the punishment ordained for each offender without pity or fear.[45]

When the lawgiver commands that the protagonist "not feel," he does not aspire to uproot sentiments that rankle in the heart, but rather bids him to restrain those feelings so as to overcome the hesitations and internal conflicts provoked by the heavy duty weighing upon him. It stands to reason that one would hesitate to execute a relative or intimate friend; it is only natural to fear harming the (charismatic) false prophet in the event that he might turn out to be a true one; and certainly one would flinch at maiming a woman. It is precisely for these reasons that the lawgiver feels a need to intervene in the protagonist's internal world and influence his state of mind. It is more difficult to understand the source of this need in the other two instances: premeditated murder and a false accusation, because neither one involves circumstances

---

43. The meaning attributed to joy in this context is inferred from the most common terms of spontaneous volition and willingness in cuneiform legal and nonlegal documents, that is, the expression *ina ḫūd libbi* ("in the joy of his heart") and its synonym *ina ṭūb libbi* (see Muffs, *Aramaic Legal Papyri*, 128–39). On love and joy as metaphors of willingness in biblical and rabbinic sources, see Muffs, *Love and Joy*, 121–38. On the motif of joy in the book of Deuteronomy, see Georg Braulik, *The Theology of Deuteronomy: Collected Essays of Georg Braulik* (trans. U. Lindblad; Dallas: BIBAL, 1994), 34–52.

44. The metaphorical use of the eye, as the organ of pity, arises from the concrete image of the compassionate gaze a person casts upon an object of pity. For the verb לחוס, see *BDB*, s.v. [חוס], 229a.

45. The injunction not to fear the false prophet refers not only to administering his punishment, but also to the rejection of his prophecies; that is, do not fear rejecting his words, even if they sound convincing (see Driver, *Deuteronomy*, 230).

that arouse pity toward or fear of the offenders; they arouse only revulsion and a desire to punish.

The answer should be sought not in a substantive reason but rather in a common element shared by both laws. Allow me to clarify. The punishments for intentional homicide as well as for false criminal accusation reflect the principle of *talio*. In the law of the false accuser this also receives linguistic expression, as it contains two talionic formulas: the first, "then you shall do to him as he had meant to do to his brother" (Deut 19:19); and the second, "it shall be life for life, eye for eye, tooth for tooth . . ." (19:21),[46] following the commandment "Your eye shall not pity." One must not exclude the possibility that this commandment or its variant, "your eye shall have no pity," was a common introduction to the *talio* formula, and that in certain cases, as in the law of homicide, the lawgiver did not reproduce the complete phrase but left only the familiar opening (this may also be the case in the law about the woman who seizes a man's private parts). If so, the commandment that seems to derive from the lawgiver's fear that the protagonist will hesitate to execute the punishments of the intentional homicide and of the false accuser, merely reflects part of the language of the familiar *talio* formula.

The transition to the next cases reflecting the lawgiver's invasive "takeover" of the psyche is marked by irony, because it is precisely when one might expect the protagonist to feel empathy toward the other that he is incapable of it. Here the lawgiver feels the need to intervene, in order to neutralize whatever feelings might prevent him from fulfilling his duty. That duty might be giving a loan to a poor person:

> [7]If there is among you a poor man . . . you shall not *harden your heart* or shut your hand against your poor brother, [8]but you shall open your hand to him, and lend him sufficient for his need, whatever it may be. [9]Take heed lest there be *a base thought in your heart* . . . and *your eye be hostile* to your poor brother, and you give him nothing, and he cry to the LORD against you, and it be sin in you. [10]You shall give to him freely, and *your heart shall not be grudging* when you give to him; because for this the LORD your God will bless you in all your work. . . . [11]For the poor will never cease out of the land; therefore I command you, You shall open wide your hand. (Deut 15:7–11)

Or the duty might involve giving of one's property to a newly released slave:

> [12]If your brother, a Hebrew man, or a Hebrew woman, is sold to you, he shall serve you six years, and in the seventh year you shall let him go free from you. [13]And when you let him go free from you, you shall not let him go empty-handed;

---

46. On the talionic formula in law and narrative, see Bernard Jackson, "Models in Legal History: The Case of Biblical Law," *Journal of Law and Religion* 18 (2002): 1–30.

¹⁴you shall furnish him liberally out of your flock, out of your threshing floor, and out of your wine press . . . ¹⁸*It shall not seem hard to you,* when you let him go free from you; for at half the cost of a hired servant he has served you six years. So the LORD your God will bless you in all that you do. (Deut 15:12–18)

Both of these laws exhibit a close connection between the world of feelings and the world of deeds, as well as the dependence of external behavior on internal dispositions.

The connection between these two realms is expressed through the metaphorical use of three body parts: the heart, the eye, and the hand.⁴⁷ The opposing actions of opening and closing the hand represent the actions of giving or withholding,⁴⁸ and the activity of the heart and the eye reflect a disposition— the unwillingness that keeps the protagonist from giving, or the unwillingness and reservations that may accompany an act of giving.⁴⁹ The lawgiver makes a distinction between these states of mind, each marked by a different level of emotional intensity and having a different effect on external behavior. He therefore deals with each one differently. The negative attitude that hinders giving is treated harshly, with a veiled threat of punishment, "and he cry to the LORD against you, and it be sin in you" (Deut 15:9b), while the reaction against reserved and unwilling giving is gentler. When the lawgiver commands "and your heart shall not be grudging when you give to him" (v. 10a); and "It shall not seem hard to you, when you let him go free from you" (v. 18a),⁵⁰ he is not demanding that the protagonist perform the act with an enthusiastic and desiring heart.⁵¹ Such a demand would not be realistic when taking into account the economic lack of profitability involved in providing a loan close to the seventh year, or of a generous gift from one's property to a released slave.⁵² The lawgiver does not present a utopian demand to perform the action with

---

47. For the metaphorical use of body organs to express inner states of mind, see Muffs, *Love and Joy,* 146–47. See also Meir Malul, *Studies in Mesopotamian Legal Symbolism* (Alter Orient und Altes Testament 221; Kevelaer: Butzon & Bercker, 1988).

48. The law of debt release makes an additional metaphorical use of the hand, where the phrase "your hand shall release" expresses forfeiting of the debt (Deut 15:3).

49. On giving reluctantly or under duress, see Muffs, *Love and Joy,* 127–29, 179–81.

50. The difficulty is not the actual release of the slave but rather the onerous condition that is attached to it. This can be inferred from the choice of the preposition "when": לא יקשה בעינך בשלחך אתו, rather than לא יקשה בעינך לשלח אותו (cf. Gen 35:16 ותלד רחל ותקש בלדתה in contrast to Exod 13:15, ויהי כי הקשה פרעה לשלחנו. In the first case the difficulty is attributed to the circumstances of birth, while in the second it is attributed to the action in general). This view differs from that of S. R. Driver, who suggests that the lawgiver is referring to the difficulty of fulfilling the duty of release, a difficulty that ultimately (as reflected in Jer 34:8ff.) leads to a complete neglect of the duty (Driver, *Deuteronomy,* 184).

51. Compare Japhet, "Manumission Laws," 82; Muffs, *Love and Joy,* 185–86.

52. The verb describing the outpouring of gifts of property, העניק, includes an adver-

utter willingness but rather wishes to persuade the protagonist to reconcile himself to the obligation of giving.[53] In order to remove his understandable reluctance, he offers an incentive—a promise of a positive reward—to show him that his current loss will eventually lead to future returns (vv. 10b, 18b).[54]

The lawgiver is not content merely to intervene in the emotional life of the law's addressee, but rather wishes to dominate his consciousness. He invades it several times, meddles with its contents, and demands that certain events be preserved therein by remembering constitutive events from the ancient past.[55] In these cases too (as in cases where the emotions are the object of intervention), the lawgiver mobilizes the inner life of the mind in order to affect the world of action, knowing that the state of consciousness that he hopes to induce in the protagonist can be used to good benefit.

The command to remember relates to three events. The most important one, of course, is the enslavement in and exodus from Egypt:

> You shall remember that you were a slave in the land of Egypt, and the LORD your God redeemed you. (Deut 15:15; 16:12; 24:18, 22)
>
> You shall eat no leavened bread with it . . . for you came out of the land of Egypt in hurried flight—that all the days of your life you may remember the day when you came out of the land of Egypt. (Deut 16:3)

The two other events are indirectly tied to it, because they occurred during the wanderings in the desert:

---

bial predicate of manner. It means to pile up generously, and its literal sense is to adorn with a necklace (see *BDB*, s.v. [ענק], 778b; Driver, *Deuteronomy*, 183).

53. The negative formulation of the demands indicates that they reflect a much more modest demand than a desiring heart (cf. Deut 10:12; 11:13; 26:16), and that in cases of lack of profitability the lawgiver demands not completeness of heart but rather reconciliation to duty. In three other laws whose topic is safeguarding the rights of the needy—the law of the pledge (Deut 24:10–13), the law prohibiting the delay of wages (vv. 14–15), and the laws of gleaning (vv. 19–22)—the lawgiver does not refer to the protagonist's state of mind, perhaps because in these laws, unlike the law of the pauper and the law of the slave, these are not clear cases of a lack of profitability, which might inhibit compliance.

54. The duty to give the slave a manumission grant also has a reason that directly addresses the issue of profitability (in addition to the historical justification [v. 15]). The law states that the profit the protagonist will earn from the slave's labor, as opposed to his profit from a hired laborer, will be more valuable than the grant (v. 18b).

55. The verb "remember" denotes cognitive activity—perception and recognition. It not only denotes knowledge that something occurred, but suggests a consistent turning of thought toward the familiar experience from the near or distant past. Its meaning is not limited to the act of remembering but includes other connotations, such as relating to, considering, paying attention.

> Remember what the LORD your God did to Miriam on the way as you came forth out of Egypt. (Deut 24:9)
>
> Remember what Amalek did to you on the way as you came out of Egypt. (Deut 25:17)

The behavioral norms, to which the commandment to remember enslavement and exodus are joined—the requirements regarding release of a slave, the enjoinders to include the impoverished elements of society in the rejoicing at the Festival of Weeks,[56] and the laws of gleaning—reveal that the main purpose of remembering is to allow the protagonist to internalize the events of the past and to impress upon him the analogy between his situation then and the situation of the impoverished in his own day. Internalization is not a rational experience but rather a branding of one's consciousness that is meant to revivify a personal experience—an experience that is meant to serve as a paradigm of the empathic treatment of needy people. In this respect, memory is an important factor that leads the protagonist toward proper conduct.[57]

The obligation to remember the exodus from Egypt that is appended to the commandment to eat unleavened bread has a different function. Here remembering is not part of a cognitive process that is meant to motivate the protagonist to perform the right actions or any other kind of action, but rather the purpose for performing that action. The consumption of unleavened bread is meant to commemorate the exodus from Egypt, for memory unto itself is the goal of the action.[58] Remembering provides the protagonist with an emotional experience and as such is part of an educational process designed to teach future generations to be conscious of their belonging to a national and religious collective.[59]

---

56. In this context Walter Brueggemann writes: "The tradition of Deuteronomy cannot imagine any devotion to YHWH that is not Exodus-oriented" (Walter Brueggemann, *Deuteronomy* [Abingdon Old Testament Commentaries; Nashville: Abingdon, 2001], 175). See also Yair Hoffman, *The Doctrine of Exodus in the Bible* (in Hebrew; Tel Aviv: University Publishing Projects, 1983), 136–37.

57. The importance of memory for preserving the correct attitude toward YHWH and the dangers involved in forgetfulness, which might lead one astray from God, are reflected in Deuteronomy 8, in what appears to be Moses' "psychoanalysis" of the children of Israel (this chapter makes intensive use of verbs of remembrance: "remember" (vv. 2, 18); "know" (vv. 3, 5, 16); "fear" (v. 6); "forget" (vv. 11, 14, 19). In this context, see Nelson, *Deuteronomy*, 107.

58. Treating memory as a goal unto itself is reflected in the commandment to make a fringe on one's garment (Num 15:39). The fringe, which is the object of the action, is supposed to remind one of God's commandments.

59. See Exod 12:26–27; 13:8–9, 14–15; Deut 6:20–25. On this subject, see Brueggemann, *Deuteronomy*, 174.

What is the purpose of the commandment to remember what Amalek did to you? Is the memory supposed to serve as a catalyst for action? Is it meant to arouse the protagonist to perform his duty and destroy Amalek? Or is memory here not a means but rather an end—to preserve in consciousness the historical experience in order to perpetuate eternal hatred toward Amalek?

Secure and peaceful dwelling in the land might cause the protagonist to forget the hardships of the past, to dull the feelings of vengeance, and ultimately to undermine the extermination of Amalek. This is why memory is needed—for it is the only function that can arouse the protagonist to fulfill his duty to blot out "the remembrance of Amalek from under heaven" (v. 19). Since this memory is meant to motivate to action, the commandment to remember Amalek is not eternal but is rather contingent on action.[60] The moment Amalek's memory is erased, so too will the memory of its actions be erased.

Finally, what is the purpose of the commandment to remember what God did to Miriam? What function does memory fulfill in this law? The answer is seemingly simple, because the protagonist is commanded to remember the disease of leprosy with which Miriam was afflicted (as described in Numbers 12), an event that is eminently suitable to serve as a precedent for a law that deals with leprosy. But the answer appears to be more complicated, for this precedent does not contribute anything substantial to the main commandment as specified in the law: "Take heed, in an attack of leprosy, to be very careful to do according to all that the Levitical priests shall direct you" (Deut 24:8). To answer this question we ought to pay heed to what the protagonist is commanded to remember. The phrase "that God did to Miriam" refers not to her sudden affliction, or to the way in which it was treated, but rather to the fact that she was punished. Since the protagonist is supposed to remember the circumstances that led to her disease, that is, her rejection of Moses' authority and God's response, this represents a sort of veiled threat to anyone who would dare reject the authority of the priests or the Levites to treat the affliction of leprosy. The commandment to remember is not meant, then, to serve as a precedent demonstrating how leprosy should be treated, but rather to remind listeners of how anyone rebelling against authority will be treated.[61] In any event, the memory is meant to support the behavioral norms to which the protagonist is beholden, and to guarantee that he adheres to them.

---

60. See Nahmanides' words: "Do not forget what Amalek did to us *until* his name is erased from under the sky." The eternal enmity toward Amalek is directed at the evil represented by Amalek as an enemy of Israel and of humanity in general, but in my opinion this enmity should not be attributed to the commandment to remember that is under discussion here.

61. See Brueggemann, *Deuteronomy,* 237–38; Phyllis Trible, "Bringing Miriam Out of the Shadows," *Bible Review* 5, no. 1 (1989): 14–25, 34.

It is time now to summarize. In the current chapter I presented a broad and diverse assembly of cases where the lawgiver refers to the mental life of his characters. At the end of the chapter, after having bandied about concepts such as "external behavior," "inner world," "functional reference," "intervention for its own sake," "narrative level," "legal plane," "the lawgiver's takeover" and others, it might appear that there is nothing more natural than to address psychological reality as part of the investigation of the pentateuchal laws. In truth, however, there is nothing more unusual than the biblical lawgiver's intensive preoccupation with the characters' mental and emotional life.[62] This preoccupation is an expression of his uniqueness in comparison both to other ancient lawgivers and to modern legislators. The biblical lawgiver not only makes extensive references to mental life in order to achieve certain ends, and not only uses diverse means, both overt and covert, to reveal the life of the mind, but accords the internal world a central place in relation to the world of deeds. He recognizes its power and the crucial influence it has on external behavior, and exhibits a surprising degree of insight in respect to its complexity, richness, and dynamism.

One of the most fascinating features of the lawgiver's approach to psychological reality (apart from merely recognizing its existence) is that in most cases he does not address it on account of a strict legal necessity, or in order to achieve a legal end. Exceptions to this are the extensive treatment of criminal intent, in the context of the laws of homicide, whose purpose is to classify the actions according to their severity and to distinguish among them in order to establish sanctions. To this can be added the quasi-functional approach to the moods and dispositions of the characters in the law of the *Sotah*, which is designed to explain the law; the description of the blood avenger's passionate feelings, which shows that inner life is taken into account as a part of the legislative considerations; the laws of "craving and desiring," in which the inner world is presented as the motive for legislation. In all other cases, the exposée of the life of the psyche contributes to the narrative and rhetorical plane of the law. Presenting the attitude of characters toward other characters or toward events as an explanation or background for their behavior belongs to the narrative plane of the law—it illuminates the world of the characters and contributes to our understanding of the human situations, but it does not have a concrete effect on the law. This is true of almost all the references to the psyche in the "laws of intimate relations," which reflect the lawgiver's great interest in the dynamic relationships of the characters.

---

62. In the course of my discussion I have referred monolithically to the "lawgiver" and will continue to do so, but it ought to be noted here that the invasion of the characters' psyche is conspicuously more common in later sources, and chiefly in the Deuteronomic legislation, in comparison to earlier sources.

Another fascinating phenomenon is, of course, what I have called the lawgiver's "takeover" of the mind's life—not a penetration of the internal world to discover what is going on inside it but rather an intervention that is supposed to influence consciousness and feeling. These cases, in which the lawgiver mobilizes the inner world for the law's purpose, provide the most distinctive evidence of his belief in how external behavior depends on internal states of mind. It is for this reason that I have entitled him the "psychological lawgiver."

5

POINT OF VIEW

Our journey through the poetics of biblical law is approaching its end. We have yet one more stop, where we encounter, hovering side by side, the consciousness of the lawgiver and the consciousness of the other characters—all in search of a narrator. This surrealistic image of "consciousness in search of a narrator" reflects the distinction in narrative text between the voice of the narrator, which presents events in the medium of language, and the perspective or angle of vision through which he reports them. The narrator may describe matters as he himself perceives them (through his senses, his intelligence, in an emotional or ideological manner), or he can give verbal expression to the perspective of one or more of the characters, or to the way in which they perceive things. The mediation between the narrating voice and the angle of vision—either the narrator's or the characters'—is defined as a "point of view" or "focalization."[1]

Every discerning reading of a narrative text is accompanied by the search for a perspective from which events are reported, and by the awareness that the narrator may switch from his own point of view to that of a certain character, and on to another character's perspective (and so on and so forth). The manner in which events are presented—whether from a neutral, supposedly objective point of view, or from an engaged, subjective point of view—may affect the content conveyed as well as the reader's attitude toward it. Perspective,

---

1. On "perspective," "point of view," "focalization," and the like, see Genette, *Narrative Discourse*, 185–89; Rimmon-Kenan, *Narrative Fiction*, 71–85; Bal, *Narratology*, 100–118; and specifically concerning biblical narrative, Bar-Efrat, *Narrative Art in the Bible*, 35–41; Polak, *Biblical Narrative*, 324–30; Gary Yamasaki, *Watching a Biblical Narrative: Point of View in Biblical Exegesis* (London: T&T Clark, 2007). Although some scholars make a clear distinction between "perspective" and "focalization" (see Bal, loc. cit.), and others prefer to use the second term, rather than the first (Rimmon-Kenan, loc. cit.), in the context of the present discussion I shall use the terms indiscriminately, because the distinction between the two concepts is chiefly theoretical and is not essential for our discussion. See, e.g., the glossary accompanying Willie van Peer and Seymour Chatman, eds. *New Perspectives on Narrative Perspective* (SUNY Series, The Margins of Literature; Albany: State University of New York Press, 2001), 357–58.

therefore, is a rhetorical device that allows the narrator to paint human experiences in different and variable colors.

Is any of the above relevant to a reading of legal texts? Is it reasonable to expect to find any wealth of perspectives within such texts? On the face of it, the answer to this question would appear to be no. In the laws, so it seems, reality cannot be presented as a relative concept that depends on the angle from which it is presented. Furthermore, we generally assume that texts determining binding behavioral rules are reported from the point of view of the one who enacts them, that the rules and norms, as well as the foundation of facts underlying them are represented from the perspective of the lawgiver. These assumptions are not valid when it comes to the casuistic laws, and it appears that differentiation of points of view is indeed relevant when analyzing these laws. Certainly, events and characters are commonly depicted from the perspective of the lawgiver—for it is he who observes them, thinks about them, considers them, and decides the case. But sometimes he opts to give expression to a personal point of view and presents events or some aspect of an event from the point of view of one of the characters involved.

In what cases does the narrator abandon his own focalization and choose to focalize the narration through the eyes of one of the characters? What purpose does a "close-up" description serve, and when is it preferable to a "distant" one? What is the lawgiver trying to achieve when, in a certain law, he adopts a multi-perspectival approach, and what is the relationship between the alternate perspectives? These are the chief questions to be discussed.

The present chapter will acquaint the reader with two verbal markers, three lawgivers-narrators, and a number of laws, which together will deepen our awareness that in reading the laws of the Pentateuch we must pay attention to the character that focalizes the legal material. One of the lexical markers that indicate that the lawgiver (like the narrator) presents things as seen through the mind of one of the characters is the use of verbs or idioms that denote sensory or cognitive perception (sight, hearing, knowing, understanding). The use of these verbs indicates that the character himself, not (only) the lawgiver, perceives and understands matters, and that the voice of the speaker chooses to hew close to his or her perceptions. Another textual marker that indicates that events are reported from a character's point of view is the use of multiple designations or appellations for other characters or for places.[2] Next to a neutral designation employed by the lawgiver, another, different designation appears that may intimate a character's personal style or position, or otherwise attest to its relationship with the focalized or designated object. Let

---

2. See Meir Sternberg, "Language, World and Perspective in Biblical Art: Free Indirect Discourse and Modes of Covert Penetration" (in Hebrew), *Hasifrut* 32 (1983): 121–23.

us begin with the first lexical marker and focus on the verb "see."³ We will explore how, through the use of this verb, we are exposed to a personal point of view and ask whether this serves the spirit of the law.

Compassion for Animals

> ⁴If you meet your enemy's ox or his ass going astray, you shall bring it back to him. ⁵If you *see* the ass of one who hates you lying under its burden, you shall refrain from leaving him with it, you shall help him to lift it up. (Exod 23:4–5)

> ¹You shall not *see* your brother's ox or his sheep go astray, and withhold your help from them; you shall take them back to your brother. ²And if he is not near you, or if you do not know him, you shall bring it home to your house, and it shall be with you until your brother seeks it; then you shall restore it to him. ³And so you shall do with his ass. . . . ⁴You shall not *see* your brother's ass or his ox fallen down by the way, and withhold your help from them; you shall help him to lift them up again. (Deut 22:1–4)

In the laws concerning help to animals, the description of events begins by noting the protagonist's act of seeing. The animals, so it seems, had buckled under their burdens, or had gone astray in a far-off field, before this was noticed by the protagonists. However, the readers learn of the animals' existence and of what befell them only from the moment they are seen through the protagonist's eyes.⁴ To understand why the lawgivers describe the events from up close, through the eyes of a person who is present on the spot—either in the field or on the road—one must define precisely what it is that he sees (since, by the same token, things could have been seen and perceived differently).

---

3. I will not discuss the uses of two other verbs of perception and recognition, "hear" and "know," except to note that the first appears in the context of the laws that protect the rights of the weak: "I will surely *hear* their cry," "And if he cries to me, I will *hear*" (Exod 22:23, 27); in the law of the idolatrous city: "If you *hear* in one of your cities (Deut 13:12); and in the law of the idolater: "and it is told you and you *hear* of it" (17:4). It should be noted that in the first example, the lawgiver indeed hears things, yet he focalizes the experiencing-self, rather than the lawgiver-self. The second verb appears, for instance, in the law concerning the protection of the rights of the sojourner: "you *know* the heart of a stranger" (Exod 23:9); in the law of a siege against a city: "Only the trees which you *know* are not trees for food" (Deut 20:20); and the law for helping animals in distress: "if you *do not know* him" (Deut 22:2).

4. In one of the two laws that deal with the return of stray animals to their owners (Exod 23:4) no verb of perception is used. However, in light of the structural and thematic similarity between the four laws of helping animals, one can assume that here too the lawgiver describes the event from the perspective of the protagonist. In any event, this is the underlying premise of my discussion.

What the protagonist sees—this much is conveyed by the four descriptions—is animals in distress. Not an ox, ass, or sheep grazing openly in the field, free from its master's yoke, but lost, stray, and helpless animals; not an ass or an ox lying down peacefully on the side of the road, resting from its day's labor, but fallen beasts, bowing under a heavy burden and unable to stand. The pitiful sights (as well as the pastoral scenes) are perceived by the one who focalizes the object not only externally but from "within." The observer, who processes this external scene of an animal lying in a certain pose, at a certain place, draws a conclusion regarding its interior state and needs. This mental processing, which is a product of the protagonist's understanding, experience, and feelings, turns a "neutral" image into a meaningful one, and more so, into an emotionally charged image. Both lawgivers adopt this manner of subjectively processing perceptions. Adopting the protagonist's point of view allows the reader to perceive and sense the animal's distress along with it, and to recognize that it is in need of help. This is the function achieved by representing the protagonist's point of view; it brings us closer to the animals' distress, and this, of course, serves the spirit of the law.

The scenes perceived by the protagonist include another internal element (apart from the animals' distress)—the animal's identity, or rather its relational status. The lawgiver does not report that the protagonist sees an ox, an ass, or a sheep (although this is what is plainly visible to the eye), but rather the ox or ass of *his enemy*, the ass of *one who hates him*; and an ass or sheep of *his brother*. It is reasonable to think that the protagonist knows to whom the bowing animals belong, since their owners are present on the site. In the first instance (Exod 23:5), he identifies him as his enemy, and in the second instance (Deut 22:4), it appears as though they have no previous acquaintance (although this cannot be ruled out), and the man, designated as "your brother," is, from his point of view, "the owner."

The use of the designation "your brother" exemplifies the way in which the text differentiates between the point of view and its verbal expression. The protagonist perceives the beast's owner, but since the report is conveyed by the lawgiver, he designates that man by a term that is acceptable to him. This distinction is even more pronounced in the two alternative situations pertaining to lost animals (Deut 22:1–2). According to the main law the designation "your brother" refers to a man the protagonist knows, while in the second law the very same designation refers to a man he does not know (and whom he cannot even locate in order to return his property). This is explained by the fact that the repeated designation reflects the standard language employed by the lawgiver.[5]

---

5. Famously, "your brother" is one of the characteristic idioms used by the Deutero-

The association of the stray animals with owners is also self-evident. In the world of the protagonist (as in our world) domesticated animals such as an ox or an ass must always belong to someone, and therefore their identity as owned animals might be thought to be somehow embedded in their appearance. But how should we understand a description in which the protagonist perceives an animal as belonging to someone specific? Can such a concrete attribution be an integral part of an external appearance? And if not, what can be learned here about the point of view? These questions are certainly relevant also to the parallel situation described in the Book of the Covenant (Exod 23:4), in which the protagonist sees animals that belong to someone who is defined as his enemy. One cannot discount the possibility that our protagonist simply knows his neighbor's animals, or that he recognizes them by special identity markers, or because they have strayed near the home or the pasture of their owner (and not of anyone else). But there is also another possibility. It could be that the look of a certain-owner's-animal is not described from the point of view of the protagonist at the moment of perception, but rather from a retrospective point of view, after having found out who its owner is.[6] In this instance the description of the beasts is indeed reported through the protagonist's eyes but from two different perspectives—the type of animal and its condition are reported from the initial point of view, and the association with its known owner is described from a slightly later point of view. This interpretation, in my view, is helpful, because it preserves the realistic aspect of the given description that was somewhat obscured in order to emphasize the law's rationale.

What is this rationale? The lawgiver includes the animal's identity, in fact the identity of its owner, in the initial scene perceived by the protagonist, even if this could seemingly mar the description's realism, since this element reflects the central normative thrust of the laws, namely, to determine rules of appropriate and inappropriate conduct in human relationships (and not only a matter of caring for animals in distress). Let us take, for example, the appearance of the enemy's animal. When the protagonist is reported to observe an animal that belongs to a person with whom he has a precarious relationship, and nevertheless offers help, this serves the spirit of the law, because it stresses that extraneous factors are irrelevant to the law.[7] The lawgiver insinuates the

---

nomic lawgiver in respect to the "other" from among the Israelites (see, e.g., Deut 15:2–3, 7, 9, 11, 12; 23:20–21; 25:3; see also Lev 19:17; 25:25, 35–37, 47).

6. Such an identification, which is almost instantaneous, should be distinguished from the comprehensive and extensive investigation that the owner must undertake to find the owners, when no "leads" exist (as described in the secondary law in Deut 22:2).

7. Both laws in the Book of the Covenant tacitly assume that the protagonist will extend help to an animal with whose owner he has a cordial relationship, and that therefore the law is meant to intervene only in "difficult" cases. The Deuteronomic laws reflect, in my

image of the enemy into the overall scene in order to emphasize that it is not supposed to have an impact on the protagonist's behavior (even if "in reality" he comes to mind only later).

FROM SEEING TO FEARING IN THE LAW OF WARFARE

> [1]When you go forth to war against your enemies, and see horses and chariots and an army larger than your own, you shall not be afraid of them; for the LORD your God is with you, who brought you up out of the land of Egypt. [2]And when you draw near to the battle, the priest shall come forward and speak to the people, [3]and shall say to them, "Hear, O Israel, you draw near this day to battle against your enemies: let not your heart faint; do not fear, or tremble, or be in dread of them; [4]for the LORD your God is he that goes with you, to fight for you against your enemies, to give you the victory." (Deut 20:1–4)

Point of view has a decisive influence on the first part of the law, because the perspective from which events are described explains the gap between the confident and promising opening words and the subsequent text, which reflects the opposite sentiments. In fact, it is point of view that is responsible for this gap between promise and realization.

At the focus of the general action of going to war stands another fateful event—an event of acquaintance—which impacts everything that follows. The protagonist sees the enemy against which he is going to war, and this sight overwhelms him with fear.[8] To understand the about-face that the protagonist experiences—from a voluntary decision to go to war, to a feeling of fear of and aversion to its prospect—we must explore what this sight holds that so diminishes his will to fight and his endurance. The manner in which the enemy is perceived by his consciousness will, presumably, explain the change in his inner world.

The description of the enemy and, more precisely, of the enemy's army includes two elements. First, the *means of war* are presented ("horses and chariots"), and next the *fighting force* ("an army larger than your own"). This presentation is neither incidental nor arbitrary but flows rather from the way in which the details are perceived from the protagonist's subjective point of view. Certainly, one could suppose that the order in which the details are communicated is a matter of the lawgiver's stylistic choices, for he is responsible

---

opinion, a more realistic view, where the duty to help animals is presented as a general obligation, which takes into account the possibility that a person might not extend help, either for selfish reasons or because of inconvenience, and not necessarily because his relations with the owner are precarious.

8. This conclusion arises, by inference, from the words of the lawgiver and the priest (vv. 1b, 3).

for the linguistic formulation of the description, even if it is delivered from another point of view. In this instance, however, I prefer to understand that the description arises from the lawgiver's conformity to the protagonist's state of mind. Why so? Because the protagonist first notices the sights that are more frightening and threatening—the horses and chariots that the enemy possesses, and which his army does not. His gaze focuses on those things that reflect the enemy's clear military superiority, which he fears he is ill-equipped to challenge; and only later does he notice the seeming multitude of enemy warriors, who appear to outnumber him. In short, because technological superiority is more threatening than numerical superiority, this aspect is the first to enter his consciousness.

Undoubtedly another, non-psychological explanation could be given for the order in which matters are presented. The fact that the scene is described from a personal point of view does not rule out the possibility that the way information is organized in the given passage is based in reality. In other words, the details of the scene become known to the protagonist not as a function of the level of anxiety that each engenders, but rather as they appear in reality; since the horses and chariots are positioned on the front line, before the infantry, he sees them first.[9] Either way, whether the protagonist perceives the facts as they are, or as they appear to him, the overall scene has a decisive influence on his state of mind.

The lawgiver's choice to describe the enemy from up close, from the point of view of the protagonist who has gone to war (the reader's knowledge of the enemy is mediated through the eyes of the protagonist) concretizes a sense of alarm and fear of military confrontation. It also explains why a law that begins with the protagonist's action and initiative does not deal at all with preparation for battle, but only with strengthening his morale and encouraging him. It is because the visual scene disrupted the normal sequence of events that would have been expected to ensue after the lawgiver's vigorous opening words.

"Is the Seer Here?" (Leviticus 13–14)

The protagonist of Leviticus 13–14, two chapters that deal with treatment of leprosy (צרעת) and other grievous skin diseases,[10] is of course the priest whose

---

9. See a similar presentation in Exod 14:9; 1 Sam 13:5; 2 Kgs 6:14. Compare the different presentation in Josh 11:4.

10. The identification of biblical צרעת with "leprosy" is unlikely, for the symptomatology provided in chapter 13 does not conform to the nature or course of Hansen's disease (leprosy). Apparently, a complex of various skin (or scale) diseases, subsumed under the category of impurity, was designated by the enigmatic term צרעת. The place of צרעת in the impurity system is due to the fact that it was associated with death; the body of the stricken,

role is to declare the stricken either pure or impure. His hands have plenty of work to do—or, better put perhaps, his eyes have plenty of work—for his craft relies most of all on the sense of sight. He looks at infections and diagnoses disease according to the symptoms he sees; he examines them a second time to determine if they were cured. The priest's use of the sense of sight is described so intensively that one might say that the lawgiver presents him as a "seer in action." Why is this significant for our discussion? Briefly stated, and before going into detailed explanations, Leviticus 13–14 presents us with a "perspectival paradise."

When one reads the laws concerning infectious diseases, one senses that the lawgiver not only reports or describes the priest's craft but actually accompanies him to his day's work—going from home to home, from one infected person to the next, from action to action. This sensation is produced through the lawgiver's incessant presentation of the things that the priest sees, and in wording that is particularly apt for this present chapter. All of the situations and events described by the lawgiver are reported literally through the eyes of the priest, from his point of view. This fact is conveyed in the multiple appearances (in chapter 13 more than in 14) of two lexical markers—the verb "to see," either alone, or the verb accompanied by the expression והנה ("and behold")—which show that the lawgiver hews closely to the perceiving mind.[11] For example:

---

like a corpse, is wasting away (see Num 12:12; Job 18:13). The afflicted person, treated as an impure substance, was therefore banished from the community (see Lev 13:46; Num 5:2–4; 12:14–15; 2 Kgs 7:3; 15:5; 2 Chr 26:21). Throughout the ancient Near East, disease, and skin disease in particular, is considered a divine punishment. Many of the biblical narratives concerning צרעת confirm its origin in God's wrath, being a punishment for sins against the deity or his messengers (Miriam [Num 12:9]; Gehazi [2 Kgs 5:27]; Uzziah [2 Chr 26:18–19]). For more on the nature of biblical "leprosy" see Levin, *Leviticus*, 75; Milgrom, *Leviticus 1–16*, 816–24; Anne Marie Kitz, "Sara'at Accusations and the Sociology of Exclusion" (Ph.D. diss., Johns Hopkins University, 1994).

11. Whereas in the Hebrew source the reference to the act of seeing is conveyed only by the verb "to see," in the JPS translation given here the verb "to look" is usually employed (the RSV prefers the verb "to examine, and the NJPS chooses to alternate between "to see" and "to examine"). Apart from the many occurrences of the verb of sight (alone, in 13:3a, 3b, 7a, 7b, 14, 15, 19, 27, 49–51, 57; 14:35, 36a, 36b; with "and behold," in 13:5, 6, 8, 10, 13, 17, 20, 21, 25, 26, 30–32, 34, 36, 39, 43, 53, 55, 56; 14:3, 37, 39, 44, 48), other words are joined to the semantic field of sight: "appearance" (13:3, 4, 12, 20, 25, 30–32, 34, 43; 14:37) and עין, an eye (13:5, 12, 37, 55). The last word is not reflected in the English translation (On the meaning of the phrases בעיניו, מראה עיני and עינו, see Milgrom, *Leviticus 1–16*, 780–81, 798.) The various colors and hues also belong to this semantic field: white, reddish, yellow, black, greenish, dark, light (13:3, 4, 6, 10, 13, 16, 17, 19–21, 24–26, 28, 30–32, 36–39, 42, 43, 49, 56; 14:37).

³And the priest shall *look* upon the plague in the skin of the flesh; and if the hair in the plague be turned *white* and the *appearance* of the plague be deeper than the skin of his flesh, it is the plague of leprosy; and the priest shall *look* on him, and pronounce him unclean. ⁴And if the *bright* spot be *white* in the skin of his flesh, and the *appearance* thereof be not deeper than the skin, and the hair thereof be not turned *white*, then the priest shall shut up him that hath the plague seven days. ⁵And the priest shall *look* on him the seventh day; *and, behold,* if the plague stay in its *appearance,* and the plague be not spread in the skin, then the priest shall shut him up seven days more. ⁶And the priest shall *look* on him again the seventh day; *and, behold,* if the plague be *dim,* and the plague be not spread in the skin, then the priest shall pronounce him clean: it is a scab; and he shall wash his clothes, and be clean. ⁷But if the scab spread abroad in the skin, after that he hath *shown himself* to the priest for his cleansing, he shall *show himself* to the priest again. ⁸And the priest shall *look, and, behold,* if the scab be spread in the skin, then the priest shall pronounce him unclean: it is leprosy. (Lev 13:3–8 JPS)

Focalization through the priest's eyes endows the description of the diseases and of the diseased with a realistic dimension and allows the reader to become intimately acquainted with the process from start to finish. The frequent use of the expression "and behold" in relation to the appearance of the objects reflects the priest's perception "here and now" and allows the reader to experience the discovery of the signs and symptoms together with him.[12] These descriptions enliven the original experience and produce an encounter with a "priestly expert in action."

Sometimes, however, the descriptions are delivered from another point of view; namely, the point of view of the lawgiver, which is revealed in the opening verses of specific laws, in the verses that report the various infections, before the priest has entered the scene. Thus, for example:

When a man shall have in the skin of his flesh a rising, or a scab, or a bright spot, and it become in the skin of his flesh the plague of leprosy, then he shall be brought unto Aaron the priest. (Lev 13:2 JPS)

When the plague of leprosy is in a man, then he shall be brought unto the priest. (Lev 13:9 JPS)

¹⁸And when the flesh hath in the skin thereof a boil, and it is healed, ¹⁹and in the place of the boil there is a white rising, or a bright spot, reddish-white, then it shall be shown to the priest. (Lev 13:18–19 JPS)[13]

---

12. On the meaning of the phrase "and behold," see McCarthy, "The Uses of wᵉhinnēh"; Berlin, *Biblical Narrative,* 62–63, 91–95; Sternberg, "Language, World and Perspective," 96–102; Simcha Kogut, "On the Meaning and Syntactical Status of 'hine' in Biblical Hebrew," *Scripta Hierosolymitana* 31 (1986): 133–54; Meir Weiss, "On Narrative Art in the Bible" (in Hebrew), in *Mikraot ke-kavanatam: An Anthology* (Jerusalem: Mosad Bialik, 1987), 293–311.

13. Other opening verses in which the lawgiver's perspective is reflected are 13:24, 29,

The lawgiver describes a variety of symptoms and changes that appear in people's bodies and in clothes, textiles, leather wares, or houses. In most instances the description is accompanied by diagnostic comments—a medical diagnosis, such as "it is leprosy," or a diagnosis concerning the infected person's status, "he is clean." This information provides the factual basis for the description of the priest's craft, but the lawgiver does not leave things here and chooses to present an additional set of facts. He does not use his own descriptions and diagnoses because he is still interested in presenting the entirety of the priest's responsibilities, including diagnosis, and in accompanying the "actual" process from start to finish. Therefore, after presenting matters from his external point of view, he states the requirement to present the infected objects to the priest. From this moment on, each one is described, almost exclusively, from the priest's perspective.

Already in the first law (13:2–8) one can notice the combination of two perspectives—the first distant and the second near. The lawgiver reports certain symptoms of the skin and diagnoses them as "the plague of leprosy." But in describing what the priest sees, he does not call it a "plague of leprosy" (although clearly this is the type of infection in question) but rather a "plague in the skin of the flesh." He thus reconstructs for us the priest's first encounter with the disease and reveals the secrets of diagnosis: self observation and an expert gaze, both capable of revealing specific signs—such as the infection's depth, the hair growing in it, or its color—that indicate its type.

Certainly, the permanent existence of both perspectives and the fact that the reader becomes aware of the infections and their types before the priest sees them load the text with surfeit information and numerous repetitions. But it is important to note that, while the description of the focalizing lawgiver is usually brief, the information reported by the priest is richer and includes elements that were not revealed before.[14] The difference between the two descriptions does not reside in any advantage that the priest has over the lawgiver; rather, in order to underscore the priest's expertise, the omniscient lawgiver withholds part of what he knows.

38, 40–42, 47–49; 14:34–36. Six other verses, which also reflect an external point of view, should be noted (13:7, 14, 16, 35, 57; 14:43). They describe new conditions that developed in the infections after they had already been inspected by the priest; they therefore can be viewed as secondary laws. I do not deal with them in the context of the present discussion.

14. The law of leprosy of a garment (13:47–59) represents an exception, for two reasons. First, the opening verses, delivered from the perspective of the lawgiver, describe the infection with a relatively high level of detail (vv. 47–49); and, second, after the infection is revealed to the priest's eyes, no further information about it is presented (v. 50). Possibly, in this instance the elliptical principle overrode the recurring pattern of a duplicate description.

The law of house leprosy is an excellent illustration of perspectival richness.

> ³⁴When ye are come into the land of Canaan, which I give to you for a possession, and I put the plague of leprosy in a house of the land of your possession; ³⁵then he that owneth the house shall come and tell the priest, saying: "There seemeth to me to be as it were a plague in the house." ³⁶And the priest shall command that they empty the house, before the priest go in to see the plague, that all that is in the house be not made unclean; and afterward the priest shall go in to see the house. ³⁷And he shall look on the plague, and, behold, if the plague be in the walls of the house with hollow streaks, greenish or reddish, and the appearance thereof be lower than the wall; ³⁸then the priest shall go out of the house to the door of the house, and shut up the house seven days. (Lev 14:34–38 JPS)

The lawgiver here "drifts" between three perspectives. First he reports the plague from the perspective of the one who is responsible for its appearance, namely, he himself; since he is the one who inflicted the disease, he knows its characteristics (v. 34). Later the perspective of the house's owner is revealed: he sees the plague but does not know what it is. The assured diagnosis of the lawgiver-focalizer—"a plague of leprosy"—is replaced by a hesitant statement that he has observed something that "seems" like a plague (v. 35b). What sort of plague? He cannot say. The third perspective is that of the priest-expert. His description, like that of the house's owner, is based on the sense of sight, but while the latter's observation is not sufficient for making a clear diagnosis, the priest's discrimination reveals the variety of symptoms that point to the infection's type: its location, special color, and its depth (v. 37). The fact that both figures employ the same sense emphasizes the difference between the perspective of the layperson and that of the expert. The man who lives in the house does not attach importance to the specific location of the infection, since from his perspective it is found in the domestic space, perceived as a totality. Lacking diagnostic skill, he does not even see the "hollow streaks," although they are present and revealed to the (skilled) eye. The additional details, which the reader learns only through the priest's discerning eyes, attest not only to expertise but to a high level of skill.

This is true of the relationship between the layperson and the expert. But what is the purpose of the "perspectival discourse" that takes place (in this law as well as in other laws) between the priest and the lawgiver-focalizer? As mentioned earlier, the reader does not receive the priest's revelations and insights as a blank slate but rather encounters them after the lawgiver has already equipped him with important details. In truth, the reader does not require the priest's perspective in order to obtain knowledge about the existence of infection or about the type of infection; it seems, therefore, that the purpose of combining perspectives is not informational. Its role, rather, is to grant credibility to the functionary's skill and expertise, because the repeated description not only reveals the difference between the two perspectives (the priest's certainly enriches the lawgiver's description), but also emphasizes the *correspondence* between them. In other words, presenting the different descriptions alongside one another demonstrates that the priest's diagnoses are always correct, and this produces complete trust in his office.

The Designations

The laws contain designations for the characters who participate in the actions. The protagonists (as well as other characters) are commonly referred to as "man," "woman" or "person" (אדם, נפש, אשה, איש);[15] their "others" are designated as "brother" or "neighbor" (עמית, אח, רע).[16] Alongside these common and "neutral" designations, the laws also employ specific designations that are tied to specific content or circumstances, such as "Hebrew slave," "pregnant woman," "murderer," "poor person," "sojourner." And in a number of instances a character is described by several designations. First the common, general designation is used, and later, the more specific one that is tied to the narrated events, explicating the character's identity and underscoring the attributes that are relevant to the legal narrative of which he or she is part. Thus is the protagonist presented in the law of corporal damage (Exod 21:18–19)—he is first called a "man," but then is described as "he that struck him," in order to distinguish him from his beaten friend. And in the law of the pit (Exod 21:33–34), for instance, in order to underscore the protagonist's liability, the lawgiver no longer refers to him as a "man" (in the apodosis) but rather points up his relationship to the dangerous site and calls him "the owner of the pit."

Neither of these examples (or others that one could cite) raises any questions in regard to perspective. The variety of perspectives is employed for emphasis, or at the very most for purposes of clarification, but not in order to produce perspectival distinctions, since the only perspective that governs the scene is the lawgiver's. But there are cases in which the multiplicity of designations also conveys multiple perspectives. How should we regard the alterna-

---

15. The Priestly legislation uniquely uses another designation, איש איש (in H it appears with the descriptor "from the house of Israel" or "from the children of Israel").

16. There would appear to be a difference between the neutral designations "man," "woman," and "person," and the designations "brother" and "neighbor," which convey a notion of brotherhood and intimacy. The latter terms do indeed reflect the lawgivers' beliefs regarding the solidarity that the laws' addressees are expected to feel toward their fellow Israelites, but even these designations are used neutrally, since any fellow Israelite is called your "friend" or "brother." It should be noted that in ancient Near Eastern laws there is no such distinction, and that Akkadian *awīlum* or Sumerian *lú* are used for the protagonists as well as for their "others."

tion between "man" and "[he] who is beating him," מכהו, the two designations of the man whose genitals are seized by a woman (Deut 25:11–12)? Might the second, specific designation be given from a perspective other than that of the lawgiver, namely, from the perspective of the woman? In my opinion, it certainly is.[17] The description of the scene combines two perspectives—the first is external and distant, and the second is subjective and involved. Each perspective is reflected in the designations given to the secondary characters (the husband and the second man). The lawgiver describes a physical confrontation between two parties who each contribute equally to the event. He therefore employs designations that do not actually distinguish between the fighting parties, but rather paint a picture of a balanced conflict: "men" fighting "one with another."[18] But when the alternate designation is introduced, turning the character from "man" or "brother" to "his smiter," this balance is disturbed, and suddenly we have a smiter and a smitten person, not two people in a fight with each other. Who, then, is capable of viewing the event in such a one-sided manner? The woman, of course, who would not have otherwise interfered to assist her husband. The lawgiver's choice to employ a designation that disturbs the balance that he himself created at the opening is meant to give voice to the woman's subjective point of view, thus offering an authentic presentation of her motives.

When determining whether a character's designation is mediated through another character's consciousness, one must distinguish between two situations. When the designation is contained in a statement delivered in direct speech, one can assume that it reflects the speaker's consciousness, as part of the quoted speech. But when it appears within the lawgiver's words, this is much harder to determine and should be decided by the context—Whom does a certain designation of a character seem to suit better, the lawgiver or one of the characters involved in the scene? Let us illustrate both situations.

These are the "names" of the two central characters in the law of the false accusation (Deut 22:13–19): first the general designations "the man" and "any man" are given, as well as the specific designations "a wife," "young woman." All of them are conveyed from the point of view of the lawgiver. These are followed by the distant designations "this woman" and "this man," conveyed by the husband, who accuses his wife, and by her father, who responds to his

---

17. In the previous chapter we addressed the way in which the lawgiver exposes the woman's motive (by penetrating her mind). I shall now discuss the linguistic marker that reflects what is occurring in her mind.

18. The designation איש ואחיו, "a man and his brother," which gives an almost idyllic air to the description of the brawl, is missing for some unexplained reason from the English translation.

son-in-law's accusation.[19] Last, we are given the intimate designation "my daughter," employed by the father. In total we encounter four neutral designations, accompanied by three subjective designations that reflect the stance of the speaker toward the designated characters.

But the law includes two other designations that relate to the woman, which deserve separate treatment: the first is contained in the father's speech when he quotes the husband's words, "... saying, 'I did not find in *your daughter* the tokens of virginity'" (v. 17); and the second as part of the lawgiver's motive clause "... because he has brought an evil name upon *a virgin of Israel*" (v. 19). The father does not quote the husband's words (in v. 14) precisely; and, among the other changes he introduces into the quoted speech, he replaces the designation "this woman," employed by the husband, with "your daughter."[20] This designation, which reflects the intimacy between them (as well as his liability for her actions), is certainly compatible with the nature of the words he addresses to the elders, but it is incompatible with the spirit of the husband's original statement. We see, therefore, that in the context of a quotation, which is supposed to reflect the mind of the quoted person, a linguistic element is introduced—the designation of a character—that reflects the point of view of the one who is quoting.[21] Elsewhere I called this feature "combined discourse"; that is, the designation turns the quotation into a combined utterance. It appears, therefore, that close attention must be paid when analyzing point of view, since even a designation that is contained within a character's speech could be questioned in regard to the point of view from which it is delivered.

And now to the woman's second designation as "a virgin of Israel." Although this designation appears as part of a motive clause supplied by the lawgiver, implying that the point of view it represents is definitive, I suggest a different possibility. Each of the woman's designations indicates a different sphere of belonging that forms a part of her identity. She is "a wife" in relation to "the man" because he took her in marriage. But from the moment the father entered the picture, the lawgiver no longer designates her as "a wife" but rather as "a young woman," to underscore her subordination to the father's authority (and in consequence, his own liability). The third designation, "a vir-

---

19. It could be thought that the designation "this man" is a neutral designation that indicates the husband's presence at the site and that therefore it is emotionally neutral. (It is also possible that it reflects standard terminology for pointing at a party to a judicial proceeding [see, e.g., Jer 26:11].) At the same time, as already mentioned elsewhere, when it appears together with the designation "this woman," it is difficult not to view it as a counter-response that reflects the father's attitude toward the man who harmed his daughter.

20. For the rest of the changes, see the discussion in chapter 3 above on representation of speech.

21. See chapter 3, n. 48 above.

gin of Israel," combines two identities—a personal-social status, and national belonging. This coupling is meant to justify the husband's corporal punishment (for he damaged the good name of a daughter of the nation) and also the level of compensation that is demanded of him (twice the virginal brideprice). Is it appropriate for the lawgiver to employ this designation in respect to the woman? Undoubtedly, but at the same time, one should not rule out the possibility that the designation also reflects the engaged point of view of those who administer the legal procedure and who are responsible for carrying out the sanctions. For the city elders, who protect society's virtues, are also (or perhaps chiefly) suited to view her as "a virgin of Israel."[22]

It is not surprising that the law of levirate marriage (Deut 25:5–10), which is concerned with the preservation of the (family) name, gives the two main characters a number of different designations. These alternating designations reflect changes in the familial and social status of the characters and in their relationships. The designations, which appear to have been carefully chosen, play an important role: they propel the plot forward and contribute to the comprehension of the legal-normative dimension of the law. Here, too, some of the designations are conveyed by the lawgiver (in which case we must examine whether they reflect his point of view) and others by the characters themselves. The widow's first designation "the wife of the dead" is tied to circumstances. It points to the change in her familial situation, from which derives the son-in-law's duty to marry her. As a result, the dead man's brother, on whom this duty is incumbent, is designated by a term that reflects this duty יבמה ("the one who performs a brother-in-law's duty for her").[23] But when the circumstances change, the designations change as well. As soon as the secondary legal procedure begins (v. 7), another, quite surprising designation for the brother-in-law is used. He is no longer designated by the duty that falls to him, nor even in respect to his familial relationships, but is simply called "the man." On the face of it, this is the general designation commonly used by the lawgiver, but since in this particular law, he makes extensive use of specific (carefully chosen) designations, one suspects that in this instance the common designation does not bear a merely plain or neutral meaning. Indeed, unlike the usual use of the designation "man," here the lawgiver chooses it precisely because, unlike other designation, it is particularly suited to the circumstances. The use of a designation that lacks

---

22. In light of the possibility that is presented here, it may be worthwhile to examine methodically whether the motive clauses are delivered only from the lawgiver's point of view, or whether sometimes they are conveyed from the perspective of a collective character who is charged with the application of the law.

23. The designation used in the English translation "her husband's brother" is infelicitous, because it refers only to their familial relationship and does not contain, as the Hebrew term does, an explicit reference to the duty to perform levirate marriage.

specification allows the lawgiver to illustrate how the protagonist has shirked his duty (and to indicate his alienation from the extended family unit). Later, the protagonist's identity becomes even more obscure (perhaps because, in spite of the fact that the law grants him the right of refusal, it does not view the exercise of this right kindly). When his summons to the city elders and their address to him are described, he receives no designation at all; the lawgiver refers to him only obliquely with possessive pronouns: "his [city]," "him," "[to] him" (v. 8). The obscuring of his identity culminates in its utter loss and the receipt of a new identity, but more about this below.

My arguments about the designation "the man" may sound convincing. Yet I am compelled to present a competing interpretation because of an additional designation that is applied to the woman. Three times (twice in v. 7 and once more in v. 9), the lawgiver designates her as יבמתו and, like the designation יבמה, this appellation too not only describes a familial relationship—the fact that she is the brother's wife (see Ruth 1:15)—but also underscores her connection to the act of levirate marriage. Why should the lawgiver employ a designation that indicates the shirking of a duty, while simultaneously using a designation that points to that very duty? Perhaps this is because a different consciousness from the lawgiver's has produced the designation "the man." Perhaps it is the character's point of view that determines that designation, for after all it is apt that the person who has shirked his duty should designate himself as someone who is not even obligated by that duty. His shirking of his duty is expressed in another, more explicit way, through the nondesignation of the widow. He does not state (in v. 8), "I do not wish to take my brother's wife [יבמתי]," but rather, "I do not wish to take *her*." By doing so he obscures the relationship between them—the relationship that is the source of his duty toward her.

The two designations in the widow's statements, which together tell the whole story, should also be noted. At the beginning of the judicial procedure (v. 7), when she is still hopeful that the city elders will persuade him to fulfill his duty, she calls him יבמי, that is, *my husband's-brother, the one upon whom the duty lies*. But in the statement that accompanies the removal of the shoe (v. 9), after she understands that he still refuses to fulfill his duty, she calls him "the man."

At first there was a "brother," who then became "the dead man's brother" and then the "one who is obligated to a brother-in-law's duty." Once he shirked his duty he became "a man," but ended up as "the house of him that had his sandal pulled off." From whose point of view is this last designation conveyed? Since it is contained in the lawgiver's statement (v. 10), nothing prevents us from saying that it reflects his thinking. Moreover, the opening words, "And the name of his house shall be called in Israel," are typical of an authoritative statement of principle on the part of the lawgiver. At the same time, it seems that a different point of view determines this designation. The audience who witnesses the procedure, with its humiliating ritual of removing the shoe, is the one who slaps the brother-in-law with the designation that perpetuates his shame. Here I invoke with appreciation the commentary of Rashi, who suggests that the designation is not to be attributed to the lawgiver's statement, but rather to the words spoken by those who were present at the trial.[24] Since, however, the law does not describe such a speech event, the view I propose, that the designation reflects the audience's point of view, provides a more appropriate solution to the problem. And perhaps the designation is in fact given by the widow (as part of the long utterance that begins in v. 9 and continues in v. 10), since it most aptly reflects her attitude toward the man.

Finally, let us briefly visit a few sites where dramatic events take place. This time, however, our chief interest lies not in the events but in the places, or more precisely, the designations of the places. Below is the law of the broken-necked heifer:

> [1]If in the land which the LORD your God gives you to possess, any one is found slain, lying in the field,[25] and it is not known who killed him, [2]then your elders and your judges shall come forth, and they shall measure the distance to the cities which are around him that is slain; [3]and the elders of the city which is nearest to the slain man[26] shall take a heifer which has never been worked and which has not pulled in the yoke. [4]And the elders of that city shall bring the heifer down to a valley with running water, which is neither plowed nor sown, and shall break the heifer's neck there in the valley. [5]And the priests the sons of Levi. . . . [6]And all the elders of that city nearest to the slain man shall wash their hands over the heifer whose neck was broken in the valley; [7]and they shall testify, "Our hands did not shed this blood, neither did our eyes see it shed" (Deut 21:1-7)

The events described take place in several sites, beginning at the place where the slain man was found and extending to the outlying space between that initial site and the surrounding places of settlement (cities). The measuring operations of the elders and the judges lead to the city nearest to the dead body; the ritual of expiation takes place outside the settlement, in a place that is designated by its geographical features, both as a "valley" and a "valley with running water."

I shall focus on three designations that entail the issue of perspective: "the land which the LORD your God gives you to possess"; "the field"; "the city which is nearest to the slain man." All three are the lawgiver's expressions, but

---

24. See chapter 3, n. 51 above.
25. According to the RSV, "lying in the open country."
26. The translation does not reflect the opening verse in the Hebrew text, "And it shall be, that the city which is nearest unto the slain man" (which is present in the JPS version).

it appears to me that only one of them represents his point of view. The first two designations refer to the place where the slain man was found, but each reflects a different consciousness. When the place is focalized by the lawgiver it is called "the land which the LORD your God gives you to possess," thus expressing the law's rationale. The lawgiver chooses a broad and general designation to stress that the place is part of a contaminated environment that must be cleansed from blood impurities. On the other hand, the designation "the field" refers not to the space in general but to the specific location where the corpse lies. This designation embodies the perspective of those who were in the field and who found the slain man, the people who saw the body with their own eyes and therefore refer to its location specifically as a bounded place.

As regards the third designation, the existence of settled places near "the field" is an objective fact, and therefore the designation "the cities which are around him that is slain" certainly reflects the mind of the lawgiver. That one particular settlement is closest to the site of the corpse is also an objective fact. Nevertheless, it does not necessarily mean that the designation "the city which is nearest to the slain man" also reflects the lawgiver's consciousness. The proximity of that specific location is discovered only after the elders and judges measure the distances. Once discovered, after long and arduous labor, they must certainly declare it as such. Therefore the stated designation corresponds to their perspective. The lawgiver even furnishes the subjective perspective with a linguistic marker, by introducing the designation with the phrase "And it shall be," which dramatizes the moment of discovery.[27]

Finally a few words of conclusion from the author's perspective. It can be claimed without hesitation, surprising as this may sound (especially to those who still believe that "law is law and narrative is narrative"), that the casuistic laws provide perspectival bounty. Undoubtedly, following the different points of view from which matters are reported, and identifying the subjective points of view enabled by the lawgivers' narration, enriches the reading experience. The lawgivers' choice to combine their perspective with other (sometimes utterly different) perspectives is motivated by their understanding that the exposition of personal and internal points of view will lead the reader to an experiential appreciation of the events and of the characters. The authors of the laws are clearly not content with a merely neutral presentation, and they therefore employ a device that enhances comprehension of the laws and shapes the reader's stance toward the characters and the events that take place in their world.

---

27. On the use of the verb "to be" (היה) as an expression of discovery or revelation, see *BDB*, s.v. היה, 225b, II.1.a

The lawgivers hew closely to the characters' own perceptions, endowing their descriptions with vitality and authenticity and enabling the reader to experience the events along with them: to feel the distress of the animals—an impression that effectively serves the spirit of the laws; to sense the intense fear of combat and recoiling from war, to understand better the need for encouragement and for placing trust in YHWH; to see the priestly specialist at work from "up close" and to know for certain that he is fulfilling his role faithfully. The lawgivers take the trouble of presenting the designations people apply to each other, so that we can divine what they are actually feeling within the welter of human emotions and drives. And we, the readers of the laws, benefit from this perspectival richness, because we find that we are taking an active role in the process of reading.

Conclusions

Having completed this journey through the nonlegal terrain in the margins of the laws, my readers have surely arrived at a few conclusions of their own. Frankly, I hope that this journey has offered more than just scholarly insight but also a different kind of reading experience. A few words must be said, however; I therefore present my own conclusions here.

The narrative reading of the casuistic laws is of very little use (if it is of any use at all) for understanding their normative dimensions; it is possible to comprehend the legal norms even without recognizing the narrative elements embedded in them. A narrative reading, however, is eminently useful for a reader in search of other types of meanings—the human meaning embodied in events in which people participate or in circumstances that may befall them. The analytic and interpretive tools offered by literary theory and narratology can open the door onto these meanings, allowing us to understand how they are constructed and what effect their mode of construction has on the addressees and readers of the laws.

Only a narrative reading, not the legal reading, can reveal the essential characteristics of the casuistic laws of the Pentateuch; this is my first conclusion. First of all, this reading extricates the laws out of the rigid framework in which they are cast—the permanent linguistic formulas and logical schemes of the casuistic pattern—and points to their narrative essence.[1] Second, it reveals that their authors "thickened" and enriched the basic narrative form and furnished it with actual stories—stories alive with concrete descriptions (even if not richly detailed) that present the reader with all the complexity of human experience.[2] Third, it teaches us that the approach guiding the ancient authors is no different from the approach that we moderns deem valid—that narrative is a cognitive instrument endowing actions and events with meaning, and that it is therefore a prime mechanism for perceiving and understanding

---

1. By this I refer, for example, to the two readings of the law of the deposit (Exod 22:26–27), in chapters 2 and 3, which demonstrated how a law formulated in the "if . . . then" form manages to present a day and a night in the life of a borrower and lender (or, rather, the story of one garment and one compassionate lawgiver).

2. For example, the law of false accusation (Deut 22:13–21), discussed in chapter 3, which describes the saga of a family steeped in conflict, passions, and emotions.

reality. They understood that employing a story, composed of concrete situations, is useful for grasping rules and abstract principles, and that the narrative medium, as a rhetorical device, is an aid to internalizing ideas, perceptions, and opinions.[3]

This brings me to an additional conclusion. The poetics of the casuistic laws are intimately tied to the function they fulfill; they are designed to enable the laws to achieve their declared end, namely, obedience to the norms they establish. The authors employed a variety of literary devices in the laws, both aesthetic and rhetorical, to impress meanings that their addressees would understand, internalize, and act upon. These "reading guidelines" can be discovered only by means of a narrative reading. Therefore, even when this kind of reading illuminates details or focuses on elements that might seem superfluous, or at least inconsequential from a legal perspective, we must understand that they still fulfill a role—they offer a depth of perspective and breadth of view that may not be strictly necessary for obtaining legal insight, but which paint a more precise picture that touches on the substance of the matter.[4]

These comments lead me to the first major characteristic of the casuistic laws, which, as we have pointed out, is revealed through the narrative reading—their mimetic quality. Despite the rigid framework, the set patterns, the brief format, and the sparse details, the laws manage to leave us with a powerful impression of reality. This is achieved primarily because the lawgivers describe events concretely, moving from one scene to another and giving the readers the illusion that they see things with their own eyes, sometimes even allowing us to hear the characters' voices. The possibility (or perhaps it should be said, the privilege) of hearing these voices not only gives an aura of realism to the events, due to the meticulous representation of personal linguistic traits, but it also dresses the events in dramatic garb. This is certainly true in the representation of external speech, but even more so in the characters' internal speech, which exposes what transpires in their heart and minds.

To this are added other varied modes of exposing the world of emotions and thought, which also play an important role in creating an illusion of real-

---

3. Recall the use that the Deuteronomic lawgiver makes of the story in the law of the firstborn's rights (Deut 21:15–17), which we alluded to in chapter 4. The story of the husband and his two wives, one loved and the other spurned, which makes him liable to prefer the son of the former over the firstborn of the latter (echoing Jacob's favoring of Rachel's sons over Leah's firstborn whom he despised), contributes to the legal understanding of the rights of the firstborn and the prohibition against evading their implementation.

4. The laws of the leper in Leviticus 13–14, discussed in chapter 5, can be mentioned in this context. These laws are replete with repetitions and emphases, presenting a multitude of perspectives, much more than would have been required for setting the legal norms.

ity. The authors accord a great deal of weight, relatively speaking, to the inner life of the characters, because of the weight such matters have in real life. The same is true of details that are immaterial to the presentation of the legal case, or irrelevant to the establishment of the legal norm. Their inclusion enhances the mimetic illusion, because the only reason they appear within the framework of the laws is that they do indeed exist in the world.[5]

Another means of achieving the illusion of reality is the internal focalization of the events and of the characters. Seeing things from the characters' vantage point, and not only from the lawgivers' external point of view, allows us to experience the events, along with the characters, in a concrete and "real" manner.[6]

The second chief characteristic of the casuistic laws is their communicative and dialogic nature. When the lawgivers invite the addressees and themselves to participate in the events portrayed in the laws, communication is open and direct (as, for example, in the law of homicide [Exod 21:13–14]). So it is when they refer to the art of legislation and reveal their own reasoning (through the use of motive clauses, for instance). The dialogic nature of the laws is conspicuous and perceptible in those cases where the lawgivers respond directly and immediately to what is going on in the inner world of their addressees, with the explicit intention of influencing it (as well).[7] Frequently, however, the dialogue that takes place in the framework of the laws is covert or indirect. This is apparent when the lawgivers intervene in the contents of the laws for the sake of the addressees, demonstrating that when they composed the laws the addressees' world and needs were in the forefront of their minds.[8] Communicative and dialogical laws not only establish binding norms; the commanding and coercive elements are not their sole, nor even their chief component. Such laws appeal to the consciousness of the addressees and invite their response to their substance.

---

5. Such, for example, is the lengthy statement made by the father of the young woman accused of having sexual intercourse before her marriage (Deut 22:16–17a), discussed in chapter 3. His statement adds nothing from the factual point of view and therefore does not contribute to the formation of the legal norm (only the presentation of the acquitting evidence—the daughter's stained garment—has legal significance). Nevertheless, it still appears in the law, since, after all, those were the father's verbatim statements.

6. We can virtually observe the fight described in the law of the woman who seized the man's genitals (Deut 25:11–12) through the woman's eyes as well (as we showed in our discussion in chapter 5).

7. Recall, for example, the law of the pauper (Deut 15:9–11), which we referred to in chapters 2 and 3, and the response of the lawgiver to the protagonist's internal speech.

8. Here one can recall, for example, the Priestly lawgiver's tendency to add "headings" and "summary comments" in some of the laws (see our discussion in chapter 2).

My following comments relate to us, the readers of the laws. I do not know whether I have fulfilled the promise I made in the introduction, that the narrative reading would be much more enjoyable than the legal reading. But I have no doubt, and this therefore is my next conclusion, that a narrative reading provides a rich and emotionally stimulating reading experience, which allows the reader to participate actively in the process of reading. The focus on events and characters, on the relationships between the characters and between the lawgivers and their addressees, invites us to experience an entire spectrum of emotions, positive and negative: identification, satisfaction, joy, relief, sorrow, anger, compassion, fear. The narrative reading does not allow us to remain affectively "neutral," because it focuses on the way the laws give voice to the feelings and responses of the characters and of the lawgivers. We fill in informational gaps, reconstruct a fuller version of the events out of the brief and elliptical descriptions, and draw analogies between the situations depicted in the laws and other human situations with which we are familiar. Is this enjoyable? For me it is.

The final necessary conclusion relates to the comparison between the casuistic laws of the Pentateuch and those of the other ancient Near Eastern law collections. I must preface my conclusion by saying that the former do not display a uniform style; we pointed out the different characteristics of the casuistic laws in each of the three law collections (the Book of the Covenant, the Deuteronomic Code, and the Priestly Code). The "foreign" law collections should also not be viewed monolithically, as each of them (Sumerian, Babylonian, Assyrian, and Hittite) has its own characteristic style and formulations. Nevertheless, one can undoubtedly point out a significant difference between the laws of the Pentateuch as a whole and the "foreign" laws, which relates to the way in which narrative means are employed. The difference is chiefly quantitative, but ultimately it reflects a qualitative difference.

The "foreign" laws are also reality-mimicking laws; they too give expression now and again to the voice of the characters. But they do not display the broad variety of narrative means that promote an illusion of reality, as the laws of the Pentateuch do. They do not, for example, contain (numerous and diverse) references to the inner life of the characters, which in addition to being a means of characterization also enhance the realism of the descriptions. Here and there the "foreign" laws do reveal the intervention of the lawgivers in the materials of the laws. But they do not contain the "intervention mechanisms" we encounter in the laws of the Pentateuch, which render them into normative-communicative texts.[9] In brief, the essential difference between the

---

9. It is sufficient here to mention the conspicuous difference between a motive clause of the *aššum* type (the "because clause"), which appears in a number of the foreign laws, and the rich and diverse motive clauses that appear in many of the Pentateuchal laws. The

narrativity of the casuistic laws of the Pentateuch and that of the ancient Near Eastern laws is defined by two parameters: the ability to enhance the mimetic illusion and the ability (or better said the desire) to conduct a dialogue by way of legal texts. The enhanced narrative qualities of the Pentateuchal laws are certainly (also) a result of the fact that they are embedded within a narrative framework; they too, serve the purpose of the biblical narrator, just as the stories do.

---

former type of clause serves as a means of emphasis (rather than a motive clause), while the latter clauses (usually) expose the positions and the views of the lawgivers, presenting the rationale of the law and serving a clear persuasive function.

Bibliography

Alt, Albrecht. "The Origins of Israelite Law." In *Essays on Old Testament History and Religion*, 79–132. Translated by R. A. Wilson. Garden City, N.Y.: Doubleday, 1967.
Alter, Robert. *The Art of Biblical Narrative*. New York: Basic Books, 1981.
———. *The Art of Biblical Poetry*. New York: Basic Books, 1985.
Anbar, Moshe. "L'influence Deutéronomique sur le Code de L'Alliance: le cas d'Exodus 21:12-17." *Zeitschrift für Altorientalische und Biblische Rechtsgeschichte* 5 (1999): 165–66.
Aristotle. *Aristotle's Poetics*. Translated by J. Hutton. New York: W. W. Norton, 1982.
Austin, John L. *How to Do Things with Words*. William James Lectures 1955. London: Oxford University Press, 1975.
Bach, Alice. "Good to the Last Drop: Viewing the Sotah (Numbers 5. 11-31) as the Glass Half Empty and Wondering How to View It Half Full." In *The New Literary Criticism and the Hebrew Bible*, edited by David J. A. Clines and J. Cheryl Exum, 26–54. JSOTSup 143. Sheffield: JSOT Press, 1993.
Bakhtin, Mikhail. "Discourse in the Novel." In *The Dialogic Imagination: Four Essays by M. M. Bakhtin*, edited by M. Holquist, translated by C. Emerson and M. Holquist, 259–422. Austin: University of Texas Press, 1981.
Bal, Mieke. *Narratology: Introduction to the Theory of Narrative*. Translated by C. van Boheemen. Toronto: University of Toronto Press, 1985.
———. "The Point of Narratology." *Poetics Today* 11 (1990): 727–53.
Bar-Efrat, Shimeon. *Narrative Art in the Bible*. Translated by D. Shefer-Vanson in conjuction with the author. JSOTSup 70. Bible and Literature Series 17. Sheffield: Almond, 1989.
Barmash, Pamela. *Homicide in the Biblical World*. Cambridge/New York: Cambridge University Press, 2005.
———. "The Narrative Quandary: Cases of Law in Literature." *VT* 54 (2004): 1–16.
Barth, John. "Tales within Tales within Tales." *Antaeus* 43 (1981): 45–63.
Bartor, Assnat. "The 'Juridical Dialogue': A Literary-Judicial Pattern." *VT* 53 (2003): 445–64.
———. "Reading Law as Narrative: A Study in the Casuistic Laws of the Pentateuch" (in Hebrew). In *Igud, Selected Essays in Jewish Studies*, edited by

B. Schwartz, A. Melamed, and A. Shemesh, 1:51–70. Jerusalem: World Union of Jewish Studies, 2008.

———. "The Representation of Speech in the Casuistic Laws of the Pentateuch: The Phenomenon of Combined Discourse." *JBL* 126 (2007): 231–49.

Bellefontaine, Elizabeth. "Deuteronomy 21:18–21: Reviewing the Case of the Rebellious Son." *JSOT* 13 (1979): 13–31.

Ben-Dov, Jonathan. "The Poor's Curse: Exodus XXII 20–26 and Curse Literature in the Ancient World." *VT* 56 (2006): 431–51.

Berlin, Adele. *The Dynamics of Biblical Parallelism*. Bloomington: Indiana University Press, 1985.

———. "Numinous Nomos: On the Relationship between Narrative and Law." In *"A Wise and Discerning Mind": Essays in Honor of Burke O. Long*, edited by Saul M. Olyan and Robert C. Culley, 25–31. Brown Judaic Studies 325. Providence: Brown Judaic Studies, 2000.

———. *Poetics and Interpretation of Biblical Narrative*. Bible and Literature Series 9. Sheffield: Almond, 1983.

———. "Shared Rhetorical Features in Biblical and Sumerian Literature." *JANES* 10 (1978): 35–42.

Bialik, Chaim Nachman. "Halacha and Aggadah." In *Contemporary Jewish Record*, vol. 7. Translated by L. Simon. New York: American Jewish Committee, 1944.

Binder, Guyora, and Robert Weisberg. *Literary Criticisms of Law*. Princeton, N.J.: Princeton University Press, 2000.

Boecker, Hans J. *Law and the Administration of Justice in the Old Testament and Ancient East*. Translated by Jeremy Moise. London: SPCK, 1980.

Borochovsky, Esther. "The Specific Meaning of Verbs: Incorporation of Arguments and Fusion of Downgraded Predicates." [In Hebrew.] Diss., Tel Aviv University, 1988.

Bosworth, David A. *The Story within a Story in Biblical Hebrew Narrative*. CBQ Monograph Series 45. Washington, D.C.: Catholic Biblical Association of America, 2008.

Bottéro, Jean. *Mesopotamia: Writing, Reasoning, and the Gods*. Translated by Z. Bahrani and M. Van De Mieroop. Chicago/London: University of Chicago Press, 1992.

Braulik, Georg. *The Theology of Deuteronomy: Collected Essays of Georg Braulik*. Translated by U. Lindblad. Dallas: BIBAL, 1994.

Brichto, Herbert C. *Toward a Grammar of Biblical Poetics: Tales of the Prophets*. New York: Oxford University Press, 1992.

Briggs, Richard S. "Reading the Sotah Text (Numbers 5:11–31): Holiness and a Hermeneutic Fit for Suspicion." *Biblical Interpretation* 17 (2009): 288–319.

Bright, John. "The Apodictic Prohibition: Some Observations." *JBL* 92 (1973): 185–204.

Brin, Gershon. *The Concept of Time in the Bible and the Dead Sea Scrolls*. Studies on the Texts of the Desert of Judah 39. Leiden/Boston: Brill, 2001.

———. "The Formula 'If He Shall Not (Do)' and the Problem of Sanctions in Biblical Law." In *Pomegranates and Golden Bells: Studies in Biblical, Jewish and Near Eastern Ritual, Law, and Literature in Honor of Jacob Milgrom*, edited by David P. Wright, David Noel Freedman, and Avi Hurvitz, 341–62. Winona Lake, Ind.: Eisenbrauns, 1995.

———. *Studies in Biblical Law: From the Hebrew Bible to the Dead Sea Scrolls*. Translated by Jonathan Chipman. JSOTSup 176. Sheffield: Sheffield Academic Press, 1994.

Brooks, Peter. "Narrativity of the Law." *Law and Literature* 14 (2002): 1–10.

Brooks, Peter, and Paul Gewirtz, eds. *Law's Stories, Narrative and Rhetoric in the Law*. New Haven: Yale University Press, 1996.

Brueggemann, Walter. *Deuteronomy*. Abingdon Old Testament Commentaries. Nashville: Abingdon, 2001.

Bruner, Jerome S. *Acts of Meaning*. Jerusalem-Harvard Lectures. Cambridge, Mass.: Harvard University Press, 1990.

———. "The Narrative Construction of Reality." In *Narrative Intelligence*, edited by Michael Mateas and Phoebe Sengers, 41–62. Amsterdam/Philadelphia: John Benjamins, 2003.

Burnside, Jonathan P. *The Signs of Sin: Seriousness of Offence in Biblical Law*. JSOTSup 364. Sheffield: JSOT Press, 2003.

Cardozo, Benjamin. *Law and Literature and Other Essays and Addresses*. New York: Harcourt, Brace, 1931.

Carmichael, Calum. *Illuminating Leviticus: A Study of its Laws and Institutions in the Light of Biblical Narratives*. Baltimore: Johns Hopkins University Press, 2006.

———. *Law and Narrative in the Bible: The Evidence of the Deuteronomic Laws and the Decalogue*. Ithaca, N.Y.: Cornell University Press, 1985.

———. *The Spirit of Biblical Law*. The Spirit of the Laws. Athens: University of Georgia Press, 1996.

Cassuto, Umberto. *A Commentary on the Book of Exodus*. Translated by Israel Abrahams. Jerusalem: Magnes, 1967.

Chatman, Seymour. *Story and Discourse: Narrative Structure in Fiction and Film*. Ithaca, N.Y.: Cornell University Press, 1978.

Chavel, Simeon. "Law and Narrative in Four Oracular Novellae in the Pentateuch." [In Hebrew.] Diss., The Hebrew University, Jerusalem, 2006.

Childs, Brevard S. *The Book of Exodus*. OTL. Philadelphia: Westminster, 1974.

Cohen, Chaim. "The Phenomenon of Negative Parallelism and Its Implications for the Study of Biblical Poetry" (in Hebrew). *Beer-sheva* 3 (1988): 69–107.

Cohen, Yoram. *Taboos and Prohibitions in Hittite Society: A Study of the Hittite Expression natta āra ('not permitted')*. Texte der Hethiter 24. Heidelberg: Universitatsverlag C. Winter, 2002.

Cover, Robert. "Nomos and Narrative." *Harvard Law Review* 97 (1983): 4–68.

Dällenbach, Lucien. *The Mirror in the Text*. Translated by Jeremy Whiteley with Emma Hughes. Chicago: University of Chicago Press, 1989.

Daube, David. *Ancient Jewish Law.* Leiden: Brill, 1981.
———. *Studies in Biblical Law.* 2nd ed. New York: Ktav, 1969.
Davies, Eryl W. *Numbers.* NCBC. London: M. Pickering, 1995.
De Vries, Simon J. "The Development of the Deuteronomic Promulgation Formula." *Biblica* 55 (1974): 301–16.
Dick, Michael B. "Job 31: The Oath of Innocence and the Sage." *ZAW* 95 (1983): 31–53.
Diengott, Nilli. *Poetics of Narrative Fiction,* vol 2. [In Hebrew.] Tel Aviv: The Open University Press, 1988.
Dion, Paul E. "Deuteronomy 13: The Suppression of Alien Religious Propaganda in Israel during the Late Monarchical Era." In *Law and Ideology in Monarchic Israel,* edited by Baruch Halpern and Deborah W. Hobson, 147–217. JSOTSup 124. Sheffield: JSOT Press, 1991.
Driver, Godfrey Rolles, and John Charles Miles. *The Babylonian Laws,* vol. 1, *Legal Commentary.* Oxford: Clarendon, 1952.
Driver, Samuel Rolles. *The Book of Exodus: In the Revised Version.* 1911. Repr., Cambridge: Cambridge University Press, 1953.
———. *A Critical and Exegetical Commentary on Deuteronomy.* ICC. 3rd ed. Edinburgh: T&T Clark, 1902.
Dworkin, Ronald. "Law as Interpretation." In *The Politics of Interpretation, Critical Inquiry* 9 (1982–83): 179–200.
———. *Law's Empire.* Cambridge, Mass.: Belknap Press, 1986.
Edwards, Derek. *Discourse and Cognition.* London: SAGE, 1997.
Eslinger, Lyle. "The Case of an Immodest Lady Wrestler in Deuteronomy XXV 11–12." *VT* 31 (1981): 269–81.
Ewen, Yosef. "Writer, Narrator, and Implied Author" (in Hebrew). *Hasifrut* 18–19 (1974): 137–63.
Farber, Daniel A., and Suzanna Sherry. "Telling Stories Out of School: An Essay on Legal Narratives." *Stanford Law Review* 45 (1993): 807–55.
Fisch, Harold. *Poetry with a Purpose: Biblical Poetics and Interpretation.* Indiana Studies in Biblical Literature. Bloomington: Indiana University Press, 1988.
Fish, Stanley. *Doing What Comes Naturally: Change, Rhetoric and the Practice of Theory in Literary and Legal Studies.* Post-contemporary Interventions. Durham, N.C.: Duke University Press, 1989.
———. "Working on the Chain Gang: Interpretation in the Law and in Literary Criticism." In *The Politics of Interpretation, Critical Inquiry* 9 (1982–83): 201–16.
Fishbane, Michael. "Accusations of Adultery: A Study of Law and Scribal Practice in Numbers 5:11–31." *HUCA* 45 (1974): 25–45.
———. "Biblical Colophons, Textual Criticism and Legal Analogies." *CBQ* 42 (1980): 438–49.
———. *Biblical Interpretation in Ancient Israel.* Oxford: Clarendon, 1985.
Fisher, Walter R. *Human Communication as Narration: Toward a Philosophy of*

Reason, Value, and Action. 2nd ed. Columbia: University of South Carolina Press, 1989.

Flavius Josephus. *See* Josephus.

Fleishman, Joseph. *Parents and Children in Biblical and Ancient Near Eastern Law.* [In Hebrew.] Jerusalem: Magnes, 1999.

Follingstad, Carl M. *Deictic Viewpoint in Biblical Hebrew Text: A Syntagmatic and Paradigmatic Analysis of the Particle Kî.* Dallas: SIL International, 2001.

Frymer-Kensky, Tikva. "The Strange Case of the Suspected Sotah (Numbers V 11–31)." *VT* 34 (1989): 11–26.

Gemser, Berend. "The Importance of the Motive Clause in the Old Testament Law." In *Congress Volume: Copenhagen 1953*, 50–66. SVT 1. Leiden: Brill, 1953.

Genette, Gérard. *Narrative Discourse: An Essay in Method.* Translated by J. E. Lewin. Ithaca, N.Y.: Cornell University Press, 1980.

Gerstenberger, Erhard S. "Covenant and Commandment." *JBL* 84 (1965): 38–51.

Gilmer, Harry W. *The If-You Form in Israelite Law.* SBLDS 15. Missoula, Mont.: Scholars Press, 1975.

Gesenius, Wilhelm, and Emil Kautzsch. *Hebrew Grammar.* Translated by A. E. Cowley. Oxford: Clarendon, 1910.

Goldenberg, Gideon. *Studies in Semitic Linguistics: Selected Writings.* Jerusalem: Magnes, 1998.

Greenberg, Moshe. "The Biblical Concept of Asylum." *JBL* 78 (1959): 125–32.

Greenstein, Edward L. "Biblical Law." In *Back to the Sources: Reading the Classic Jewish Texts,* edited by Barry W. Holtz, 83–103. New York: Summit Books, 1984.

———. "Direct Discourse and Parallelism" (in Hebrew). *Studies in Bible and Biblical Exegesis (Presented to Uriel Simon)* 5 (2000): 33–40.

———. "A Forensic Understanding of the Speech from the Whirlwind." In *Texts, Temples, and Traditions: A Tribute to Menahem Haran,* edited by Michael V. Fox et al., 241–58. Winona Lake, Ind.: Eisenbrauns, 1996.

———. "Introduction and Annotations to the Book of Exodus (Shemot)." In *The HarperCollins Study Bible: A New Annotated Edition by the Society of Biblical Literature,* edited by Wayne A. Meeks et al. New York: HarperCollins, 1993.

———. "On the Genesis of Biblical Prose Narrative." *Prooftexts* 8 (1988): 347–54.

———. "The Poem on Wisdom in Job 28 in Its Conceptual and Literary Contexts." In *Job 28: Cognition in Context,* edited by Ellen van Wolde, 253–80. Biblical Interpretation Series 64. Leiden: Brill, 2003.

———. "Presenting Genesis 1, Constructively and Deconstructively." *Prooftexts* 21 (2001): 1–22.

———. "The Syntax of Saying 'Yes' in Biblical Hebrew." *JANES* 19 (1989): 51–59.

———. "The Torah as She Is Read." In *Essays on Biblical Method and Translation,* edited by Edward L. Greenstein, 29–51. Brown Judaic Studies 92. Atlanta: Scholars Press, 1989.

Gunn, David M., and Danna N. Fewell. *Narrative in the Hebrew Bible.* Oxford Bible Series. Oxford: Oxford University Press, 1993.

Halberstam, Chaya. "The Art of Biblical Law." *Prooftexts* 27 (2007): 345–64.

Halivni, David W. *Midrash, Mishnah, and Gemara: The Jewish Predilection for Justified Law.* Cambridge, Mass.: Harvard University Press, 1986.

Hallo, William W. "Biblical Abomination and Sumerian Taboos." *JQR* 76 (1985): 21–40.

———. "The Slandered Bride." In *Studies Presented to A. Leo Oppenheim, June 7, 1964,* edited by R. D. Briggs and J. A. Brinkman, 95–105. Chicago: Oriental Institute of the University of Chicago, 1964.

Held, Moshe. "The Action-Result (Factitive-Passive) Sequence of Identical Verbs in Biblical Hebrew and Ugaritic." *JBL* 84 (1965): 272–82.

Hertzig, Hanna. *The Fictional World: Mimesis vs. Artifice.* [In Hebrew.] Tel Aviv: The Open University Press, 1989.

Hoffman, Yair. "The Conception of 'Other Gods' in Deuteronomistic Literature." *Israel Oriental Studies* 14 (1994): 103–18.

———. *The Doctrine of Exodus in the Bible* [In Hebrew.] Tel Aviv: University Publishing Projects, 1983.

———. "'Pseudoepigraphic Constraints' in the Book of Deuteronomy" (in Hebrew). *Shnaton* 5–6 (1981–82): 41–54.

Hoffner, Harry A., Jr. *The Laws of the Hittites: A Critical Edition.* Documenta et monumenta Orientis antiqui 23. Leiden: Brill, 1997.

Houtman, Cornelis. *Exodus,* vol. 3. Historical Commentary on the Old Testament. Leuven: Peeters, 2000.

Humbert, Paul. "'Etendre la Main': Note de Lexicographie Hébraïque." *VT* 12 (1962): 383–95.

Hurowitz, Victor Avigdor. "'His master shall pierce his ear with an awl' (Exodus 21.6): Marking Slaves in the Bible in Light of Akkadian Sources." *Proceedings—American Academy for Jewish Research* 58 (1992): 47–77.

———. *Inu Anum ṣirum: Literary Structures in the Non-Juridical Sections of Codex Hammurabi.* Occasional Publications of the Samuel Noah Kramer Fund 15. Philadelphia: University Museum, 1994.

Isser, Stanley. "Two Traditions: The Law of Exodus 21:22–23 Revisited." *CBQ* 52 (1990): 30–45.

Jackson, Bernard S. "The Ceremonial and the Judicial: Biblical Law as Sign and Symbol." *JSOT* 30 (1984): 25–50.

———. *Law, Fact, and Narrative Coherence.* Legal Semiotics Monographs 1. Roby, Merseyside, U.K.: Deborah Charles, 1988.

———. "Literal Meaning: Semantics and Narrative in Biblical Law and Modern Jurisprudence." *International Journal for the Semiotics of Law/Revue International de Sémiotique Juridique* 13 (2000): 433–57.

———. "Models in Legal History: The Case of Biblical Law." *Journal of Law and Religion* 18 (2002): 1–30.

———. "Narrative Theories and Legal Discourse." In *Narrative in Culture: The Uses of Storytelling in the Sciences, Philosophy and Literature*, edited by Cristopher Nash, 23–50. London: Routledge, 1994.

———. "The Problem of Exodus 21: 22–5 (Ius Talionis)." In Bernard S. Jackson, *Essays in Jewish and Comparative Legal History*, 75–107. Studies in Judaism in Late Antiquity 10. Leiden: Brill, 1975.

———. *Studies in the Semiotics of Biblical Law*. JSOTSup 314. Sheffield: Sheffield Academic Press, 2000.

———. *Theft in Early Jewish Law*. Oxford: Clarendon, 1972.

———. *Wisdom-Laws: A Study of the Mishpatim of Exodus 21:1–22:16*. Oxford: Oxford University Press, 2006.

Jacob, Benno. *The Second Book of the Bible: Exodus*. Translated by Walter Jacob. Hoboken, N.J.: Ktav, 1992.

Japhet, Sara. "The Relationship between the Legal Corpora in the Pentateuch in Light of Manumission Laws." *Scripta Hierosolymitana* 31 (1986): 63–89.

Jeon, Jaeyoung. "Two Laws in the Sotah Passage (Num. V 11–31)." *VT* 57 (2007): 181–207.

Jepsen, Alfred. *Untersuchungen zum Bundesbuch*. Beiträge zum Wissenschaft vom Alten und Neuen Testament 3.5. Stuttgart: Kohlhammer, 1927.

Joosten, Jan. "Do the Finite Verbal Forms in Biblical Hebrew Express Aspect?" *JANES* 29 (2002): 49–70.

———. "The Predicative Participle in Biblical Hebrew." *Zeitschrift für Althebräistik* 2 (1989): 128–59.

Josephus. *Antiquities*. Vol. 4 of *Josephus in Nine Volumes*, translated by H. St. J. Thackeray. Loeb Classical Library. Cambridge, Mass.: Harvard University Press, 1962–65.

Joüon, Paul. *A Grammar of Biblical Hebrew*. Translated and revised by Takamitsu Muraoka. Subsidia biblica 14.1–2. Rome: Pontificio Instituto Biblico, 1996.

Kahn, Paul W. *Law and Love: The Trials of King Lear*. New Haven: Yale University Press, 2000.

Kitz, Anne Marie. "Saraʿat Accusations and the Sociology of Exclusion." Ph.D. diss., Johns Hopkins University, 1994.

Klein, Jacob, and Yitschak Sefati. "The Concept of 'Abomination' in Mesopotamian Literature and the Bible" (in Hebrew). *Beer-Sheva* 3 (1988): 131–48.

Kogut, Simcha. "On the Meaning and Syntactical Status of 'hine' in Biblical Hebrew." *Scripta Hierosolymitana* 31 (1986): 133–54.

Kruger, Paul A. "The Removal of the Sandal in Deuteronomy XXV 9: A Rite of Passage?" *VT* 46 (1996): 534–39.

Kugel, James L. *The Idea of Biblical Poetry: Parallelism and Its History*. New Haven: Yale University Press, 1981.

Lambert, Wilfred G. *Babylonian Wisdom Literature*. Oxford: Clarendon, 1960.

LaRue, Lewis H. *Constitutional Law as Fiction: Narrative in the Rhetoric of Authority*. University Park: Pennsylvania State University Press, 1995.

Levine, Baruch A. *Leviticus-Va-yikra: The Traditional Hebrew Text with the New JPS Translation.* JPS Torah Commentary. Philadelphia: Jewish Publication Society, 1989.

———. *Numbers 1-20: A New Translation with Introduction and Commentary.* AB 4. New York: Doubleday, 1993.

Levinson, Sanford. "Law as Literature." In *Interpreting Law and Literature: A Hermeneutic Reader,* edited by Sanford Levinson and Steven Mailloux, 155-73. Evanston, Ill.: Northwestern University Press, 1988.

Licht, Jacob. "The Biblical Claim of Establishment" (in Hebrew). *Shnaton* 3-4 (1980-81): 98-128.

———. *A Commentary on the Book of Numbers, 1-10.* [In Hebrew.] Jerusalem: Magnes, 1985.

Liss, Hanna. "Kanon und Fiktion: Zur literarischen Funktion Biblischer Rechtstexte." *Biblische Notizen* 121 (2004): 7-38.

Loewenstamm, Samuel E. "Exodus 21: 22-25." *VT* 27 (1977): 352-60.

Lohfink, Norbert. *Das Hauptgebot: Eine Untersuchung literarischer Einleitungsfragen zu Dtn. 5-11.* Analecta Biblica 20. Rome: Pontificio Instituto Biblico, 1963.

Mabee, Charles. "Jacob and Laban: The Structure of Judicial Proceedings (Genesis 31, 25-42)." *VT* 30 (1980): 192-207.

Malul, Meir. *Knowledge, Control, and Sex: Studies in Biblical Thought, Culture, and Worldview.* Tel Aviv/Jaffa: Archaeological Center Publication, 2002.

———. *Studies in Mesopotamian Legal Symbolism.* Alter Orient und Altes Testament 221. Kevelaer: Butzon & Bercker, 1988.

Manley, George Thomas. *The Book of the Law: Studies in the Date of Deuteronomy.* London: Tyndale, 1957.

Marcus, David. "Juvenile Delinquency in the Bible and the Ancient Near East." *JANES* 13 (1981): 31-52.

Mayes, A. D. H. *Deuteronomy: Based on the Revised Standard Version.* NCBC. 2nd ed. Grand Rapids: Eerdmans, 1981.

McCarthy, Dennis J. "The Uses of wᵉhinnēh in Biblical Hebrew." *Biblica* 61 (1980): 330-42.

McEvenue, Sean E. *The Narrative Style of the Priestly Writer.* Analecta Biblica 50. Rome: Biblical Institute Press, 1971.

Meier, Samuel A. *Speaking of Speaking: Marking Direct Discourse in the Hebrew Bible.* SVT 46. Leiden: Brill, 1992.

Milgrom, Jacob. *Leviticus 1-16: A New Translation with Introduction and Commentary.* AB 3. New York: Doubleday, 1991.

———. *Leviticus 17-22: A New Translation with Introduction and Commentary.* AB 3A. New York: Doubleday, 2000.

———. *Numbers-Be-midbar: The Traditional Hebrew Text with the New JPS Translation.* JPS Torah Commentary. Philadelphia: Jewish Publication Society, 1990.

———. "Sancta Contagion and Altar/City Asylum." In *Congress Volume: Vienna 1980*, edited by J. A. Emerton, 278–310. SVT 32. Leiden: Brill, 1981.
Miller, Cynthia L. *The Representation of Speech in Biblical Hebrew Narrative: A Linguistic Analysis*. Harvard Semitic Monographs 55. Atlanta: Scholars Press, 1996.
Mitchell, W. J. Thomas, ed. *On Narrative*. Chicago: University of Chicago Press, 1981.
Moran, William L. "Ancient Near Eastern Background of the Love of God in Deuteronomy." *CBQ* 25 (1963): 77–87.
Muffs, Yochanan. *Love and Joy: Law, Language and Religion in Ancient Israel*. New York: Jewish Theological Seminary of America, 1992.
———. *Studies in the Aramaic Legal Papyri from Elephantine*. Leiden: Brill, 1969.
Nash, Cristopher, ed. *Narrative in Culture: The Uses of Storytelling in the Sciences, Philosophy and Literature*. Warwick Studies in Philosophy and Literature. London: Routledge, 1994.
Nasuti, Harry P. "Identity, Identification and Imitation: The Narrative Hermeneutics of Biblical Law." *Journal of Law and Religion* 4 (1986): 9–23.
Nelson, Richard D. *Deuteronomy: A Commentary*. OTL. Louisville: Westminster John Knox, 2002.
Noth, Martin. *Exodus: A Commentary*. Translated by J. S. Bowden. OTL. London: SCM, 1962.
Nussbaum, Martha C. *Poetic Justice: The Literary Imagination and Public Life*. Boston: Beacon, 1995.
Paran, Meir. *Forms of the Priestly Style in the Pentateuch*. [In Hebrew.] Jerusalem: Magnes, 1989.
Patrick, Dale. *Old Testament Law*. Atlanta: John Knox, 1985.
———, ed. *Thinking Biblical Law*. Semeia 45. Atlanta: Scholars Press, 1989.
Paul, Shalom M. *Studies in the Book of the Covenant in the Light of Cuneiform and Biblical Law*. SVT 18. Leiden: Brill, 1970.
Peer, Willie van, and Seymour B. Chatman, eds. *New Perspectives on Narrative Perspective*. SUNY Series, The Margins of Literature. Albany: State University of New York Press, 2001.
Phillips, Anthony. *Ancient Israel's Criminal Law: A New Approach to the Decalogue*. Oxford: Blackwell, 1970.
———. "The Laws of Slavery: Exodus 21:2–11." *JSOT* 30 (1984): 51–66.
Philo. *Philo*, vol. 7, *On the Special Laws*. Translated by F. H. Colson. Loeb Classical Library. Cambridge, Mass.: Harvard University Press, 1950.
Polak, Frank. *Biblical Narrative: Aspects of Art and Design*. [In Hebrew.] Jerusalem: Bialik Institute, 1994.
———. "The Style of the Dialogue in Biblical Narrative" (in Hebrew). *Teʿuda* 16–17 (2001): 47–102.
———. "The Style of the Dialogue in Biblical Prose Narrative." *JANES* 28 (2002): 53–95.

Polzin, Robert. *Moses and the Deuteronomist: Deuteronomy, Joshua, Judges.* A Literary Study of the Deuteronomic History 1. New York: Seabury, 1980.

Posner, Richard. *Law and Literature: A Misunderstood Relation.* Cambridge, Mass.: Harvard University Press, 1988.

Prince, Gerald. *A Grammar of Stories: An Introduction.* De proprietatibus litterarum, Series maior 13. The Hague: Mouton, 1973.

———. *Narratology: The Form and Functioning of Narrative.* Janua linguarum, Series maior 108. Berlin: Mouton, 1982.

Propp, William H. C. *Exodus 19–40: A New Translation with Introduction and Commentary.* AB 2A. New York: Doubleday, 2006.

Rimmon-Kenan, Shlomith. *Narrative Fiction: Contemporary Poetics.* New Accents. London: Methuen, 1983.

Rofé, Alexander. *Introduction to the Book of Deuteronomy.* [In Hebrew.] Jerusalem: Academon, 1988.

———. "The Laws of Warfare in the Book of Deuteronomy: Their Origins, Intent, and Positivity." *JSOT* 32 (1985): 23–44.

Roth, Martha. "The Because Clause: Punishment Rationalization in Mesopotamian Laws." In *Veenhof Anniversary Volume: Studies Presented to K. R. Veenhof on the Occasion of His Sixty-Fifth Birthday,* edited by W. H. van Soldt, 407–12. Leiden: Nederlands Instituut voor het Nabije Oosten, 2001.

———. "Hammurabi's Wronged Man." *JAOS* 122 (2002): 38–45.

———. *Law Collections from Mesopotamia and Asia Minor.* 2nd ed. SBLWAW 6. Atlanta: Society of Biblical Literature, 1997.

Sarna, Nahum. *Exodus-Shemot: The Traditional Hebrew Text with the New JPS Translation.* JPS Torah Commentary. Philadelphia: Jewish Publication Society, 1991.

Savran, George W. "The Character as Narrator in Biblical Narrative." *Prooftexts* 5 (1985): 1–17.

———. *Telling and Retelling: Quotation in Biblical Narrative.* Indiana Studies in Biblical Literature. Bloomington: Indiana University Press, 1988.

Schwartz, Baruch. *The Holiness Legislation: Studies in the Priestly Code.* [In Hebrew.] Jerusalem: Magnes, 1999.

Seebass, Horst. "Noch Einmal zum Depositenrecht Ex 22, 6–14." In *Gottes Recht als Lebensraum: Festschrift für Hans Jochen Boecker,* edited by Peter Mommer et al., 21–31. Neukirchen-Vluyn: Neukirchener Verlag, 1993.

Sekuler, Robert, and Randolph Blake. *Perception.* 2nd ed. New York: McGraw-Hill, 1990.

Simon, Uriel. "The Poor Man's Ewe-Lamb: An Example of a Juridical Parable." *Biblica* 48 (1967): 207–42.

Simon-Shoshan, Moshe. "*Halachah Lema'aseh:* Narrative and Legal Discourse in the Mishnah." Ph.D. diss., University of Pennsylvania, 2005.

Sonnet, Jean-Pierre. *The Book within the Book: Writing in Deuteronomy.* Biblical Interpretation Series 14. Leiden: Brill, 1997.

Sonsino, Rifat. *Motive Clauses in Hebrew Law: Biblical Forms and Near Eastern Parallels.* SBLDS 45. Chico, Calif.: Scholars Press, 1980.
Sprinkle, Joe. *"The Book of the Covenant": A Literary Approach.* JSOTSup 174. Sheffield: JSOT Press, 1994.
Sterne, Laurence. *The Life and Opinions of Tristram Shandy, Gentelman.* 1767. World's Classics. Oxford: Clarendon, 1983.
Sternberg, Meir. "Between the Truth and the Whole Truth in Biblical Narrative: The Rendering of Inner Life by Telescoped Inside View and Interior Monologue" (in Hebrew). *Hasifrut* 29 (1979): 110-46.
———. "Language, World and Perspective in Biblical Art: Free Indirect Discourse and Modes of Covert Penetration" (in Hebrew). *Hasifrut* 32 (1983): 131-88.
———. *The Poetics of Biblical Narrative: Ideological Literature and the Drama of Reading.* Indiana Literary Biblical Series. Bloomington: Indiana University Press, 1985.
Thompson, Leonard L. *Introducing Biblical Literature: A More Fantastic Country.* Englewood Cliffs, N.J.: Prentice-Hall, 1978.
Tigay, Jeffrey H. *Deuteronomy-Devarim: The Traditional Hebrew Text with the New JPS Translation.* JPS Torah Commentary. Philadelphia: Jewish Publication Society, 1996.
Trible, Phyllis. "Bringing Miriam Out of the Shadows." *Bible Review* 5, no. 1 (1989): 14–25, 34.
Wallace, Martin. *Recent Theories of Narrative.* Ithaca, N.Y.: Cornell University Press, 1986.
Walsh, Jerome T. "'You Shall Cut Off Her ... Palm'? A Reexamination of Deuteronomy 25:11-12." *JSS* 49 (2004): 47–58.
Waltke, Bruce K., and M. O'Connor. *An Introduction to Biblical Hebrew Syntax.* Winona Lake, Ind.: Eisenbrauns, 1990.
Ward, Ian. *Law and Literature: Possibilities and Perspectives.* New York: Cambridge University Press, 1995.
Watts, James W. *Reading Law: The Rhetorical Shaping of the Pentateuch.* Biblical Seminar 59. Sheffield: Sheffield Academic Press, 1999.
———. *Ritual and Rhetoric in Leviticus: From Sacrifice to Scripture.* Cambridge: Cambridge University Press, 2007.
Weinfeld, Moshe. *Deuteronomy and the Deuteronomic School.* Oxford: Clarendon, 1972. Repr., Winona Lake, Ind.: Eisenbrauns, 1992.
———. "The Loyalty Oath in the Ancient Near East." *Ugarit-Forschungen* 8 (1976): 379–414.
———. "The Origin of the Apodictic Law." *VT* 23 (1973): 63–75.
———. "The Temple Scroll or 'The Law of the King.'" In Moshe Weinfeld, *Normative and Sectarian Judaism in the Second Temple Period,* 158–85. Library of Second Temple Studies 54. London: T&T Clark, 2005.
Weisberg, Richard. *Poetics and Other Strategies of Law and Literature.* New York: Columbia University Press, 1992.

Weiss, Meir. *The Bible from Within: The Method of Total Interpretation*. [In Hebrew.] Jerusalem: Mosad Bialik, 1962.

———. "On Narrative Art in the Bible" (in Hebrew). In *Mikraot ke-kavanatam: An Anthology*, 293–311. Jerusalem: Mosad Bialik, 1987.

West, Robin. *Narrative, Authority, and Law*. Law, Meaning, and Violence. Ann Arbor: University of Michigan Press, 1993.

Westbrook, Raymond. "Biblical and Cuneiform Law Codes." In *Folk Law: Essays in the Theory and Practice of Lex Non Scripta*, edited by A. D. Renteln and A. Dundes, 1:485–94. 2 vols. Madison: University of Wisconsin Press 1995.

———. "Lex Talionis and Exodus 21, 22–25." *RB* 93 (1986): 52–69.

———. "The Deposit Laws of Exodus 22, 6–12." *ZAW* 106 (1994): 390–403.

———. "The Female Slave." In *Gender and Law in the Hebrew Bible and the Ancient Near East*, edited by Victor H. Matthews et al., 214–38. JSOTSup 262. Sheffield: Sheffield Academic Press, 1998.

———. "A Matter of Life and Death." *JANES* 25 (1997): 61–70.

———. *Property and the Family in Biblical Law*. JSOTSup 113. Sheffield: JSOT Press, 1991.

White, Edward J. *Commentaries on the Law in Shakespeare*. 2nd ed. St. Louis: F. H. Thomas Law Books, 1913.

White, Hayden. *The Content of the Form: Narrative, Discourse and Historical Representation*. Baltimore: Johns Hopkins University Press, 1987.

White, Hugh, ed. *Speech Act Theory and Biblical Criticism*. Semeia 41. Decatur, Ga.: Scholars Press, 1988.

White, James Boyd. *The Legal Imagination: Studies in the Nature of Legal Thought and Expression*. Boston: Little, Brown, 1973.

Wilson, John A. "The Oath in Ancient Egypt." *JNES* 7 (1948): 129–56.

Yamasaki, Gary. *Watching a Biblical Narrative: Point of View in Biblical Exegesis*. London: T&T Clark, 2007.

Yaron, Reuven. "Stylistic Conceits: The Negated Antonym." *JANES* 22 (1993): 141–48.

———. "Stylistic Conceits II: The Absolute Infinitive in Biblical Law." In *Pomegranates and Golden Bells: Studies in Biblical, Jewish and Near Eastern Ritual, Law, and Literature in Honor of Jacob Milgrom*, edited by David P. Wright, David Noel Freedman, and Avi Hurvitz, 449–60. Winona Lake, Ind.: Eisenbrauns, 1995.

Zakovitch, Yair. "The Book of the Covenant Interprets the Book of the Covenant: The 'Boomerang Phenomenon'" (in Hebrew). In *Texts, Temples, and Traditions: A Tribute to Menahem Haran*, edited by Michael V. Fox et al. Winona Lake, Ind.: Eisenbrauns, 1996.

Index of Authors

Alt, Albrecht	6, 9, 26	Cassuto, Umberto	26, 61, 62
Alter, Robert	12, 14, 72	Chatman, Seymour	4, 24, 51, 52, 163
Anbar, Moshe	28	Chavel, Simeon	12
Aristotle	5	Childs, Brevard S.	33, 95
Austin, John L.	93	Cohen, Chaim	72
		Cohen, Yoram	81
Bach, Alice	115, 146	Cover, Robert	2
Bakhtin, Mikhail	111, 125, 129		
Bal, Mieke	4, 5, 163	Dällenbach, Lucien	21
Bar-Efrat, Shimeon	12, 163	Daube, David	12, 26, 55, 61, 80, 110
Barmash, Pamela	12, 29		
Barth, John	18, 20	Davies, Eryl W.	116, 117
Bartor, Assnat	12, 67, 128	De Vries, Simon J.	50, 53
Bellefontaine, Elizabeth	100	Dick, Michael B.	114
Ben-Dov, Jonathan	127	Diengott, Nilli	18, 27
Berlin, Adele	8, 12, 14, 18, 71, 72, 171	Dion, Paul E.	81, 125, 129, 130
		Driver, Godfrey Rolles	58
Bialik, Chaim Nachman	2	Driver, Samuel Rolles	29, 42, 75, 76, 100, 103, 124, 143, 154, 156, 157
Binder, Guyora	3		
Blake, Randolph	135		
Boecker, Hans J.	32, 95		
Borochovsky, Esther	135	Dworkin, Ronald	3
Bosworth, David A.	21		
Bottéro, Jean	6	Edwards, Derek	4
Braulik, Georg	154	Eslinger, Lyle	149, 151
Brichto, Herbert C.	14	Ewen, Yosef	52
Briggs, Richard S.	146		
Bright, John	6	Farber, Daniel A.	5
Brin, Gershon	28, 31, 39, 53, 79	Fewell, Danna N.	81
Brooks, Peter	5	Fisch, Harold	14
Brueggemann, Walter	158, 159	Fishbane, Michael	61, 75, 76, 78, 79
Bruner, Jerome S.	4	Fisher, Walter R.	4
Burnside, Jonathan P.	110	Fish, Stanley	3
		Fleishman, Joseph	101
Cardozo, Benjamin	3	Follingstad, Carl M.	97, 114
Carmichael, Calum	12, 21	Frymer-Kensky, Tikva	146

Gemser, Berend	59	Kogut, Simcha	171
Genette, Gérard	4, 24, 163	Kruger, Paul A.	110
Gerstenberger, Erhard S.	40	Kugel, James L.	14, 72
Gesenius, Wilhelm	152		
Gewirtz, Paul	5	Lambert, Wilfred G.	47
Gilmer, Harry W.	9, 27, 40	LaRue, Lewis H.	5
Goldenberg, Gideon	96, 109	Levine, Baruch A.	113, 115, 117, 135, 146
Greenberg, Moshe	29		
Greenstein, Edward L.	1, 11, 18, 19, 21, 55, 70, 89, 97, 114, 123, 145	Levinson, Sanford	3
		Licht, Jacob	53, 111, 115, 117, 146
		Liss, Hanna	12
Greimas, A. J.	13	Loewenstamm, Samuel E.	65, 66
Gunn, David M.	81	Lohfink, Norbert	68
Halberstam, Chaya	13	Mabee, Charles	12
Halivni, David W.	57	Malul, Meir	135, 156
Hallo, William W.	81, 103	Manley, George Thomas	68
Held, Moshe	72	Marcus, David	100
Hertzig, Hanna	98	Mayes, A. D. H.	39, 54, 100
Hoffman, Yair	36, 52, 129, 158	McCarthy, Dennis J.	104, 171
Hoffner, Harry A., Jr.	28	McEvenue, Sean E.	77
Houtman, Cornelis	26, 62	Meier, Samuel A.	96
Humbert, Paul	152	Miles, John Charles	58
Hurowitz, Victor Avigdor	18, 58, 89	Milgrom, Jacob	30, 31, 32, 56, 57, 82, 103, 111, 112, 113, 115, 117, 135, 170
Isser, Stanley	65		
Jackson, Bernard S.	5, 7, 13, 14, 27, 28, 38, 39, 62, 64, 65, 66, 67, 76, 80, 83, 89, 93, 95, 114, 136, 144, 155	Mitchell, W. J. Thomas	5
		Moran, William L.	90
		Muffs, Yochanan	7, 63, 154, 156
		Nash, Cristopher	5
		Nasuti, Harry P.	7, 11, 17, 22
Jacob, Benno	26, 33, 34	Nelson, Richard D.	77, 82, 129, 158
Japhet, Sara	26, 156	Noth, Martin	29, 62
Jeon, Jaeyoung	79, 117	Nussbaum, Martha C.	3
Jepsen, Alfred	26		
Joosten, Jan	52	O'Connor, M.	119, 153
Josephus	65		
Joüon, Paul	153	Paran, Meir	77
		Patrick, Dale	10, 26, 27, 28, 90, 95
Kahn, Paul W.	2		
Kautzsch, Emil	152	Paul, Shalom M.	26, 28, 29, 61, 63, 65, 89
Kitz, Anne Marie	170		
Klein, Jacob	81	Peer, Willie van	163

Phillips, Anthony	26, 62, 151	Sterne, Laurence	52
Philo	65		
Polak, Frank	97, 106, 163	Thompson, Leonard L.	7
Polzin, Robert	20, 53, 55	Tigay, Jeffrey H.	42, 99, 109, 129, 138
Posner, Richard	3		
Prince, Gerald	4, 8	Trible, Phyllis	159
Propp, William H. C.	66, 144		
		Wallace, Martin	126
Rimmon-Kenan, Shlomith	8, 9, 20, 21, 24, 67, 85, 86, 126, 163	Walsh, Jerome T.	149
		Waltke, Bruce K.	119, 153
		Ward, Ian	3
		Watts, James W.	11, 13, 14, 20, 22, 35, 69
Rofé, Alexander	39, 91		
Roth, Martha	6, 28, 58, 59, 87	Weinfeld, Moshe	6, 41, 47, 68, 90, 91
Sarna, Nahum	27, 29, 33, 62, 65	Weisberg, Richard	3
Savran, George W.	18, 87	Weisberg, Robert	3
Schwartz, Baruch	12, 13, 56, 67	Weiss, Meir	12, 171
Seebass, Horst	95	Westbrook, Raymond	6, 62, 63, 66, 72, 96, 108, 114
Sefati, Yitschak	81		
Sekuler, Robert	135		
Sherry, Suzanna	5	West, Robin	3
Simon-Shoshan, Moshe	7	White, Edward J.	2
Simon, Uriel	12, 19	White, Hayden	5
Sonnet, Jean-Pierre	55	White, Hugh	93
Sonsino, Rifat	31, 35, 49, 57, 59	White, James Boyd	2
Sprinkle, Joe	12, 13, 26, 28, 29, 60, 62, 65, 66, 95	Wilson, John A.	114
		Yamasaki, Gary	163
Sternberg, Meir	12, 69, 87, 104, 120, 126, 145, 147, 150, 164, 171	Yaron, Reuven	34, 72
		Zakovitch, Yair	28

Index of Passages

Ancient Near Eastern Texts

Ana Ittishu III:10–16	99	LH 131	79
		LH 131–132	111
Hittite Laws		LH 132	79
HL 3–4	28, 136	LH 133b	72
HL 17–18	65	LH 136	59
HL 75	87	LH 137	59
HL 187–195	80	LH 141	61
		LH 142	87, 142
Laws of Eshnunna		LH 148	63
LE 6	136	LH 162–163	59
LE 8	6	LH 168	99
LE 12–13	72	LH 168–169	99
LE 22	87	LH 170	87
LE 24	83	LH 194	59
LE 26	83	LH 206	114
LE 28	72	LH 206–207	87, 135
LE 33	136	LH 207	28
LE 36	71	LH 209–214	65
LE 37	87, 114	LH 210	66
LE 54	64	LH 212	66
LE 58	83	LH 214	66
		LH 227	135, 136
Laws of Hammurabi		LH 229	48
LH 7	83	LH 232	59
LH 9	83, 87, 96, 97, 98	LH 251	64
		LH 265	136
LH 13	83	LH 282	89
LH 20	114	LH xlvii 59–78	51
LH 29	64	LH xlviii 3–19	58
LH 37	65	LH xlviii 59–94	51
LH 44	72		
LH 55	48	Laws of Lipit-Ishtar	
LH 61	72	LL 28	63, 144
LH 107	59	LL d–f	65
LH 126	87	LL e	66

Middle Assyrian Laws		MAL A 23–24	135
MAL A 5	87	MAL A 33	83
MAL A 8	151	MAL A 40	89
MAL A 12	87	MAL A 44	89
MAL A 18–19	87	MAL A 47	87
MAL A 22	87, 114	MAL A 50	66
MAL A 23	83	MAL A 50–52	65

Scripture

Genesis		42:38	66
1:31	126	43:4–5	113
3:14	113	44:29	66
4:10	32		
12:6	29	Exodus	
13:3	29	1:13–14	55
13:17	113	2:23	32
16:6	44	3:21–22	55
17:17	118	4:4	152
19:10	152	7:14	108
19:19	38	9:15	152
20:4	103	12:26–27	158
21:16	118	12:43	19
21:17–18	113	13:8–9	158
22:10	152	13:13	31
24:3	117	13:14–15	158
24:49	113	13:15	156
24:58	100	13:19	117
24:65	100	14:9	169
27:41	118	20:11	21
28:8	145	20:13	6
34:19	109	20:19–23:19	10, 24, 25
35:16	156	20:22–21:1	19
37:15	126	20:23–26	25
38	110	20:25b, 26b	61
38:7	145	21–23	1
41:3	144	21:2	25
41:4	144	21:2–6	1, 59, 86, 88, 141
41:19	144	21:4	26, 89
41:20	144	21:5	88
41:21	144	21:5a	34
41:27	144	21:7	63
42:4	66	21:7–11	60, 76
42:15–16	113	21:8	61, 62, 63, 141

INDEX OF PASSAGES

Exodus (*cont.*)		22:11	25
21:9	60	22:11a	34
21:10	63	22:12a	34
21:11	31, 63	22:17b	61
21:12	28, 29	22:18–19	28
21:12–14	27	22:21	21
21:13	29	22:21–22	147
21:13–14	28, 29, 185	22:21–27	31, 58
21:13a	136	22:21b	61
21:13b	136	22:22	34
21:14	30, 136	22:23	165
21:15	9	22:23–24	31
21:15–17	28	22:23b	33
21:17	101	22:24	23
21:18	66	22:25–26	86
21:18–19	67, 85, 174	22:25–27	33
21:18–21	25	22:26–27	126, 183
21:20b	34	22:27	165
21:21b	61	22:27a	61
21:22	34, 135	22:27b	34
21:22–23	23	22:29	75
21:22–25	26, 65	22:29–31	25
21:22b	26	23:4	165, 167
21:23–25	26	23:4–5	27, 76, 165
21:23b-25	26	23:5	166
21:24–25	26	23:7	6, 35
21:26b, 27b	61	23:7b	61
21:28	34	23:8b	61
21:28–32, 35–36	64	23:9	21, 165
21:28–36	25	23:9b	61
21:29	64	23:11	75
21:31	61	23:12b	61
21:33–34	48, 174	23:14–15	25
21:36	64	23:15b	61
22:2–3	49	23:18	25
22:3a	34	32:1	100
22:4	135	34:11–26	10
22:5	135	34:17	152
22:5–6	25	34:22	152
22:6	6	34:24	21
22:6–7	95		
22:7	95, 110, 114	Leviticus	
22:8	86, 95	4:1–2	19
22:9–10	95	4:2	135
22:10	95, 110, 114	4:3–17	61

INDEX OF PASSAGES

4:13	135	13:20	80, 170
4:22	135	13:21	170
4:27	135	13:23	80
5:10	61	13:24	171
5:15	135	13:24–26	170
5:18	135	13:25	80, 170
6:2–6	61	13:26	170
6:9	78	13:27	80, 170
6:14	78	13:28	170
6:20	78	13:29	171
6:25	78	13:30	80
7:1	78	13:30–32	170
7:11	78	13:34	170
7:35	78	13:35	172
7:37	78	13:36	80, 170
9:16	61	13:36–39	170
11:46	23	13:37	80, 170
11:46–47	78	13:38	172
12:7b	78	13:39	80, 170
13–14	79, 169, 170, 184	13:40	80
13:2–8	172	13:40–42	172
13:2 JPS	171	13:41	80
13:3	80, 170	13:42	170
13:3–8 JPS	171	13:43	170
13:3a	170	13:44	80
13:3b	170	13:45	117
13:4	170	13:46	80, 170
13:5	170	13:47–49	172
13:6	80, 170	13:47–59	172
13:7	172	13:49	170
13:7a	170	13:49–51	170
13:7b	170	13:50	172
13:8	170	13:51	80
13:9 JPS	171	13:53	170
13:10	170	13:55	80, 170
13:11	80	13:56	170
13:12	170	13:57	170, 172
13:13	170	13:59	78
13:14	170, 172	14:2	78
13:15	170	14:3	170
13:16	170, 172	14:32	78
13:17	80, 170	14:34	21, 173
13:18–19 JPS	171	14:34–36	172
13:19	170	14:34–38 JPS	173
13:19–21	170	14:35	170

INDEX OF PASSAGES

Leviticus (*cont.*)

Passage	Page
14:35b	173
14:36a	170
14:36b	170
14:37	170, 173
14:39	170
14:43	172
14:44	80, 170
14:48	170
14:54–57	78
14:57	79
15:32–33	78
17	56
17–26	56
17:5–7	56
17:9–10	32
17:10	56
17:11–12	56
17:12a	56
17:14	56
17:14b	56
17:15–16	31
18:2	56
18:3	56
18:4–5	56
18:6	82, 103
18:6–23	80
18:7–8	82
18:10–17	82
18:14	103
18:17	80
18:18	110
18:19	103
18:22	80
18:23	80
18:30	56
19:2–4	56
19:4	152
19:6–8	31
19:10	56
19:12	56
19:12a	56
19:13	147
19:17	167
19:17–18	153
19:30	56
19:33	153
19:34	153
19:36	56
19:36–37	56
20:2	9
20:2–6	32
20:3	56
20:5–6	56
20:7–8, 24, 26	56
20:9	49, 101
20:9–21	80
20:11	82, 103
20:14	80
20:16	103, 110
20:17	80, 82
20:18	103
20:19–21	82
20:20	103
20:21	80
20:22	56
20:22–24	56
20:23	56
20:24	21, 56
20:26	56
21:8, 12, 15, 23	56
21:23b	56
22:2–3, 8–9	56
22:2b	56
22:14	135
22:31	56
22:33	56
23:2b	56
23:4	78
23:10	56
23:15	152
23:22, 43	56
23:29–30	32
23:30	56
23:40	152, 153
23:43	21, 56
24:10–23	19
24:19–20	26
24:22	56
25:2	56

25:8	152	6:21	78
25:18	56	9:1–14	19
25:19–22	124	12	159
25:20	86, 124	12:9	170
25:21	124	12:12	170
25:25	167	12:14–15	170
25:35–37	167	13:33	38
25:38	56	15:22–29	135
25:42	56	15:32–36	19
25:43	55	15:39	158
25:44	128	16:15	114
25:47	167	19:1–2	19
25:55	56	27:1–11	19
26:1	152	27:4	108
		31:27–30	19
Numbers		34:9–34	29
5:2–4	170	35:9–34	29
5:11–31	111	35:11	136
5:12–13	78	35:15	136
5:12–31	1, 86	35:16–18	82, 136
5:12b–13a	116	35:19	29
5:12b–14	112	35:19–24	99
5:13	111, 146, 148	35:20–21	82
5:13–14	145	35:20–23	136
5:14	79, 111, 116, 141	35:21	29
5:16	146	35:25–28	83
5:17	116		
5:18	116, 146	Deuteronomy	
5:19–20a	112	1:5	68
5:20	146	4:1	68
5:21	116	4:2	50
5:22b	112	4:5	68
5:23	111, 116	4:8	68
5:24	116	4:14	68
5:24a	116	4:34	38
5:26b	116	4:40	50
5:27	116, 146	4:41–43	29
5:27–28	112	5:7	129
5:27a	116	5:28	68
5:28	115	6:1	68
5:29	78, 146	6:6	50
5:29–30	78	6:13	43
5:29–30a	112	6:14	129
5:30	79	6:20–25	158
6:13	78	7:4	129

Deuteronomy (cont.)

Passage	Page
7:11	50
7:17	118, 128
7:17–19	124
7:22	47, 128
8	158
8:2	158
8:3	158
8:5	158
8:6	43, 158
8:11	50, 158
8:14	158
8:16	158
8:18	158
8:19	129, 158
9:4–5	128
10:12	157
10:12–13	43
10:13	50
10:20	43
11:10	123
11:13	43, 157
11:16	129
11:23	128
11:28	129
11:32–12:1	50
12–26	10
12:5	29
12:5–8	36
12:6	51
12:7	153
12:11	51, 52
12:12	153
12:14	51, 52
12:15	120, 139
12:15–16	118
12:18	153
12:20	21
12:20–21	118, 139
12:20–28	39, 40, 86, 118
12:28	51
12:29	21
12:29–30	56
12:29–31	86
12:29–31	39, 40, 86, 123
12:30	86, 128, 152
12:31	129
12:32	51, 52
13	86
13:1–5	39, 40, 42
13:1–6	129
13:2–6	125
13:2b	129
13:3b	125
13:4	43
13:5	81
13:6	129, 147
13:6–11	39, 40, 42
13:7–12	125, 129
13:7b–8	125
13:8	154
13:8a + 8b	44
13:8c + 9a	44
13:9	39
13:9b+c+10a	44
13:12	165
13:12–13	129
13:12–18	39, 73
13:13	147
13:13–19	40, 125, 129
13:14	81, 125
13:18	51, 52
13:22	43
14:3	71, 81
14:3–21	71
14:4–8	71
14:11	71
14:12–18	71
14:26	139, 153
15:2–3	167
15:2a	78
15:3	156
15:4	54
15:5	51, 52
15:7	167
15:7–9	31
15:7–11	39, 40, 44, 45, 86, 121, 155
15:9	32, 81, 167
15:9–11	185
15:9b	45, 54, 156
15:10a	156

15:10b	45, 54, 157	18:9–14	39, 40, 41
15:11	53, 167	18:12	56
15:12	9, 167	18:14	128
15:12–18	39, 40, 44, 45, 86, 88, 127, 156	18:15	23
		18:15–18	36
15:12a	76	18:15–22	39, 40, 41, 87, 124
15:15	46, 53, 157		
15:16–17	46	18:20	129
15:16–17a	75	18:21	118, 124
15:17b	76	18:22	124, 154
15:16a	88	19:1–3	29, 40
15:16b	90	19:1–13	29, 39
15:17b	75	19:2–3	137, 152
15:18a	156	19:2–7	137
15:18b	46, 157	19:4	136, 138
16:1	36	19:4a	78
16:3	36, 157	19:5	136
16:3a	72	19:6–7	53, 138
16:9	152	19:7	138, 152
16:11	153	19:7–10	40
16:12	157	19:9	51, 52, 152
16:13	152	19:10	30, 49
16:14–15	153	19:10b	54
16:18	152	19:11	136, 138
16:21	152	19:12	29, 99, 138
16:21–22	152	19:13	39, 154
17:1	81	19:19	155
17:2	81	19:19–21	26, 38
17:2–7	39, 40, 125	19:21	154, 155
17:3	129	20:1	91
17:4	81, 125, 165	20:1–4	168
17:5	81	20:1–9	39, 40, 86, 91
17:8	146	20:1b	168
17:8–11	40	20:2	92
17:8–13	39	20:2–3	91
17:14	119, 128	20:3	138, 168
17:14–15	40	20:3–4	35, 86, 91
17:14–20	39, 46, 87	20:5	91
17:16	39	20:5–8	86, 91, 93
17:16–20	47	20:8	91, 138
17:17	138	20:9	91
17:20	138	20:9b	91
18:3a	78	20:10	86
18:6	139	20:10–14	75
18:9	56, 81	20:10–18	39
18:9–11	71	20:10–20	41

INDEX OF PASSAGES

Deuteronomy (cont.)
Reference	Pages
20:14	71
20:15	72, 75, 76, 128
20:16–18	76
20:16b–17a	72
20:19–20	39
20:20	165
21:1	146
21:1–7	179
21:1–9	37, 70
21:3–4	70
21:10–14	1, 39, 40
21:11	141
21:14	109, 141
21:15	141
21:15–17	36, 184
21:18–21	37, 44, 86, 99
21:22–23	38
22:1–2	75, 166
22:1–4	165
22:2	76, 146, 165, 167
22:3	75, 76
22:4	166
22:5	81
22:6–7	39, 41, 73
22:8	39, 41, 48
22:11	23
22:13	141
22:13–19	36, 102, 175
22:13–21	86, 183
22:14	176
22:14a	103
22:16–17a	185
22:17	176
22:19	176
22:20–21	37
22:21	81
22:22	37, 69
22:24	38
22:28–29	36, 85
23:5	36
23:7	153
23:8	153
23:10–15	39, 41
23:18	81
23:20–21	167
23:22–24	39
23:24	139
23:24–25	74
23:25–26	39, 41
24:1	141
24:1–4	37
24:3	141
24:5	36
24:7	37, 69
24:8	159
24:9	36, 158
24:10–13	39, 40, 157
24:10–15	74
24:14–15	140, 157
24:15a	75
24:15b	34, 75
24:17–18	53
24:18	53, 157
24:18b	54
24:19	147
24:19–22	39, 40, 74, 157
24:19b	54
24:20–21	147
24:22	53, 157
25:1–2	37
25:1–3	37, 148
25:3	167
25:5	150
25:5–6	106
25:5–10	36, 86, 106, 177
25:6	108
25:7	86, 141, 177, 178
25:7–10	31, 106
25:8	85, 86, 178
25:9	86, 178, 179
25:10	178, 179
25:11–12	149, 175, 185
25:12	38, 39, 154
25:16	81
25:17	158
25:19	159
26:11	153
26:16	157

27		117	22:15		114
27:1		50	22:17		152
28:14		129	25:21–22		118
28:36		129	27:1		118
28:64		129	30:25		19
30:17		129			
30:20		43	2 Samuel		
31:3		128	1:14		152
31:18		129	1:16		49
31:20		129	3:29		49
			12:11		38
Joshua			13:11		88
2:17		117	13:14–15		104
2:24		97			
11:4		169	1 Kings		
15:18		44	2:31–33		49
			9:1		109
Judges			20:6		97
1:14		44	21:15		108
7:3		94	21:25		44
7:4b		97	22:33		126
9:24		49			
10:18		94	2 Kings		
14:15–17		43	5:11		118
16:4–17		43	5:27		170
19:23–24		100	6:14		169
21:5		94	6:16		32
21:8		94	7:3		170
			8:3		32
Ruth			8:18		44
1:15		178	10:9		110
			15:5		170
1 Samuel			17:15		128
8:19		108	18:28		110
10:27		100			
12:3		114	1 Chronicles		
13:5		169	13:9		152
16:12b		97			
16:14–15		145	2 Chronicles		
16:23		145	26:18		110
17:8		110	26:18–19		170
18:1		44	26:21		170
18:3		44			
18:21		118	Nehemiah		
21:16		100	5:12		117

Nehemiah (*cont.*)
5:13   117
8   117
8:6   117

Esther
1:12   108
2:14   109
7:5   97

Job
18:13   170
19:7   32
31   114

Psalms
13:4   72
24:10   97
29:5   71
41:9   121
41:14   117
72:4   32
72:19   117
78:10   108
89:53   117
101:3   121
137:5–6   113

Proverbs
6:24   145
6:34   145
23:20–21   100

Ecclesiastes
1:16   118

Isaiah
1:20   108
8:3   103
26:12   29
40:27–28   124

Jeremiah
5:19   124
7:16   100
8:8–9   124
26:11   100, 176
26:16   100
28:6   117
34:8ff.   156
38:17–18   113

Ezekiel
48   108

Hosea
6:7   61

Micah
7:5–6   43

Habakkuk
1:2   32

Zechariah
13:3   44

1 Maccabees
3:55–56   94

Index of Subjects

addressee
  active participation in execution of punishment, 38
  full participation of, 39, 40
  integration of, 35
  passive participation in law of corporal punishment, 37, 38
  role in executing justice, 30
afterthoughts: and analogical extensions, 75, 76
aggadah, 11
Amen: as confirmation of oath, 117
analogical extensions, 75
animals
  compassion for: and sensory perception, 165–68
  relieving distress of, 27
annotated laws, 69
apodictic law. *See* law, apodictic
assertive *ki*, 113, 114
authority: of lawgiver, 50–55

behavior: and emotional life, 153, 154, 155, 156
blood avenger, 29
  inner life of, 137, 138, 139
body parts, metaphorical use of, 156
Book of Holiness
  lawgiver's permanent presence in laws of, 56
  participation of lawgiver in, 56–58
Book of the Covenant, 10, 12, 32, 34, 35, 36, 88
  apodictic law in, 31
  lawgiver of, 24
  oath-taking procedures in, 110
  participation of lawgiver in, 25–35
  perceptibility of lawgiver in, 59–68
  small, 10

Book of the Law (Book of *Mishpatim*), 17

characters, mental life of, 15
cities of refuge: and inner life of blood avenger, 137, 138, 139
clarifying contrast, 72, 73, 74, 75
close reading(s), 12, 13
combined discourse, 15, 86, 125–31, 176
criminal intent. *See* mens rea

designations/appellations
  multiple, 164, 165, 174–80
  for participant characters, 174–80
Deuteronomic Code, 10
Deuteronomic law(s), 20
  combined discourse in, 128–31
  participation of lawgiver in laws of, 35–55
  perceptibility of lawgiver in, 68–77
Deuteronomic law collection: educational and sermonizing nature of, 40
diagnosis form, 80, 82, 83
dialogue: between lawgiver and addressee, 70, 76, 93, 123, 124, 127, 175
diegesis, 85
direct speech, 19, 87–117
  in judicial procedure, 98–110
  in laws of enticement to idolatry, 125
  in legal confrontations, 95–98
  and revelation of inner thought, 88, 89
discourse: and narrative reading of law, 8
Divine self, 30, 32, 33, 34
  as lawgiver, 30

ear, piercing of, 89
elliptical utterances, 97
embedded laws: as interpretive guide to frame story, 22
embedded stories, 14, 17–22

INDEX OF SUBJECTS

emotions, intensities of, 142, 143, 144
epic situation: of legislative act, 52
Eshnunna, law of, 6
ethical dative, 152
eye: as organ of pity, 154, 155

family: as source of law, 40
father-son relationship, 40, 41
focalization. *See* point of view
formulas: introducing laws, 19
frame story, 14, 17–22
free indirect discourse, 125–31
future events: as frame story, 21

gender: and inner life of characters, 142
generality, principle of, 98

halakha, 11
Hammurabi, Law(s) of, 18, 51
    and participation, 58
headings and summaries
    as common convention of ancient Near Eastern scribes, 79
    of Priestly lawgiver, 78, 79
heart: as seat of feelings, 139, 140
historical events: as frame story, 18, 19, 20, 21
Holiness Code, 32
homicide, law of, 27, 28, 29, 30
hortatory speeches, in Deuteronomy: legal elements extracted from, 68, 69
human weakness: recognized by lawgiver, 31
husband and wife, inner world of, 145, 146

if-you legal formulations, 27, 39, 40, 48, 91, 130
    as models of familial relationships, 40
imitatio dei: and legal norms, 21
imitation: use in narrative, 85, 86
informational redundancy, 69–73
inner life
    of characters, 137–41, 185
    shaping by lawgiver, 153–61
interior speech, 117–25
    as elliptical, 119, 120, 121, 122
    as a verisimilar construction, 119, 120, 122

interrogative clauses: purpose of, 94
interrogatives: in internal speech, 123, 124
intervention: of lawgiver, 62, 63, 65, 67, 68, 69, 70, 76, 77, 79, 80, 81, 83, 84, 143, 147, 160, 161, 186
intervention mechanism: of Priestly lawgiver, 77, 186
intimate relationships: and laws of Pentateuch, 141–49
intrapsychic world: as dynamic space, 142
irony, 155

judicial procedure, 98–110
jurisprudence, contemporary trends in, 1, 2, 3

laws(s)
    as communicative acts, 84
    communicative and dialogic, 185, 187
    concrete elements of, 7, 11
    as embedded stories, 18
    general and particular statements in, 70, 71
    modern: and mental states, 133
    narrative reading of, 7–11
    and role in advancing plot, 20
    as mirrors of narrative, 21
    as object of literary study, 13, 14
law(s), ancient Near Eastern, 18
    exculpatory oaths in, 114, 116, 117
law(s), apodictic, 6, 8, 9, 11, 26, 40, 53
law(s), biblical
    narrative reading of, 1, 2, 3
    participation as distinguishing feature of, 84
    poetics of, 14
    rhetoric of, 13
    semiotics of, 13
law(s), casuistic, 6, 8, 9, 10, 11, 26, 27, 31, 95
    in Book of the Covenant, 26, 27, 31
    communicative and dialogic nature of, 185, 187
    mimetic quality of, 184, 187
    as mini-stories, 7, 8
    narrative reading of, 183–84, 186
    of Pentateuch, and ancient Near Eastern law collections, 186, 187

INDEX OF SUBJECTS

pentateuchal: within narrative frame, 17, 18, 19
  and perspective, 180
  poetics of, 184
  and point of view, 164
  as reality-mimicking texts, 85, 184, 186
  as social literature, 2, 3
  and surrounding narrative, 11, 12
  transmission of, 50
law(s), pentateuchal
  criminal intent in, 135, 136
  as embedded stories, 14
  and historical events, 17
  and intimate relationship, 141–49
  as mini-stories, 17
law(s) about leprosy: and sensory perception, 169–74
law and literature: history of research, 2, 3
law and literature school, 1, 2, 3
law as literature school, 3
law codes/collections, ancient Near Eastern, 6, 40
  and participation, 58
  and principle of vicarious punishment, 61
law collections, close reading of, 12, 13
law of building a parapet: and laws dealing with negligence, 47, 48, 49, 50
law of centralization of cult: and authority of lawgiver, 50, 51
law(s) of homicide
  and criminal intent, 135, 136
  and inner life of characters, 137
law of impure touch: and inner world of women, 149–52
law of lending to poor, combined discourse in, 126–27
law of levirate marriage: direct speech in, 106–10
law of profane slaughter, inner speech in, 118–20
law of the jealousy ordeal, 111–17
law of the king: and protagonist as independent figure, 46–47
law of the male and female slave: father-son relationship in, 46
law of the pauper: father-son relationship in, 44–45

law of the poor brother, inner speech in, 121–23
law of the prophet: father-son relationship in, 41–44
law of the rebellious daughter: direct speech in, 101–6
law of the rebellious son: direct speech in, 98–101
law(s) of warfare, 91
  and sensory perception, 168–69
law(s) on idolatry: combined discourse in, 129, 130, 131
law prohibiting Canaanite cults: combined discourse in, 128, 129
law prohibiting delay of wages: and emotional intensification, 140, 141
law prohibiting imitation of Canaanite cult practices, inner speech in, 123–25
lawgiver
  authority of, 50–55
  personality of, 23, 24
lawgiver, Deuteronomic, 24
  interventions of, 69, 81
lawgiver, Priestly, 24
  approach to psychological reality, 160, 161
  and inner life of characters, 137–41
  and inner world of men, 142, 143
  and inner world of women, 147, 148, 149–52
  intervention mechanism of, 77
  as narrator, 14, 15
  as pedagogical, 77, 78
  as psychologist, 15, 161
  self-conscious, 52
  sensory perception of, 171, 172
  and shaping inner life, 153–61
  and substance of laws, 24
lawgiver self, 30, 32, 33, 165
legal and notational discourse: in Deuteronomic laws, 69
legal confrontation, statements made during, 87, 95–98
legal norms: as *imitatio dei*, 21
legal texts
  and point of view, 164

legal texts (*cont.*)
   narrative elements in, 5–7
legislation
   act of, 35, 51, 52
   art of, 51, 52, 55, 56, 185
levirate marriage, 106–10
linguistic style: of Priestly writer, 77
Lipit-Ishtar, Law of, 18
love: and loyalty oaths, 90
loyalty oaths, 82, 90

magic: 39, 40, 41, 53, 61, 111
maiming of the ear: as punishment, 89
master and female slave: inner world of, 143, 144
memory, 158, 159
men, inner world of: and lawgiver, 142, 143
mens rea (criminal intent), 134, 135, 136, 137
mental states: and modern law, 133
Middle Assyrian Laws, direct speech in, 87, 88
military speech acts, 91–94
mimesis, 85
mise en abyme, 21
Moses: as narrator, 18, 19, 20, 23
motive: and justification of actions, 151, 152
motive clauses
   in Laws of Hammurabi, 58
   in laws of Pentateuch, 35, 37, 38, 44, 45, 48, 49, 53, 54, 57, 59, 61, 62, 66, 68, 72, 80, 82, 84, 90, 93, 94, , 126, 127, 140, 176, 177, 185, 186, 187
   in Middle Assyrian Laws, 58

narrative reading: of casuistic laws, 183, 184, 186
narrative, 4
   and cognitive psychology, 4
   use of imitation in, 85, 86
   in legal texts, 5–7
   and psychic life, 134
   and story, 7
narrative unit, 9

narrator
   lawgiver as, 15, 23–85
   role of, in embedded laws, 19
   self-conscious, 51, 52

oath(s), 110–17
   assertory (declaratory), 114, 116, 117
   exculpatory, 114, 115
   of guilt, 115
   promissory, 114, 116, 117
ordeal
   and husband-wife relationships, 146, 147, 148
   ritual, 111

parallelism: in legal formulation, 63, 64, 70, 71, 72
participation
   of the addressee, 36–41
   criterion of, 15
   as distinguishing feature of biblical law, 84
   of lawgivers, 24, 25–58
Pentateuch
   law collections in, 6, 9, 10; and ancient Near Eastern law, 11, 24
   laws and narrative in, 17, 18, 19
   See also law(s), pentateuchal
perceptibility
   as common to all ANE law codes, 84
   criterion of, 15
   of lawgivers, 24, 59
performative speech acts, 93, 94
personal statement: in legislation, 53, 54, 55
perspectival discourse, 173, 174
perspective(s)
   and casuistic laws, 180
   and multiple designations, 174, 175, 176, 177, 178, 179
   multiple, 171, 172, 173
   See also point of view
place, multiple designations of, 179, 180
poetics: of biblical law, 14
point of view, 15, 163–81
   internal: and illusion of reality, 185
   retrospective, 167
Priestly Code, 10, 12

Priestly laws, 19
Priestly legislation: perceptibility of lawgiver in, 77–83
promulgation formula, 50
protagonist: point of view of, 165, 166, 168, 169, 170, 171
Proverbs: father-son relationship in, 42
psyche
   life of: and relationships between men and women, 141–49
   as seat of feelings, 139, 140
psychic life: and literary reading, 134
psychology, cognitive
   and deciphering cultural narrative, 4
   and narrative, 4

rabbinic literature: and narrative reading of law, 10, 11
readers: participation in laws' narrative scenes, 36, 37
reality, illusion of, 184, 185, 186
   and speech acts, 87, 88, 92, 93, 94
relationship: of lawgiver and addressee, 57, 58
remembering, 157, 158, 159
removal of the shoe: as symbolic act, 107, 110
repetition: in Deuteronomic laws, 69, 70, 71, 72, 73
responses, lawgiver's, 75, 76

second person, use of, 25, 26
seeing, semantic field of, 170
self, experiencing, 27
self-identification formulas, 56, 57
semio-narrative method, 13

sensory/cognitive perception: and point of view, 164, 165
slave-master relationship, 89, 90
speech acts/events, 15
spitting: as symbolic act, 110
story
   and narrative, 7
   and narrative reading of law, 8
   See also narrative

talion, principle of, 26, 27, 33, 38, 39, 149, 155
text: and narrative reading of law, 8
textual excess: in law of going out to war, 93
textual superfluity, 69, 70, 71, 72, 73
"this day," 52
time: and Deutronomic legislation, 52
Torah, public reading of, 13

Ur-Namma, Law of, 18

validation: and self-identification formulas, 56, 57
verba solemnia, 87, 88–94
verbal acts, 85, 86
vicarious punishment, principle of, 61
voice of character: incorporated into lawgiver's discourse, 126, 127
voice of lawgiver: insinuated into utterances of characters, 128–31

weak, laws protecting rights of, 30–35
women, inner world of, 147, 148, 149–52

YHWH: as narrator, 18, 19, 23

www.ingramcontent.com/pod-product-compliance
Lightning Source LLC
Chambersburg PA
CBHW021840220426
43663CB00005B/336